To: Steve
" Best Wishes"
Rick & Dick
Hoyt
2002

"Dad, when I'm running it feels like I'm not even handicapped."

in another cheer, Donna, Alan and I lifted our glasses and joined in.

I don't recall whether the commentator appeared during the entire broadcast, but during his opening voiceover, the man gave an impassioned narration about the immense challenge and the dedication required to prepare for an Ironman. They followed his presentation with film clips and human-interest stories, each one featuring an athlete who would be competing in this most recent Ironman, along with several other athletes who had competed in past events.

York Summerville, a mountain-biking Mad Dog in my age division, impatiently demanded, "We want to see Rue Morgan! We want Morgan! We want Morgan!"

The commentator ignored his demands, but instead profiled a slender actress from Baywatch who had taken a nine-month hiatus from filming to train and compete in this prestigious event. They went to a rugged septuagenarian next, and followed him with a former professional football player I had never heard of. These were the headliners that the Ironman producers hoped would capture our attention and keep us glued to the tube for the next two hours. That's all we would get, two hours, even though it would take some of the athletes as long as twenty hours to reach the finish line, if they reached it at all.

Donna turned to me and said, "If it takes over seventeen hours, they don't make the cutoff time. They did all that work for nothing."

I shrugged. "They'll get to enjoy the scenery longer. That's not a bad consolation."

The commentator got a cheer when he anointed the event as *The Super Bowl of triathlons*. "This is Ironman Hawaii," he said. "Every triathlete's goal."

The man was way off base about it being "every" triathlete's goal. It certainly wasn't one of mine. I preferred the shorter triathlons, like the sprint and international distances.

"An Ironman is overkill," I told Donna. "It's like changing a Super Bowl from one hour to six hours."

Since Donna and Alan had been preparing for an Ironman in Panama City, Florida, Donna promptly refuted my analogy. She frowned at me, shook her head and scoffed, "It isn't overkill. You're just a wuss."

The Baywatch babe was an interesting touch, I thought. She got plenty of hoots and howls from the male dogs among us. I ogled her for a moment, but when the commentator started telling us about the Hoyts, he had my full attention. Alan nudged me with his elbow when the spotlight landed on the man who had carried his son the entire race. He said, "That's the guy right there. That's Dick Hoyt."

The Mad Dogs became uncharacteristically silent when we were introduced to Dick and Rick Hoyt, two warriors who had crossed the Pacific to challenge the Ironman. These guys were not your typical triathletes. Rick was born with cerebral palsy, and as a non-vocal quadriplegic, he had been confined to a wheelchair for his entire life. Dick was a burly man with a square jaw and reddish-blonde hair so thick it looked like a full wig.

I looked over at Alan, who was now holding hands with Donna, his future wife, and asked, "Are you kidding? He actually does this with his son?"

Without taking his eyes off the TV, Alan said, "Just keep watching."

"He does," Donna interjected, "but not in today's race. This is video from last year's Ironman Hawaii. I think the Hoyts did it in 1988 or 1989."

Alan said, "It was 1989."

The commentator continued. He told us, in essence, that the Hoyts refused to let a little inconvenience like cerebral palsy deny them their dreams. So at the urging of young Ricky, they began their career when they entered a five-mile charity race, but soon graduated to Ironman triathlons and cycling across the United States together.

The swim began from a deep-water start. We watched in awe while Dick methodically worked his way through the flailing arms and rolling waves. He somehow managed to swim the two-point-four miles with his son tethered behind him in a rubber boat. Next, with a bicycle customized to carry Rick in front of him, Dick peddled out onto the hot, mountainous lava fields to complete the 112-mile adventure ride. Then they showed clips of the Hoyts as Dick pushed his son in a *running* chair for the final 26.2 miles, a full marathon. The Hoyts sprinted across the finish line to the delight of screaming spectators and teary-eyed Mad Dogs. This amazing team had completed Ironman Hawaii. It was an emotional experience, one I would not soon forget.

As the broadcast neared conclusion, it occurred to me that Americans everywhere had been watching much more than the simple chronicling of two determined athletes participating in a rigorous event. They were also witnessing a love story. A story about a father who had so much love for his son that he refused to partake in life's fruit unless his son was at his side to feast right along with him, regardless of the obstacles. Their story was about a personal triumph against staggering odds, a story about accomplishing goals so unimaginable that no one had even considered it before. Dick and Rick Hoyt touched my heart that day. When the telecast ended, I asked Donna a very serious question: "Why have I never heard of them before?"

A couple years and many sprint races later, I read an article in *Inside Triathlon* about the Hoyts completing the 1999 Hawaii Ironman. The article reminded me that I had not heard a word about these incredible men since that day at the Bar and Grill. As a writer, I wondered why. Was there a movie in the making? Had a book been written? If that were the case, surely I would have heard about it from one of my friends. After all, it was truly an inspirational story, a story that needed to be told in its entirety.

I fired up my Packard Bell, clicked on AOL, and sent off an e-mail to USAT, the governing body of American triathlons. The

Hoyts, I assumed, would be members. I gave them my USAT number, told them I was a writer, and said I wanted to contact Dick Hoyt. I requested his phone number or an e-mail address. About one week later, Tim Yount, an official from the USA Triathlon organization, responded. Not surprisingly, he said it was against USAT policy to give out phone numbers of members, so at that point, it looked like a dead end.

One evening nearly a month later, I came home from a workout, sat at my computer, opened the E-mailbox and checked my messages. There were several, including one from Dick Hoyt. I peered down at the monitor and quickly realized that the only thing he had written was his e-mail address. Yount had delivered the message, after all. I typed a brief response, which began with adulation for his accomplishments. I told him a little about myself and I asked if anyone had ever approached him to write a screenplay about his life. I thanked him for his time and hit the send button. He got back to me three days later. Again, his message was succinct.

"Disney has the rights to the screenplay, but we can talk about a book."

He included his telephone number and the best time to reach him. When I called the following evening, we engaged in casual conversation before eventually getting around to the purpose of my call. He told me all about the contract with Disney, which would expire within a year, and that he was frustrated because they were dragging their feet on the project. He also mentioned something about an invitation to appear on the Oprah Show, but had decided to wait until they had a book ready for her to read, hoping she would be inclined to promote it.

"At all our speaking engagements, they ask for our book," Dick lamented. "But we don't have one yet. One hasn't been written."

"Would a book conflict with your contract to Disney?" I asked.

"No. They only have the movie rights."

Less than one month later, I took a Southwest flight to Massachusetts by way of Hartford, Connecticut, where Dick Hoyt would meet me at the airport. When I got off the plane, I had no idea what to expect from my host. But there I was, a stranger, about to invade his home for the next nine days. I learned during the telephone conversations that Dick was fifty-nine-years old and Rick was thirty-eight. He had given me a little background, including information about cerebral palsy, but beyond that, I knew only that Dick Hoyt had a lot of heart, one that overflowed with love for his son. I also knew the man had incredible fortitude and dedication, and, of course, he was one hell of an athlete.

As I bound down the steps to the baggage claim, I realized that Dick would have no way of identifying me. After all, it wasn't my face they flashed all around the world on the television screen. But I spotted him immediately, standing alone at the bottom of the stairs, checking each passenger as they went by to pick up their luggage. Before I could speak, he smiled, stuck out his hand and put me at ease.

With a Boston accent as thick as any I had ever heard, he said, "I knew it was you right away. You're the only one who looks like a triathlete."

IT'S ONLY A MOUNTAIN

Dick and Rick Hoyt, Men of Iron

CHAPTER 1 — IRON MEN

*I have thought long and hard about what I would
do if I wasn't in a wheelchair. I really don't know
what I would do first. I love sports, so maybe I
would play hockey, baseball or basketball. But
then I thought about it some more and what I
would probably do first is tell my dad to sit down
in the wheelchair and now I would push him.*

—Richard Hoyt, Jr.

Dick and I left Holland, Massachusetts, on Saturday, under
threatening clouds and an occasional drizzle. It was cold that
morning. Fifty degrees in the month of June felt pretty darn cold
to someone who lived in Florida. Dick had purchased a new S-10
pickup, but since it hadn't been delivered yet, we made the trip in
his red Ford Escort. A sudden downpour on the Massachusetts

Turnpike slowed us for several miles, but the sun hit us hard by the time we drove through Boston. The 75-minute trip put us in Brookline at ten o'clock.

Dick shared several anecdotes along the way, and as we neared our destination, he recounted one about the fortieth President of the United States. With a boyish grin, Dick said, "When I got on the phone, it was President Reagan. After congratulating us, he asked me to call him if we ever got back to California. So when we were in Los Angeles, I did, and he invited us over." Dick smiled and said, "A *People Magazine* crew was in his office interviewing him, but he kicked them out and asked us in."

Dick was proud to share that story. Although he generally avoided discussing politics, it was obvious he respected our former president, the man who was Commander in Chief during eight years of Dick's military career. We rounded a corner and drove down a residential street lined with brick homes and apartments. Most of them were two or three stories high, but as we approached a brown, seven-floor apartment building, Dick pointed to it and said, "Rick lives there, on the Fifth floor."

Rick was Dick's oldest son, the younger half of the now world-famous Ironman and marathon team, "Team Hoyt." We would be taking him back to Holland with us, and on the following morning, all three of us would compete in a sprint triathlon in Marlboro. Rick was a 38-year-old quadriplegic who could not speak or feed himself. How, I wondered, could a person with such a severe disability possibly live alone in an apartment? And how could he compete in all those grueling endurance races with his father? Many before me had asked those questions about the Hoyts, and my objective was to find the answers. At that moment, however, the anticipation of meeting Rick stirred an anxiety I had not expected.

Dick parked the car in a reserved slot at the front of the building. We walked around to the back, where he pulled out a key and unlocked the security door. Once inside the building, the

2

elevator whisked us up to the fifth floor. The walls in the narrow hallway were a blanched gray, with all the doors painted green. Many of the elderly residents were of Russian descent and very polite to strangers. It was a quiet complex, with a safe and comfortable ambience. Dick pulled out a second key and unlocked the door to Rick's one-bedroom apartment.

"Morning, Rick," he said cheerfully.

There may have been a response, but I didn't hear it. We went to the living room where Dick slid back the blinds.

"It's too warm in here," he observed, then opened a window and walked over to the hallway. "Are you ready to get up, Rick?" he asked, and glanced in the direction of the bedroom.

Again, no response. "He likes to sleep late," Dick said, as I followed him down the hall.

Posters of the New England Patriots and the Boston Red Sox lined the walls in Rick's bathroom. An autographed picture of Bobby Orr – the man considered by many as the greatest hockey player to ever wear a Boston Bruin uniform – hung by the door. In the great Northeast, natives revered their hockey teams, and Rick Hoyt, apparently, was no exception.

Dick dropped a plug in the tub, turned on the water, stuck his hand under the spigot, and held that position until he had the water temperature adjusted to his satisfaction.

"Rick likes it hot," he said.

I observed the steam. "Sure looks hot to me."

Dick picked up a small, inflatable, horseshoe-shaped pillow, put it to his mouth and blew several blasts of air through the nozzle. When the pillow felt firm, he tossed it in the tub.

"This is all standard procedure," Dick informed me. "When Rick's PCAs are here, they do all this for him."

"What is a PCA?" I inquired.

"Personal Care Attendants. They're students employed by Rick. They work on scheduled shifts to help him do his shopping and laundry, provide transportation, or whatever needs to be done. They bathe him, dress him, everything."

3

Dick led me into the bedroom where I saw Rick lying face down on his waterbed, under a sheet that covered him to the neck. "He's comfortable sleeping in that position. That's the way Yoel, his attendant, left him last night."

"Oh."

"Oh" was often my response over the next nine days. The things I saw and learned left me speechless at times.

A cloth banner from the Hawaii Ironman hung majestically above Rick's bed. Printed in bold, black letters was the date: October 21, 1989. The time it took them to complete that championship race also appeared: fourteen hours, twenty-six minutes, and four seconds. They were impressive numbers by anyone's standard. However, perhaps of even greater importance, juxtaposed on the wall next to the Ironman banner, Rick's college diploma was in full view. He had received a Bachelor of Science degree from Boston University, and considering his disability, that accomplishment suddenly impressed me more than his participation in the Ironman.

Dick yanked the sheet from Rick's naked body. "You plan to sleep all day?"

Rick's body tightened and he let out a groan and a laugh. It looked to me as if he were trying to roll over to face his father, but it was not to be.

"Quit complaining," Dick told him playfully. "Tomorrow you have to get up at five. This will our first Triathlon of the new millennium. You want to start it with a win, don't you?"

Rick wailed again, protesting even louder. This was playful bantering between the two men. Dick teased his son about always wanting to sleep late, but they both knew it would not be a problem on race morning. Rick looked forward to racing with his dad, and even though he never admitted it, he had no qualms about sacrificing a few hours of sleep.

"How did you sleep?" Dick asked. "Okay?"

Rick made another sound that was unintelligible to me, but one I concluded to mean "Yes," therefore assuring his dad that everything was fine. This was the spoken word between father and son, which was all very intimidating to me because my intentions were to communicate with Rick, and I did not have sufficient time to learn his esoteric method.

As Dick stepped over to the closet, he said, "Sam is here."

"Hi, Rick. Good to meet you."

The young man did not respond, of course. Dick had prepared me for this on our drive into Boston; he told me to grab Rick's hand just as I would anyone else. "He can't shake your hand, but he knows. He understands."

I was eager to greet Rick with my normal handshake, but with him lying flat on his stomach, the opportunity did not present itself. While I glanced curiously around the bedroom, Dick selected clothes for Rick to wear that day. Sports posters, pictures and awards adorned the walls; emergency telephone numbers and a list of people to contact had been taped on the door. It was impossible for Rick to call for help should the need arise, but the phone numbers were for the attendants or anyone else who might be visiting if an emergency occurred.

The most unusual object I noted in the bedroom was a black wheelchair with a covered box attached to the armrest. The box, I learned later, contained Rick's computer, the one he used to express himself via the written word on a monitor, or when necessary, with the aid of a voice synthesizer. This marvelous device gave him the ability to communicate, and to share all the wisdom and thoughts that were otherwise hostage inside his fertile mind.

Dick tossed the clothes down on the bed and asked, "Are you ready to go?"

When Rick acknowledged he was ready, Dick bent down and gently lifted his smiling, 110-pound son up from the bed, and then carried him off to the bathroom where the bath water was still running. The tub was not yet full, but Dick had timed it perfectly, so it would be ready about the same time they finished with other business. When he took Rick over to the toilet, I

5

discreetly returned to the living room and left them alone to conduct the most private step in their personal procedure.

Rick's living room motif resembled something of a sports buffet. Autographed pictures of Dick and Rick hobnobbing with famous athletes hung from nearly every wall. He had a very impressive collection, which included awards, trophies, photos and posters. One wall was covered with a huge quilt made from T-shirts he had received at various races and events from all over the world. Numerous mementos were on display, with each one proclaiming that the Hoyts were well respected and appreciated, not only for their athletic accomplishments, but also for the humanitarianism and the inspiration they provided to disabled people throughout the world.

My attention was drawn to an autographed picture of Ronald Reagan standing together with Dick, Rick, Judy and Russell Hoyt. Rob Hoyt, the middle brother, could not be with them on that particular trip to California. At the bottom of the picture, the former President had written these words: *With great admiration, every good wish, and warm regards.*

When the toilet flushed, I returned to the bathroom to observe Dick carefully place Rick down in the tub, which had now filled with hot water and a layer of bubbles. Referring to the water temperature, Dick asked, "How is it, Rick? Okay?"

With a response barely discernable to me, Rick affirmed that the water was fine. Dick submerged him in the tub, making sure his head stayed on the inflatable pillow, safely above the water level. What a powerful moment. Here was Dick Hoyt, a burly athlete with a barrel chest and muscular arms, down on his knees exhibiting all the caring and gentleness of a mother cat licking life into her newborn kittens. His first-born child, his adult son, was lying motionless in the soothing water, totally at ease, while at the same time he was as helpless and vulnerable as an infant. In silence, I witnessed the unwavering trust that Rick held in his father.

"Is that okay, Rick?" Dick asked again.

6

At some point during that poignant exchange between father and son, my vision became somewhat blurred, a lump swelled in my throat, and I felt a tug at my heart. It became clear that learning and writing about the Hoyts would be a greater challenge than I had realized.

With Rick's head cradled in one hand, Dick used the thumb of his other hand to pop open the top of a shampoo bottle. He squeezed a portion of the contents onto Rick's short, brown hair, and then scrubbed his head clean, ever careful that the soapy water drained to the back of his head rather than down the front of his face. Rick coughed several times, which prompted Dick to pause before continuing the meticulous cleansing process.

When finished with the shampoo, Dick rested his son's head on the pillow. He shook up a can of shaving cream and spread it across Rick's stubble, and with due care, shaved his face clean, ear to ear. There wasn't a nick or a trace of blood. Then, while holding Rick's head in one hand, he used his free hand to rinse away the shampoo and the shaving cream. With a washrag and a bar of soap, he washed Rick from neck to toe. With that chore completed to his satisfaction, Dick stood, turned to me and said, "He likes to soak a while."

While Rick relaxed on the pillow, soaking in the hot water, Dick went into the bedroom and spread out a large towel on the side of the bed. He tidied the room first, then picked up soiled clothes and stuffed them inside a plastic bag along with other items that required laundering. Finally, he moved the wheelchair out of the way and returned to the bathroom.

"You ready, big guy?" he asked.

Rick nodded slightly. Dick lifted his son's slippery body from the tub and carried him back to the bedroom. As he laid him down on the towel, Rick looked up at his father through bright, penetrating brown eyes and laughed. I didn't catch the humor, but Rick found it somewhere.

"What's so funny now?" Dick asked, and briskly rubbed the towel over his son's emaciated, unusable legs.

"He has a strong upper body," I observed honestly.

"Yeah, he's solid. He's spastic, so his muscles tighten up a lot. He gets real tight. He can't control it. That's what we mean when we say 'spastic' quadriplegic."

"Oh."

Due to my own sensitivities, I did not pursue the subject any further. Even though it was the reason for my visit, some of my questions seemed too personal.

Dick offered another anecdote. "One night Rick knocked the plug out of his waterbed with his toe. The water dripped through the floor so the people below him called the manager." Rick laughed when he realized which story Dick was telling. "When the manager came in and found Rick alone, lying in the water, he assumed something was wrong, panicked, and rushed Rick to the hospital." Rick laughed again. "He thinks it's funny because I had to drive all the way over here at three in the morning."

Dick dried him completely, but the effects from the hot bath lingered and Rick continued to perspire heavily.

"I'll let him cool down a few minutes," he said, and during the time that Rick relaxed and cooled, Dick kept on working.

When he went back to clean the tub and the bathroom, I strolled around the apartment. I found a picture of Dick pushing Rick in the *running chair* while they carried the Olympic torch in 1996, and next to it, framed lyrics of a song about running. His brother, Herb, had written the song, and it previewed during a live telecast at the finish line of Boston's most famous race. The Hoyts had just completed their 20th consecutive Boston Marathon, and Dick was leaning on the running chair, gasping to catch his breath when he heard the song for the first time.

I stopped to read a poem inscribed on a plaque above Rick's desk. It was titled: *Look to this Day.*

Yesterday is already a dream, and tomorrow is only a vision, but today well lived makes every yesterday a dream of happiness and every tomorrow a vision of hope.

When Dick had completed various cleaning tasks, he went back to the bedroom, toweled Rick a second time, and then dressed him in shorts and a Team Hoyt T-shirt. "You look good," he said, as he unrolled a pair of white socks and put them on Rick's feet. Next came his boots, which were made of a soft material similar to what surfers wear when the water is too cold for their bare feet. With those tasks completed, he loaded Rick into the wheelchair and strapped him down.

"We've been training hard this week," Dick told his son while pushing him into the living room. "How about you?"

Rick craned his neck around as far as possible, allowing a closer, expressive look at his father's face. He had some control over the muscles above his shoulders, which enabled him to move his head around fairly well. That, I learned, gave him the ability and mobility to operate the computer.

"Yeah, yeah, I know," Dick quipped. "You quit eating candy and cake so I won't have to work so hard. Right?"

Dick looped a large, blue bib around Rick's neck and administered his medication of several different pills, mostly muscle relaxers. The pills were taken one by one. Because of an anomaly called a "reverse tongue," the pills had to be shoved far down Rick's throat, and during the procedure, he nearly choked on every pill. It was uncomfortable just to watch.

Rick's tongue did not work like a normal tongue. Rather than holding the food and moving it backward, he pushed everything forward. Without help, eating and drinking were impossible. Everything involving Rick required a tremendous amount of patience, and feeding him was no exception. They washed down the pills with a glass of orange juice, and several times during the tedious and messy process, it sounded like Rick was choking.

Dick would always ask, "Are you okay?"

With each pill, Dick watched and listened, always vigilant that Rick was only coughing, not choking. The process evolved slowly, but in an effort to minimize the painful spasms that Rick experienced every day of his life, it was something that simply had to be done.

Dick wiped the orange juice from Rick's face and looked over at me. "This is all he gets to eat for now. He can't have any food until later."

"Oh? That's a pretty lousy breakfast," I commented.

Rick laughed, so I assumed he agreed with my sentiments about the distasteful meal. Once the last pill had disappeared and the juice was gone, Dick placed the empty glass on the kitchen counter and left the room.

Since Rick and I were now alone, I walked over to the side of his wheelchair, and said, "Well, Rick, all these awards are mighty impressive."

His inability to respond in a way I could understand him only enhanced my discomfort. Fortunately, Dick promptly returned with Rick's toothbrush and a layer of toothpaste. "Open up."

Using short, horizontal strokes, he brushed Rick's teeth, including the gap in front where two were missing.

"His two front teeth got knocked out playing soccer," Dick said with a chuckle. "That's what he says, anyway."

Rick found humor in his dad's comment, and each laugh become more easily discernible to me. Once Dick finished with the teeth, he cleaned Rick's face. The bib went to the trash bag and the towel to the laundry bag. Rick gradually slid lower in the wheelchair, so Dick unfastened the waist strap and propped him up in the chair, where he would be more comfortable.

"Anything you need to tell me?" Dick asked. Rick gestured that he did have something he needed to tell his father. "Can you tell me without the computer?"

Another gesture told him the computer would not be necessary. As the two men held eye contact, communication continued with Dick enumerating vowels. With a slight pause between each vowel, Dick said, "*A-E-I-*" Rick nodded, which stopped the sequence at the letter *I*.

"Is it *I* itself?" Dick asked.

When Rick gestured it was not the pronoun "*I*," Dick continued the alphabet. "*I-J-K-L-M-*"

Rick stopped him again, indicating he wanted an *M*. The alphabetical quizzing continued until Dick determined what Rick wanted to tell him. "You want me to read the mail?" That was it. Dick then flipped on the television so Rick would be entertained while he read all the mail. It didn't surprise me when ESPN popped up with a recorded baseball game currently in progress. Rick was an ESPN junky who loved all sports, no question about that.

"Let's see what you have," Dick said, and pulled the mail from a large manila envelope pinned on a cork bulletin board. He took it to the dinning table and sorted it out. "Oh, this is June second, Rick. Don't forget about the payroll." Rick nodded but kept his eyes on the game. Dick continued reading. "Yoel won't be able to work next Wednesday. You will have to get someone else. Do you want to call Shelly?"

Rick cooed affirmatively. He had the final say in all business matters, including the decisions regarding the hiring, firing and scheduling of PCAs.

"Rick likes Shelly," Dick teased. "He can't keep his hands off her butt."

Rick snorted and gave his characteristic, wide-mouthed grin. Judging from his reaction, he was rather fond of Shelly, and darn proud of it. He seemed to enjoy being teased about his many fictitious exploits with the ladies.

Rick's government funds, SSI, covered most of his expenses, which helped him to achieve a greater independence than anyone could have ever expected. He was a very determined man, one who had battled since birth to be in control of his own life. When queried for a TV show called *West 57th Street*, Rick told the interviewer, "If I had to give up control, I might as well be dead."

When Dick finished scrutinizing all the mail and paperwork, he stuffed everything in the envelope and pinned it back on the wall. "Have Yoel call Shelly on Monday," he said to Rick.

11

Rick acknowledged with a smile.

Dick looked around the room and concluded he had taken care of everything. "Looks like we're ready." He clicked off the television, grabbed the laundry bag and trash bag, and aimed the wheelchair toward the door.

"Let me take one of those," I offered.

He handed me the trash bag and we left the apartment. When we reached the lobby downstairs, I dropped the bag in a large trash container. An elderly gentleman with a pronounced limp nodded and held the door for us. Dick thanked the man and we exited through the rear entrance.

"This is Rick's van," Dick said, as we walked to the parking slot closest to the door.

I looked through the van window and saw the dark-blue running chair stashed in the back. Rick always traveled in the van, and since the running chair came out only for racing or training, there was no reason to keep it elsewhere. Dick kept the inflatable raft and the customized bike stored at his house in Holland, both items critical for their triathlons.

Dick unlocked the side door and tossed the laundry inside the van. He flipped a switch and the hydraulic lift lowered the chair platform to the ground. After securing the wheelchair to the platform, Dick climbed inside the cargo door and hit another switch. Once the wheelchair was lifted into the van, Dick used Velcro straps to anchor it securely behind the driver's seat.

"We're ready," he announced, looking at Rick. "Remind me to get some more pills at the pharmacy, okay?" Rick nodded. Dick looked at me and said, "He has a great memory. All I have to do is ask him, and he remembers."

The return trip took us past Boston University – Rick's alma mater – and along sections of the route used for the Boston Marathon. Dick pointed out some of the landmarks. Before long, we were on the highway, dodging traffic back to Holland. When we neared the street where they needed to stop, Rick made noises and jostled his chair around to get Dick's attention, prompting

12

him to make eye contact through the rearview mirror. "What is it, Rick? Can it wait?"

Rick rattled the chair again. Dick peered into the mirror a second time before he finally realized this was the reminder he had requested.

"Oh, yeah, right," Dick said. "The pharmacy. Thanks."

"Well done," I told Rick.

Dick turned off at the next light and parked in front of a drugstore. While inside, I told Rick I was looking forward to racing with them in Marlboro.

"I might be able to keep up with you in the swim and bike," I said. "But you guys are too darn fast in the run."

Rick appreciated the compliment.

"We'll be back in Holland in about 20 minutes," Dick said when he returned to the van with the pills. "I think there'll be a surprise waiting for us."

"A surprise?" I echoed.

He did not volunteer what sort of surprise I should expect. During the remainder of the trip, Dick enumerated some of the tasks awaiting his attention at home, and also those that needed to be done in the morning before the race. All the equipment had to be checked out and loaded onto the van. He had yard work to finish and he needed to follow-up on a number of phone calls, including one to find out when their new bike would be ready for delivery. Rick watched sports on TV, but he still required Dick's attention from time to time: he needed liquids, more pills, comfort adjustments, questions answered, things like that. And, of course, that "surprise" would be waiting.

The triathlon started early in the morning, which meant Rick would have to be coaxed and lifted out of bed, taken to the toilet, dressed, fed, and stuffed with more of those horrible pills.

For most triathletes, preparation is a simple routine. Our greatest concern is getting up early enough to make it to the race on time, and then finding an open porta-potty before the swim starts. It was not quite that simple for Rick and Dick Hoyt. A

13

considerable amount of time and labor was required for their preparation. It was a labor of love; a love between a man and his son — a man who had patience equaled only by his son's courage.

During my time with the Hoyts, I viewed many videos. On one, a man named Peter Henderson succinctly expressed my feelings regarding Rick Hoyt. In a story he produced for a television show called *Our Times*, Henderson said, "Ricky can not speak, but his courage and spirit will make your ears ring."

My first full day with the Hoyts had not yet ended, but my ears were already ringing.

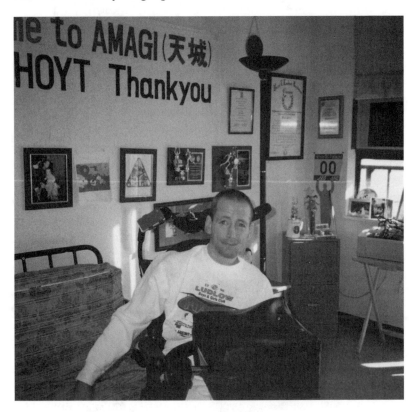

Rick relaxing in his apartment.

CHAPTER 2 — A TRIATHLON

I have to remind myself, he has to make mistakes and take risks like everyone else. That's just the way it works.

—Judy Hoyt

Since Holland is on the southern border of the state, a sign on the median said, "Welcome to Connecticut," but once we left the four-lane highway and took the blacktop into Holland, we were right back in Massachusetts. As we crossed the causeway over a small lake, Dick's ranch-style home and waterfront property came into view. Towering pines and evergreens surrounded the house and gave it the look of a Kodacolor picture puzzle, quiet and serene, with a distinct rural flavor.

In 1985, Dick and Judy Hoyt bought the property and aging cottage that rested on it. At the time, Dick was a major in the Air National Guard, stationed at nearby Westfield, but soon to be transferred to Wellesley. Since their three sons had flown the nest, they wanted a retirement home. Considering Dick's lifestyle, this was the perfect choice. Before they had settled in, he rolled up his sleeves and started overhauling the cottage. First, he built a ramp and a patio to accommodate Rick's wheelchair. In no time at all, he raised the living room ceiling, rebuilt the kitchen, put in a skylight, cleared the land, and even constructed a sturdy, wooden dock. They had an exceptional view of the lake – which was actually Hamilton Reservoir – where Dick could go fishing or boating alone or with his family. He could even swim laps in the lake if he wanted. Although he did not know how to swim at the time, his two younger sons were exceptional swimmers, and they could surely teach him if necessary.

Holland consisted of many part-time residents, which meant the population varied somewhere between 1,000 and 10,000, determined by the time of year and who you asked. The heart of commercial Holland consisted of one downtown intersection and a handful of businesses: the Auto Center, the Four Corners Package Store, a small real estate office, and a Pizzeria. They had an on-call police and fire department. The Hoyts did most of their grocery shopping at the Holland Market, about half a mile west of their property.

Most triathletes and bicyclists would describe the roads through and around Holland as "rolling hills," and they provided a perfect landscape for Dick to do his road training. He generally trained without Rick, but he would compensate for the weight difference by running up and down the hills with a 100-pound bag of cement tied down in the wheelchair. It was a lousy substitute for his son, but it helped produce the desired results.

Dick chuckled to himself when he told me, "Whenever I pushed the cement bag, all the neighbors thought I was loony."

Judy agreed with the neighbors. In fact, she eventually concluded that all the training and racing consumed him to the point where he lost sight of his objectives regarding Rick and his disability. Dick did not see it that way, and the conflicting opinions widened over time, which took them on a painful, convoluted course that contributed to their marital demise. They stayed together as long as they could; however, the union between high school sweethearts that began over thirty years earlier eventually ended in divorce. Dick was a man who always finished what he started, but divorce was not the finish he had planned. Judy was his partner, his family, the mother of his sons, and in his mind, he had failed. It was a difficult transition, but everyone made the necessary adjustments, and in 1994, Dick and Judy went on to pursue their respective goals alone.

First thing I remember seeing when we pulled onto the Hoyt property was a green banner hanging on the front porch. It displayed a colorful painting of a man pushing a young boy in a running chair. At one of their races, the woman who presented it to them said, "I just want to thank you guys for all you have done." They learned later that the grateful stranger was the mother of a child with cerebral palsy. As kindred spirits, they understood. At the side of the porch, a gray squirrel feverishly helped himself to a hearty breakfast from a bird feeder. On a wire six feet away, a tiny finch chirped disdainfully while he waited for the squirrel to move along so he, too, could get a shot at the free meal. Although I was in a town called Holland, everything seemed to whisper, "Welcome to Hoytville."

It was more of the same inside the house, where two adults and four excited children waited to surprise "Granda." Everyone shouted in unison: "Happy birthday, Granda!"

The kids rushed up and gave him hugs. It turned out that Dick's birthday was on the first day in June, the day before I arrived. A huge balloon with the number *60* floated above the dinner table. The number itself meant nothing to Dick, but as a serious triathlete, it gave him the right to compete as one of the "youngsters" in his new age division, 60-64. Dick iterated a philosophy espoused by many triathletes when he said, "It's one of the few benefits of aging."

The first person I met was Rob Hoyt, Dick's 36-year-old son, one of the two adults who had planned the surprise party. Two of the children were Rob's sons, Dick's grandsons. Jayme, the nine-year-old, was a big kid with a never-ending smile and a ton of personality. His brother Cameron was four years younger and a bit on the shy side. Both boys were polite, well-behaved kids, and very fond of their Granda.

As a teenager, Rob spent a lot of time working and playing at a camp for disabled children, and while there, he became attached to a small boy named Jamie.

17

"The boy had cerebral palsy and was abandoned by his parents," Rob told me. "I became very attached to him, and promised that one day I would have a son and name him Jayme."

The other adult at the birthday party was Heather Grey, a pretty, slender woman with long, sandy-brown hair. She and Dick had met two years earlier at the Auburn Health Club, where they both worked out with the exercise equipment. The two other youngsters – a boy named Dakota and a girl named Haley – were Heather's children.

Dick's youngest son, Russell, lived over an hour away in Billerica. He and his wife had prior plans and couldn't make it to the birthday party. Dick had spoken with Russell earlier that day, however, and had scheduled a trip to Billerica where we would meet for dinner with Russ, his wife, and their two-year-old son.

The birthday party was a great success. Everyone ate pizza and told stories. Back in high school, Rob was one of the elite swimmers in the New England area, so he needled his dad about his swimming prowess — or lack of it. He had tried to teach Dick how to use his legs properly, but with no perceptible success. According to Rob, his father's beefy legs just trailed along behind him and created excess drag.

"Cut them off and you will swim faster," Rob quipped.

That comment got a laugh, especially from Rick. In fact, his raucous reaction proved more humorous than Rob's crude hyperbole. Dick frowned at Rick and said, "What are you laughing at, Bud? I always beat you out of the water." That profundity stopped Rick cold. Apparently, he had never looked at it that way, and for once, the joke was on him.

Prior to dinner, food became the topic of our conversation, and some titillating information regarding Rick's attraction to the ladies got tossed into the mix.

"Hooters is Rick's favorite restaurant," Dick informed me.

Rob corrected him. "Hooters *are* his favorite. They come in pairs, you know." Rick laughed. "It's his favorite restaurant," Rob added, "but it has nothing to do with what's on the menu."

Before the bantering and teasing ended, Dick offered a story about a former acquaintance of his. "One night she decided to fix salmon, but she burned it so badly we couldn't eat it. I asked her why she cooked it so long, and she said, 'I was waiting for it to turn white.'"

He insisted the story was true, that the woman was serious. This was typical humor for the Hoyt boys. Many anecdotes, plenty of laughs. They had a good time, but with the triathlon looming the next morning, the night ended early. Heather rounded up her kids, and like most youngsters their age, they were in no hurry to leave a party. They objected, but a stern look from Mom resolved any conflict and they headed home.

Rob and his sons stayed at Granda's house that night. Dick stayed up to answer questions and set up the VCR so I could view videos from his racing career. Trophies, ribbons, pictures and awards covered his walls and tables. Some were the same as those Rick had displayed, but there were many others, including pictures with Bob Hope, Alberto Salazar, Bill Rogers and another one of President Reagan. He had colorful posters from races in Japan and Canada. One unusual item was an authentic machete imbedded in a red, felt base and mounted on a wooden frame, a gift from an official who had invited the Hoyts to compete in the San Salvador Triathlon. The impressive accumulation had the aura of a shrine, a tribute to their amazing success.

Something I referred to as a "bib tree" filled one corner of the guest room. Each of the bibs — race numbers — represented a race in which the Hoyts had entered and completed. According to Dick, he had more than eight hundred. Photo albums were stacked on the floor, each one overflowing with letters, pictures and news clippings. A large picture of Dick's parents, Alfred and Anne Hoyt, hung prominently on a wall in the den.

"I was very close to my parents," Dick said. "They raised ten children, but always found time for each one of us.

When asked for details, Dick fondly recalled stories about fishing and hunting with his father.

Alfred Hoyt expected big things from his young son, and he believed Richard had the talent and drive to be successful. "He suspected it might be in athletics," Dick reminisced. "He told me, 'You will know you made it as an athlete when you're on Wide World of Sports.'"

Although his statement was prophetic, Alfred never got to share the experience. Dick made the big show in 1989, but his father passed away before it happened. Alfred Hoyt left this world confident that his son would leave his mark somewhere, and when he died, Dick and Rick were already off and running toward fulfillment of those high expectations. In memory of his father, Dick made a special plaque and placed it on his headstone. The inscription went straight to the point, to the heart: *We did it for you, Dad.*

Although her mind has slowly slipped away, Anne Hoyt still enjoys the success of her son and grandson. "She is a strong woman," Dick said of his mother. "Whenever we got out of line, she wouldn't wait for Dad to come home, she just picked up the broomstick and chased us around the house. It was a good thing I could outrun her." Dick chuckled at the thought, but then he turned melancholy. "She was a very dedicated mother. She raised ten healthy children, and she had a lot of pride and love for every one of us."

Dick woke me early the next morning, exactly as planned, five o'clock. He prepared a breakfast of plain, non-fat yogurt over granola, covered it with a variety of fruit slices, and chased it with orange juice and ginger tea. It was a typical meal by Chef Hoyt – tasty, satisfying and healthful.

Dick roused Rick out of bed and cared to all his needs, including more of those muscle relaxers. The dinghy, air pump and life preserver had been loaded the night before, so Dick only had to throw the bikes on the bike rack and strap them down. After he lifted Rick inside the van and secured the wheelchair, we headed north to Marlboro for the Wet and Wild Triathlon, the first of the year 2000 for Team Hoyt.

Dick sipped his tea as he drove. "Heather will be at the race," he told Rick. "Haley and Dakota will be with her."

Rick enjoyed having young ones around him, even though they crawled up on his lap and tugged on his ears. It made him feel important being their "Uncle Rick," and the look on his face indicated he approved of Heather bringing her kids along.

Dick looked over at me and said, "Heather's been to some of our races. She's a lot of help."

"Easy on the eyes, too," I responded honestly.

Dick smiled, but made no comment.

Rick overheard our brief exchange about one of his favorite subjects — women. He laughed and rattled his wheelchair.

Dick peered at him through the rearview mirror. "Better watch it, you." He looked over at me. "His ears work fine. He hears everything."

The two men communicated better than most fathers and sons even though Rick was non-vocal. They used their eyes, gestures and emotions. It came from the heart, not the vocal cords.

The drive to Marlboro took less than an hour. A perfect morning greeted us, cool and clear, and not a trace of wind. We arrived on schedule, one hour before the start time. With all the teasing about Rick sleeping so much, I thought he might sleep the entire trip, but he remained alert and attentive, and he enjoyed the male bonding.

Many of the eager athletes had arrived at the race site ahead of us. The registration and transition area was in a small parking lot, where some of the competitors were already setting up all their equipment. A large man with a baseball cap and a salt-and-pepper beard led us to a parking spot next to the transition area. Dick spoke briefly with the man before we continued over to the registration desk to visit with the race directors, Bill Fiske and his daughter, Wendy.

We picked up our race packets. Dick received bib number 43, one number greater than mine. When I had registered on the

Internet, I told Fiske about the book and that I wanted to start the race in the same wave as the Hoyts. He honored my request.

Heather and her kids arrived ten minutes later. It was the first time Haley and Dakota had been to a race. They entertained Rick while Dick and I had our numbers marked on our arms and legs, then we hauled all the equipment out from the van. I took mine over to the transition area, where I pinned one bib on the frame of the bike and snapped another to my race belt.

"Dick and Rick Hoyt are here," an observant triathlete said to his leggy girlfriend.

It took only a minute to strip down to my faded biking shorts, toss my T-shirt and walking shorts inside my gym bag, and my routine was nearly completed. Nothing to it when you go solo. I pulled the yellow swimming cap from my race packet, grabbed my goggles, and took off to observe the Hoyts.

At that moment, I heard a familiar voice. "Hi, guys," Donna Tudor said.

Donna and Alan, the St. Pete Mad Dogs who first told me about the man who "carried his son in an Ironman," and who were now married to each other, had flown from Florida to Massachusetts to visit friends and take pictures of the race.

"What do you want us to shoot?" Alan asked.

"You guys are the experts," I told him. "Aim them at the Hoyts."

The Tudors were skilled with the cameras and needed no advice from me. Armed with a video camera and a waterproof still camera, they set out to catch Team Hoyt in action.

Several other athletes stopped by to wish the Hoyts a good race. David Laprise, a bearded man in the 55-59 age division, told me he had competed in many races with Dick and Rick, and they had earned his deepest respect. Shaking his head admirably, David said, "Watching them race always chokes me up. I guess they have that effect on everyone."

Dick placed the running chair strategically at the start of the run course, but out of the path of the other runners who would be scrambling from the transition before them. Heather and her kids walked along as Dick pushed Rick to the top of a hill near the lake, to an area convenient for the switch from swim to bike. I pitched in by carrying their inflatable boat, a nine-foot Boston Whaler with a brown stripe down the side. Across the bow were three colorful decals that promoted Team Hoyt's primary sponsors: *Saucony, United Airlines* and *Fleet Bank*. Off to the side of the decals, the words "Hoyt's Boat" had been inscribed with a black marker.

It took a second trip back to the van to get their customized bike, a Counterpoint Opus with a "Recumfortable Stoker Seat." A sturdy, cushioned seat molded to the frame and handlebars provided a safe ride for Rick. The rig weighed nearly eighty pounds, which meant that during the races, Dick pedaled more than 180 pounds of bike and son, which was ten pounds more than his own weight of 170. It took a third trip up and down the hill to get Rick's life preserver, beanbag, and the air pump.

At the edge of the lake, Dick pumped the dinghy full of air while sharing a laugh with David Laprise. The Tudors snapped pictures while Rick, Heather and the kids looked on. When the boat was firm and ready to launch, Dick tossed the green, oversized beanbag inside. Curious and supportive triathletes watched in disbelief when he took Rick from the wheelchair, carried him to the boat, and placed him down on the beanbag. Some stopped to wish them a safe race, but most were reluctant to speak. To others, the Hoyts looked out of place at a triathlon, and they simply did not know how to address Rick. I could relate to all of them.

Dick slipped an orange life vest over Rick's neck, fastened it snugly around his torso, and told him, "The water is great today." They held eye contact momentarily, and Team Hoyt appeared ready for action.

As race time approached, Dick and I went for a short swim. He was right on target about the water temperature. It was perfect. Back on shore, Dick picked up his harness — one he had made from discarded parachute straps — and locked himself in. Using a metal ring attached to the back of the harness, he tethered himself to the rubber dinghy. He dragged the raft into the water when Bill Fiske approached with a bullhorn. Fiske welcomed the 200-plus athletes to his race, gave brief instructions and outlined the course.

"The Hoyts will start two minutes before the first wave," he announced, then paused while the athletes gave a respectful applause. "The second wave goes two minutes after the first." As an afterthought, he said, "The two other people in the water are writing a book about the Hoyts."

Donna edged closer to me with her camera and said, "I'm not a writer, I'm the photographer."

"Well," I said, "show him your equipment."

When Fiske started the race, the athletes cheered. Dick pushed off and went into his unilateral breathing routine, dragging his feet and towing his son behind him. Rob may have had the birthright and the sense of humor to make fun of his father's inefficient swimming technique, but no one could fault Dick's strength and resolve. He knew how to get the job done.

As the Hoyt Express rounded the first orange buoy, the second wave of swimmers charged into the lake. The elite swimmers splashed past the raft at the midpoint buoy. Chopping kicks sprayed shots of water into the boat, but Rick did not care in the least. It was a wonderful day for a race, and he was content to mentally hold the reigns and prod his dad to swim faster.

Dick surged out of the water and strained to pull the boat up on shore. As other swimmers arrived and shot past him, he slipped out of his harness and removed Rick's life vest. In a flash, he gathered Rick in his arms and dashed toward Heather and the bike.

"You want a drink?" he asked Rick, while squeezing him into the bike seat.

A subtle gesture told him "No." Dick wiped the wet sand from his feet with a towel and slipped into his biking shoes. The helmets came next, followed by sunglasses. When Dick tried to pull his T-shirt over his helmet, he realized the mistake. "Shirt first," he scoffed, poking fun at himself. "Shirt first, then the helmet. I should know that by now."

Heather straightened Rick's sunglasses and said, "You look cool, Rick."

Dick drank from a water bottle and said, "Ready, Rick?"

When Rick indicated he was ready, Dick pushed the bike into the street and mounted up. He threw his right leg over first, straddled the bike for balance, locked his left shoe into the pedal and started rolling. Amid the shouts of encouragement, he locked his right foot in the right pedal and took off down the hill, past the bike transition. The Team Hoyt transition took over five minutes, while their competition did it in two minutes or less.

Our loyal camera crew shouted, "Way to go, Team Hoyt!"

They hustled over to their rented car, and drove out on the bike course to shoot more pictures. Bringing up the rear, I hopped on my 20-pound road bike and took off to catch Team Hoyt as quickly as possible.

Rick and Dick were acutely aware that biking was the most hazardous aspect of racing. They had fallen before, once even smashing Rick's helmet, and had reached speeds as great as 45 miles an hour when descending some of the longer hills. Dick had expressed concern over the aging bike, which they had been riding the entire fifteen years of racing. Apparently, some of the sponsors promised a new bike would be ready before June; now June had come, but no bike. Although always an optimist, Dick had good reason to be disappointed. He had committed to Ironman Germany and it was only four weeks away.

"I'm a little worried," he confessed.

Why wouldn't he be worried? With 112 hilly miles of German roadways to cover, he and Rick needed time to prepare on the new bike.

While pumping hard to catch up with them, I crested a hill and zoomed down the opposite side. Several people were standing around a car parked near the bottom. I whizzed past, faster than common sense should have allowed, and at the last moment caught sight of someone lying on the road next to a twisted bike. I touched my brakes, took a second look and knew it wasn't the Hoyts. This was not the first time I had seen an accident on a bike course, so I sped on and never gave it a second thought. My objective was clear – catch up with Team Hoyt.

Dick stood on the pedals and muscled his way up a short hill as I approached from behind. My photography team had already found them, and I could see Donna peering out from the sunroof with a camera flush against her face. Many of the local residents had lined up along the roadside, and they all cheered when the athletes rode by. A car was forced to wait while the bikers passed by, but rather than being impatient or upset, the driver reached out the window and clapped hard when the Hoyts passed by.

"Awesome, man!" he shouted. "You guys are awesome, totally awesome!"

After twenty years of training, of running or riding up hills with either Rick or a 100-pound bag of cement, Dick had developed an impressive set of quads, calves and hamstring muscles. They flexed in unison as he powered his teammate to the top of another hill, and had I been able to hitch a rope, he could have towed me right along with him. As I watched Dick climb that hill, it reminded me of the video of him and Rick conquering a mountain in Kona, Hawaii. I recalled the one where someone asked him how he accomplished such an incredible feat. Dick shrugged humbly and told the interviewer, "I get my strength from Rick. He motivates me."

The spectators gave an appreciative cheer when the Hoyts swept in from the bike ride. In the transition area, Heather held onto the bike while Dick removed Rick's helmet, lifted him out of the bicycle seat, and eased him into the running chair. Using the Velcro bindings attached to the frame, he tied him down, torso first, then his legs. A woman ran up to offer Dick a cup of water. Without hesitation, he said, "Give it to my son."

Dick tossed his helmet on the ground and quickly switched from biking shoes to running shoes. Next came his elbow pads, the ones he wore to absorb the constant pounding and rubbing from the heavy running chair. Finally, he applied a protective layer of sun block to Rick's face.

"I'm ready, Rick, are you?"

He grabbed a quick gulp from a water bottle while Heather helped Rick drink from a paper cup. Dick wiped his son's mouth and off they went, out from the transition area and onto the run course. They shot past other runners. The added weight slowed him on the uphill, but they blew past everyone on the down side. His thick running shoes produced a staccato clomping sound as he raced through the tree-lined streets of a middle-class neighborhood. A woman with a small child in her arms shouted, "Keep going, Ricky!"

The camera crew got a great shot of Dick when, without missing a stride, he reached around with a hand towel and wiped the drool from Rick's face. I strained hard to stay up with them, and although running was the strongest part of my race, they gradually pulled away.

Dick finished the run with a strong kick, but I had narrowed the gap and followed closely enough to hear the roar of the crowd and to watch Rick's arms shoot out to the sides like a glider on landing. It took them only 19 minutes and 32 seconds to run the three-mile course, a feat that was even more meaningful when the posted results revealed they had completed the run faster than anyone over the age of forty. Remarkably, Dick gave the runners an advantage of 20 years or more, pushed his son and a wheelchair, but still outran them. Team Hoyt was off to a great start in the new millennium and in the new age division. Since they had notched a win, Dick wheeled his proud teammate up to accept their matching medals.

Before the ceremony ended, Fiske picked up a microphone and made a disconcerting announcement. "I want to address the rumors about the bike accident before they get any worse." The crowd chatter ceased. "An elderly woman thought she could beat the rider across the road, but she didn't make it. A triathlete crashed into her car. He's at the hospital, but he's doing okay. I repeat, he's okay."

During the ensuing silence, Dick made eye contact with his son. Accidents were not strangers to them. They knew of the dangers in racing. "We've fallen about five times," Dick told me, with a dismissive shrug. "Once, we broke the bike frame 30 miles from home. So far, there's been nothing broke on us." In a more serious and defensive tone, he added, "Rick and I know there is danger. But let's face it, there is danger walking across the street. Risk is a part of the game, a part of life."

Regarding risk, Judy had always agreed with her husband. She was realistic about her goals of equality for the disabled, and had publicly stated the Hoyt attitude. "I always have to remind myself," she said, referring to what a doctor had told them years earlier, "Rick has to make mistakes and take risks like everyone else. That's just the way it works."

Not everyone understood Dick's motivation. In fact, when being interviewed for a television program, the interviewer started many of her questions with, "Some people will say that..." And, "What do you say to people who ask you...?"

The woman questioned Dick in the third person, that way her cynicism regarding his motivation would be construed as coming from someone other than herself.

"She was very negative," Dick said. "She thought I was *exploiting* my son."

Dick placed emphasis on the word "exploiting."

It was a sensitive issue, understandably, and when outsiders questioned his integrity and motivation, it greatly offended him.

Where, he wondered, did these people think Rick should be if not out enjoying life and taking risks with his father? While lying on a comfortable beanbag, he floats freely over some of the most stunning lakes, rivers and oceans the world has to offer. He marvels at the beauty of a rising sun and witnesses the serenity of nature in many forms. He races and flirts with young ladies in swimsuits and tight shorts. Although he might be safer, no one could possibly believe Rick would be happier sitting and watching another mundane television program, or spending the day gazing lifelessly at others who are disabled and protected from "risk."

Rick rides in relative comfort on a bicycle propelled by his father. They communicate. As father and son, they explore the countryside. Rick monitors his teammate's labored breathing as they ascend a long, winding hill. He hears the fans shout "Way to go, Rick!" and "You're the man, Rick!" He sits up tall in his running chair and chases the wind, and hears it whistle past his face. He feels the rush of success when he crosses the finish line, and the sweet thrill of victory is his.

Rick lives life to the fullest. With his father as his guide, he has inhaled the crisp, sparkling air at the top of the Rocky Mountains, navigated the deep-blue Pacific in Kona, Hawaii, and raced along the cobbled streets of Montreal. His name is shouted over and over as he runs marathons from Boston to Long Beach. He is admired in Japan and adored in El Salvador, and he has rubbed elbows with celebrities from around the world. If this is someone's definition of *exploitation*, the meaning of the word has been forever changed by the Hoyts.

One day, long after that discouraging interview, Dick received a letter from that same woman. Although she never used the exact words, she apologized for her attitude the day of the interview. Her views had changed when a member of her family gave birth to a disabled child. She could see Dick from a view less lofty, and had respectfully enclosed a two thousand dollar donation to the Hoyt Fund.

Rick and Dick beating the author in Marlboro.

CHAPTER 3 — THE PERFECT FAMILY

He was a big, strong, beautiful baby. When I saw him lying on his stomach, it looked like he was doing pushups. Instead, he was having spasms.

—Dick Hoyt

Alfred Hoyt became a member of the Hoyt family at a time when transportation meant hitching a horse to a buggy and doctors made house calls to deliver children. In the small town of Merrimac, near the Merrimac River and three miles south of the New Hampshire border, Alfred made his debut. Anne Jaworski greeted the world one year later in the coastal town of Salem. When they ultimately met and united, it lasted a lifetime. Alfred and Anne lived most of their married life on Meade Road in North Reading, a town twelve miles west of Salem and fifteen miles north of downtown Boston. Over a period of 40 years, they raised ten healthy children.

Alfred and Anne named their sixth child Richard Eugene Hoyt, and they introduced him to the family on the first day of June, 1940. Richard inhaled his first breath at Winchester Hospital in Winchester, but he lived the next nineteen years in North Reading. He grew up to be an ambitious young man, and at the age of ten, Dick landed his first job.

"I was paid 75 cents an hour to work for a local farmer," he said. "From that time on, I was never without work."

Dick attended the North Reading school system until the eighth grade. He worked hard and became an outstanding student. Dick played football, basketball, and baseball, and at the end of his eighth year, the school awarded him with a gold medal for

31

being the best all-around student, both academically and athletically.

The North Reading area had no high school at that time, so Dick transferred to a high school in Reading. During his junior year, he dropped out of school and went to work full time as a mason's tender for three dollars an hour.

"After one year of that," Dick reflected, "I returned to the new high school in North Reading because I realized how important it was to finish high school."

Dick worked various jobs throughout high school. He developed a good work ethic, and some days put in as many as twelve hours. For a dollar and a half an hour, he worked farm labor, where he weeded the vegetable crops, put up hay, shoveled manure, or whatever the employer required. At the local filling stations, he greased cars, changed tires, and pumped gasoline for a buck and a quarter an hour.

There were times when Dick did cleanup and handyman jobs at the high school. Sometimes he did "soft" work, like when he was a soda jerk at Price's Drug Store in North Reading. For that, he earned one dollar an hour, and he would bristle at anyone who dared refer to him as "The Jerk." Dick earned respect and he demanded it be given.

Through all the years he performed manual labor, he found that masonry gave him the most pleasure. "That's the work I liked best," he stated positively. "Working with my hands was very rewarding to me."

Dick was well liked and popular among his peers all the way through high school. They elected him to many offices: vice president of the Student Council, president of the Leader's Club, vice-president of the Boy's Club, business manager of the Year Book, and even a Junior Rotarian.

"I always brought home good grades," Dick said honestly. "I got A's and B's, even after I discovered that girls were a lot more fun than studying."

Dick excelled at nearly everything he attempted, and his achievements in athletics were impressive. His teammates elected him captain of the football and baseball teams, and he once landed a tryout for the Yankees as a catcher. He played basketball, hockey, softball, and even bowled whenever he found the time. Dick loved all sports, and as his father later predicted, it was the vehicle by which he would eventually make his mark.

Since Dick was a dutiful, hard working young man, his father gave him plenty of freedom. When he crossed the threshold of puberty, he discovered the "thrill of the chase" — girls. He recalled a time when his responsibilities included the irrigation chores on a local farm.

"I would get the irrigation started," Dick said with a devilish grin. "Then I'd go to Hampton Beach with my friends so we could pick up girls. I'd come back, finish the irrigation, then go hunting with my dad. I never got any sleep."

Judy Lieghton also attended school in North Reading. Although Dick had known her since the seventh grade, the mutual attraction did not begin until later in high school.

"She was a beautiful girl," Dick said. "Bright, outgoing, ambitious."

Like Richard Eugene Hoyt, Judy had many friends, and the other students elected her their class secretary. Since she exhibited plenty of energy and athleticism as a cheerleader, they voted her captain of the squad. There was nothing shy about Judy Lieghton, and when she took a fancy to the quiet, scholarly athlete named Richie Hoyt, she made no pretenses about her objectives.

"I chased Dick for many years," she admitted with a hint of embarrassment. "I chased him through the bushes and got runs in my nylons." Judy was very assertive and confident, and she told an interviewer, "That's the guy I wanted; that's the guy I'm going to have."

Friday night dances were popular to North Reading teens, and, not coincidentally, whenever Dick went, Judy showed up.

"She always tried to dance with me," Dick said. "But I wasn't really interested in her at that time, so I had all my friends come up and cut in on us. Then I wouldn't have to dance with her for very long."

The time eventually came, however, when Dick and Judy started dating. They became high school sweethearts, first love for both of them. In the 1959 Yearbook, they were voted Class Couple, and written next to their photos were the sophomoric words: *Judy and Richie are like coffee and tea. One without the other you will rarely see.*

When Dick turned sixteen, he bought his first car with the money earned from his many jobs. Before the ink dried on the pink slip, he took Judy out for a ride. When Judy asked to drive the new car, Dick pulled over to let her get behind the wheel. Unfortunately, they did not get far before she had an accident and started to panic.

Dick volunteered to take the fall. "Slide over here. We'll switch places."

According to Massachusetts law, it was not the right thing to do, of course, but young Hoyt sure knew how to impress a girl.

"I used to let her do my homework," Dick confessed. "But I still got better grades than she did. I think that upset her a little."

Although a very good student, continuing his education beyond high school did not interest Dick. After graduation in 1959, he went back to his mason's job, but the following year, he entered a six-month Army program and joined the Massachusetts Army National Guard. His first military order sent him to basic training at Fort Dix, New Jersey.

"I got the highest physical-training award," Dick admitted humbly. "And I graduated at the top of my outfit."

Upon completion of basic training, the Guard ordered Dick to a guided-missile school for advanced training at Fort Bliss, Texas. While there, he immediately received an appointment to platoon sergeant. Four months later, they shipped him to the Milton Nike Site, where he worked full-time as a grade NGW-6 on the Nike Ajax System before he transferred back to North

Reading. The military put Dick's talents to good use. They promoted him to NGW-10 and assigned him to additional training in El Paso, Texas, on the Nike Hercules system, then sent him to Lincoln, Massachusetts.

"I was very mobile," Dick said. "Guess I always have been." While Dick traveled and learned advance electronics in military schools, Judy remained in Reading. She graduated from secretarial school and worked for General Electric. When Dick returned as a full-time soldier and a part-time mason, the Class Couple decided to take the next step. On February 18, 1960, after five years of playing cat and mouse with youthful romance, Dick Hoyt leaped headlong into marital bliss with his childhood sweetheart, Judy Lieghton, the beautiful, outgoing cheerleader. They were a happy team, and looked forward to a wonderful future. A more auspicious beginning to any relationship would be hard to find.

As practical people, Dick and Judy understood the wisdom of saving money and buying a house before adding children to the family. Since they had both begun new careers, and the military kept Dick moving around for additional training, they prudently agreed to wait. That plan only worked for about a year, however, and their lives changed in late March, 1961.

"Then something happened," Dick remembered. "Judy got pregnant."

The expectant parents rejoiced from day one. They bought a home on Burditt Road in North Reading for $11,000. Dick could finally do all the handy work he loved so much. In preparation for the blessed event, Judy quit her job and worked at home.

With enthusiasm, Dick reminisced. "I did my own masonry, and I built a fireplace and put in a picture window. We needed a cellar, so I invited my brother and some buddies over. We put jacks under the house and started digging."

Respectfully, Judy said, "When Dick made up his mind to do something, he just did it. Nothing stopped him."

When working on the roof one day, Dick slipped and fell into the uncovered hole they had dug for the cellar entry. Judy wanted to rush him to the hospital, but he refused.

"I'm fine," he insisted. "I'm fine. Nothing broke." Dick had a lot of work to do and would not let a little tumble slow him down. He simply applied a bandage to the injury and climbed back on the roof. Before long, the young man had built his family a lovely home and even the neighbors were impressed.

"That was a very exciting time for us," Judy recalled. "We were very happy. Everything seemed to be perfect."

"I had everything I wanted," Dick added.

Dick and Judy were growing from a couple into a family, and their greatest thrill was right around the corner. "I always loved kids," Judy said. "I had often fantasized about the day I would finally have a child of my very own."

Dick looked at it from a male perspective. "As a man who loved sports, I dreamed that our first child would be a son. He'd be strong and beautiful, and he'd love sports as much as I did."

As the day drew near, everything went perfectly. However, the baby came two weeks late. Somewhere between three and four a.m., the nurse wheeled Judy into the delivery room at Winchester Hospital, the same hospital where Dick was born 21 years earlier.

"It was exhilarating," Judy remembered vividly. "We were confident our first baby would be everything we expected: a happy, healthy baby. A champion of life."

The excitement quickly diminished when their perfect dream took an unexpected jolt of reality. It started when the hyperactive baby moved into a face-delivery position.

"What that meant," Judy explained, "was instead of coming out the way he should, so he could breathe the way babies do when they're born, he was turned the other way."

The doctors had to manipulate the baby in order for him to be born at all, and in the process, the lives of both mother and child were in serious danger. During the birth, the umbilical cord became twisted around the baby's neck and oxygen flow to the brain was briefly blocked. The doctors scrambled, but it took precious moments for them to get the cord untwisted.

The baby fought like the true champion Judy expected, and without the slightest whimper, Richard Eugene Hoyt, Jr. came into this world on the tenth day of January, 1962. However, the lack of oxygen had caused irreparable damage to the motor control area of Ricky's brain. Judy spoke sullenly. "All our joy and elation turned to fear."

"In those days," Dick recalled, "the father was left in the waiting room. I was told only that my wife and son were having trouble, and they would keep me posted. After what seemed like forever, the doctor finally explained to me that some sort of complication had occurred."

"This could mean he will be fine," the doctor told the anxious parents. "He'll be just like all other babies. Or it could mean he might have some kind of disability."

It took seven intense hours before Judy talked with Dick to confirm what the doctor had said about complications.

"The doctor said he will be fine," Judy kept repeating. "He will be fine. He will be fine."

She embraced those words.

It wasn't until after the baby had been transferred to an incubator that the doctors finally allowed Dick to have a look at his newborn son. To Dick, that meant they had resolved all and any problems and everything was going to be fine from then on.

Wistfully, Dick said, "He was a big, strong, beautiful baby. When I saw him lying on his stomach, it looked like he was doing pushups. But instead he was having spasms."

The young parents remained optimistic and Dick went back to work. Judy returned home a few days later, but it was two weeks before the doctors released Ricky. The Hoyts had many questions, but they weren't getting answers from anyone at the hospital. The doctors always claimed to be busy, and they avoided any contact with the Hoyts.

"We knew something had gone wrong," Dick said. "We just didn't know what it was."

Judy added, "Ricky was not developing. He wasn't doing any of the things the other babies were doing."

The Hoyt and Lieghton families were devastated. They had a difficult time accepting what they were told about the situation. After giving birth to ten normal, healthy children, Anne Hoyt simply could not understand how this had happened or why the doctors were so evasive. She made many phone calls and demanded to know what was wrong. Everyone wanted to know what went wrong. Through all their disconsolation, Dick and Judy tried to maintain a positive attitude, and they refused to believe their son was abnormal.

"Our baby is going to wake up and he will be okay," Judy insisted, repeating her faith. "He will be just like all the other babies. Our dream is not going to change. Our dream is going to stay just the way we want it to be."

Her faith did dim at times, though. As their first son, Dick had planned to name him Richard Hoyt, Jr., but Judy thought he might want to reconsider.

"Do you still want to?" Judy asked him solemnly.

Without hesitation, Dick replied, "You bet your life I do."

Time marched on without mercy, and contrary to their dreams, Ricky's condition did not improve. Their hopes eroded when Rick simply "did not do the things normal babies do."

Judy confessed that she felt cheated. "I continued to deny the obvious fact that my baby was different from all the other babies born that same day," she admitted. "I prayed for my baby to die. I wanted God, that external force, to take his life so I would not have to deal with being the mother of a child with a handicap."

Her painful confession continued.

"I hated Dick, and I hated all the mothers in the hospital and all my friends who were mothers of babies that were not handicapped. My feelings kept seesawing from hate to denial for months after we brought Rick home from the hospital. He

38

couldn't suck and he couldn't cry, he couldn't even open his little clenched fists. He was tight, tight, tight. We had to force him to eat every two hours just to keep him alive. We would wake him up by pinching the bottom of his feet."

Dick and Judy received emotional support from their parents and families, but even their friends and neighbors thought the Hoyts were fooling themselves, that they were wasting time, energy and emotion on a retarded child.

"I often reminded myself of something my Grandad had told me," Judy said quietly. "He told me many times, 'Nothing in life that is worthwhile is easy.' Nothing."

All the words of wisdom and consolation were of little help. Reality of their helpless situation seeped through and reared its unforgiving head.

"I started doing moonlighting," Dick said. "I worked extra hours to help defray the rising medical bills."

On her good days, Judy went to bed at night with the belief that when dawn arrived her infant son would be okay, that he would be able to eat and cry and lift his head. On the bad days, neighbors stopped by her house with their own children, and they invited Judy to go out for walks with them. Instead, she cringed, and made up excuses: she had to wash the curtains, clean the oven, do the laundry, scrub the floors, do the dishes, or anything she could think of.

"That way I didn't have to look at their babies," she said. "I had the cleanest house in Massachusetts at the time."

Judy took Ricky for walks after the other mothers had gone home, that way no one could say she didn't walk with her baby. In her own way, she gradually accepted the fact that her son was different. "The anger and hate are what finally made me admit it to myself," Judy said. "It was that emotion, I think, that forced me to get on with life and learn how to accept my own son. I decided I would be the best Mom that I could possibly be."

Seven months after Ricky's birth, Dick and Judy sat together, looked each other directly in the eyes, and for the first time openly admitted that their baby was different, and that they needed to do something about it, if at all possible. "We made an appointment with a pediatrician in Medford," Judy said, still clinging to hope. "One who specialized in birth trauma."

With the weight of the world on their shoulders, they braced themselves. They feared the worst and hoped for the best; their determination kept them focused and strong.

With their precious eight-month-old child nestled in their protective arms, Dick and Judy headed to Medford, seeking help from a higher authority. In their minds, the journey would lead them to the healing power of God, but in their hearts, they knew the person they would see was only a pediatric specialist. A human being. A mere mortal, not a miracle worker.

Dick's parents, Anne and Alfred Hoyt.

The Class Couple united.

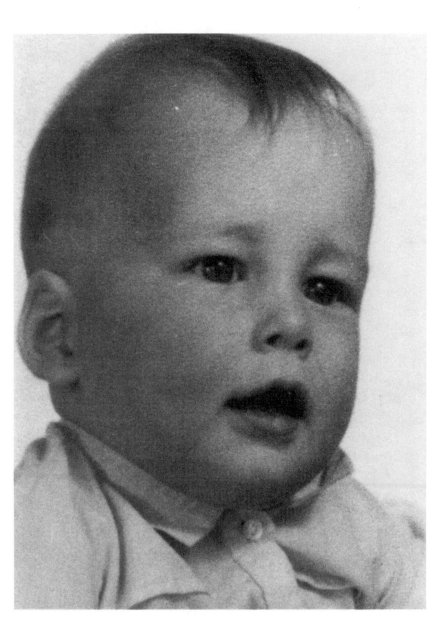

Richard Eugene Hoyt, Jr.

CHAPTER 4 — THE "VEGETABLE"

When Rick was eight months old, we took him to a specialist who said our son was a vegetable and would bring us nothing but grief. He told us our son was a spastic quadriplegic who would never speak, that we should put him in an institution and forget about him.

—Judy Hoyt

Dick Hoyt was a low-key, unassuming man with a proclivity for understatement, even at times when it was completely unexpected. And now, as he forged the watershed that would alter his life in ways he could never imagine, that did not change.

"The doctors ran all kinds of tests," Dick said, and shook his head in despair. "The results weren't good."

In reality, the results of the extensive medical tests and evaluation were *devastating*. The doctor sat them down and said the following words: "Your son has cerebral palsy." Those, and the numbing words that ensued, ripped out the hearts of North Reading's perfect couple. This medical expert, a mere mortal, informed them that their beautiful baby boy was a "vegetable."

"Put him in an institution and forget him," the doctor recommended stoically. "Go home and have other children." With a nod of his head, the highly educated man then reassuringly told them, "The chances of this happening again are about one in a million."

The doctor assumed that his statistical comment would be helpful during their recovery and survival. It wasn't. At that moment, there would be no consolation.

43

"We were horrified," Judy said. "We felt as if we had been put in the bottom of a black hole and someone had just put a cover over our dreams and snuffed them out."

The young parents had never before heard the words *cerebral palsy*. In fact, they didn't recall ever knowing anyone confined to a wheelchair. The middle-aged doctor went on to explain to them what having cerebral palsy meant, the facts about brain damage, about motor and neural skills. He told them everything. Dick and Judy came away from that meeting totally enlightened about a medical condition they wish they had never heard of.

After months of trying to be positive, holding onto hope, building their courage, they had been slammed against the wall. They had to start all over. But how, they wonderd. "We cried all the way home from Medford," Judy said. "When we got home, I didn't even go out to take the clothes off the line because I didn't want to talk to any of the neighbors. I did not want to say to anybody, 'Our son is different from other babies, his life is going to be different.'"

In stark contrast, however, their son *was* different. He could not cry, roll over, suck, or even open his tiny hands.

"His eyes were so bright," Judy said. "You could tell there was intelligence inside, but he wasn't doing anything physically."

The very thought of placing the child they loved inside an institution chilled them to the bone. The Hoyts knew they had to find another option, to go elsewhere for advice. They reached out to a Godly man, their minister, the wise and trusted man who united them in marriage. In their greatest time of need, they gave him a call.

"We want you to come over here because we're stuck," Judy told the minister. "We are really, really stuck. How can we go on? How can we continue?"

Overwhelmed by the family's passionate plea, the minister rushed to their aid, to see if he could help put it all in perspective for them.

"He gave us excellent advice," Judy said. "Excellent."

After listening to their story, after seeing their son lying in silence, motionless in his crib, the minister looked into Judy's sad, pleading eyes. In a firm voice, he said, "You have but two choices. You can put your son away and forget about him."

The medical specialist had already suggested that repugnant option, which is why the Hoyts had contacted him, a minister.

Dick asked, "What is the second option?"

The minister solemnly continued. "You can take it one day at a time. You can love and nurture and care for him, and give him the same experiences as any other baby. You can deal with his progress day by day."

The second option was clearly the one they would take, but regarding the details of how to go about it, they didn't have a clue. And since the minister offered no help with that, they would have to find a way themselves.

With pride, love, and determination, Judy spoke for the entire Hoyt family when she proclaimed, "There is no way we will ever put our son away. We love him. He is ours. We will work with him and bring him to the place where he can reach his greatest potential." In tears, she concluded, "We will never, never put him away simply because he is *different*."

Although it may have seemed like the only option, the young couple knew it would change their lives profoundly. Dick and Judy made the supreme commitment of love to their disabled son. They decided to raise him, and to treat him the same as they would any other child.

"From that point on," Judy said, "I became an advocate of people with disabilities. I became a cheerleader for them and for my son. I became society's conscience within communities that do not allow disabled people in."

The Hoyts never had doubts about their son being bright. At a very early age, Ricky knew when his father was due home from work, and he gazed out the window while he waited. When Dick came through the front door, a huge smile appeared. Whenever he wanted a drink, he stared at the refrigerator to let them know he was thirsty. Things that excited any normal child also excited Ricky, and he always laughed when he heard something humorous. He may have been born physically disabled, severely disabled, and he could not talk, but his mind worked fine, regardless what the so-called experts told his family.

Dick and Judy believed unequivocally that Ricky had normal intelligence, but convincing the rest of society wouldn't be easy. On the other hand, Judy had not forgotten what her sage Grandad told her about things worthwhile: They are never, never easy.

With guidance from the compassionate, young minister, the momentous decision had been made. They embarked on a family journey that destiny would fill with pain and heartache at times, down roads that would often be bumpy, and sometimes permanently blocked. Obstacles that could never be removed. But there would also be rewards. Love always has its rewards. Their journey began in earnest, as a family, and there was no looking back.

* * *

The United Cerebral Palsy organization could provide little help at that time, early in the sixties. Speech therapy offered no value to Rick, either, and there were strict limitations on therapy for the physically and mentally handicapped. In-home isolation and discrimination based on an individual's type of disability certainly was not what the Hoyts had in mind. They wanted Rick mainstreamed into the community, not isolated from it. For their son to live his life like everyone else, he had to be included.

Visits to Children's Hospital in Boston paid great dividends for the Hoyts. They took Rick every week, and eventually had the good fortune to make contact with Doctor Fitzgerald, a psychologist who was a polio victim and used a wheelchair to move about. According to Dick, the doctor practiced family therapy long before it became popular, but the fact that he was "totally honest" is what made him successful.

Doctor Fitzgerald listened intently to the Hoyts, and valued what they had to say. He shared his feelings and ideas, and suggested ways to go about normalizing their relationship with Rick. Fitzgerald encouraged them to experience "risks" in ways they had not thought about, and since Rick could not go to the environment, they should bring it to him. The doctor told them to take him sledding, to roll him down the grassy hill, to take him swimming and throw him in the pool, to take him boating and fishing. In other words, *treat him like any other child.*

"Dick worked as many as three jobs to keep up with the medical bills," Judy said. "I spent my time with Ricky so he could learn and develop and experience the things that our friends' babies were experiencing."

To achieve maximum success required a team effort. The Hoyts got help wherever they could find it. It took time, but eventually even the skeptical neighbors offered support. The neighborhood children accepted Rick and included him in all the backyard games right along with them. Doctor Fitzgerald also networked Dick and Judy into a support system with other parents of kids with cerebral palsy, where they could all express their views and share individual and community success stories.

The doctor offered two other suggestions that had a profound impact on their lives. He looked them squarely in the eyes and issued a challenge. "If you truly believe your kid is bright, then you must figure out a way to teach him the alphabet."

"So I did," Judy stated pointedly. "I cut out sandpaper letters and had Rick feel them. I took his finger and ran it around the letter, and showed them to him every day. We posted signs on every object in the house. On the window, refrigerator, the door."

To teach Rick the meaning of the word "hard," Judy ran his fingers over a piece of wood. For the word "soft," she used fur. The Hoyts received great rewards for all their difficult and tedious work. In a surprisingly short time, Rick did, in fact, learn the alphabet.

Proudly, Dick said, "Rick showed his understanding of each letter through his bright eyes, and he would indicate *yes* and *no* by a slight head movement."

The Hoyts gathered empirical proof to offer the cynics, those obstinate naysayers who might try to discredit them in their upcoming battles for inclusion. They could prove their son had normal intelligence, perhaps even above normal. The second challenge offered by the good doctor went straight to the heart of one of their greatest fears, a fear they found difficult to talk about with anyone but family. Understandably, they had great concern over the possible consequence of having another child.

"The doctor helped us overcome that fear," Dick said. "He told us that siblings would make us a healthy, balanced family that would not dote on the severely disabled child."

It sounded good in theory, so they set aside their trepidation and got busy with the proper procedures to conceive another child. It did not take very long before Judy got pregnant a second time. They worried about the new baby, of course, but on April 17, 1964, in the same hospital where his father and brother first appeared, Robert Stanley Hoyt popped into this world and demanded that everyone in Massachusetts pay attention; he screamed to the top of his tiny lungs. The Hoyts had another beautiful boy, a healthy, hungry, and vocal bundle of motion and energy. His muscles worked perfectly. He had a strong grip, and as Judy quickly learned, he could suck hard. Robbie was all boy, a big boy, and Ricky Hoyt now had a baby brother. Being the older brother, he also had the accompanying responsibility. After all, someone would have to teach the noisy little rascal how to control those sirens he had for lungs.

Dick and Judy had two handsome, young sons, but with very different requirements. Robbie needed a stroller; Ricky needed a wheelchair. Accepting that fact required another major step in Judy's personal development. Friends and strangers could see the contrast between a hyperactive child in a stroller and an ever-passive child in a wheelchair. There were questions and curious glances everywhere she went, but Judy never faltered. She always took the challenge head on.

"Yes, this is my child," she told them. "My child is different. He lives in a wheelchair."

Since feeding Ricky was such an awkward and messy process, many unprepared observers were repulsed by what they saw. In restaurants, people simply got up and walked out. Judy remembered one time when the family dined at a local restaurant, where a young boy boldly marched up to their table and said, point blank, "He makes me sick."

Dick and Judy remained calm. She smiled at the boy and told him the first thing that came to her mind. "Yes, but be nice to him. His parents recently died."

Hurdles such as that were easily cleared by the Hoyts.

The day came when Robbie crawled the floors and pounded the walls. He kept growing, learning and exploring. That was expected and desired, certainly, but the Hoyts did not want Ricky left behind. Their goals had not changed. They wanted him to be talked to and treated like his brother, just like any other child, and they worked diligently to make it happen.

"Rick understood everything said to him," Judy asserted. "We knew he could do all the work, he just did it in a different way." She went on to say, "We could use communication devices, but other people had to be his arms and legs."

"The challenge for us," Rob explained, "was how can we make it work for Rick?"

Since the love and desire were a given, the answers always seemed to follow. Dick constructed a vehicle he called the *Creeper*, which consisted of a metal basket mounted on wheels. He added a pillow. When placed on the pillow in the prone position, Ricky provided his own propulsion. He required the arms and legs of a caring adult to pick him up and mount him on the tot-transporter, but once Rick mastered the concept, he found himself scooting around with Robbie in no time. Another small hurdle cleared.

Next came an innovation called the *Earth Ball*. It was nothing more than a large rubber ball, but it served a dual

49

function. When someone placed Rick on top of the ball, it stretched out his tight body and massaged him with the bouncing motion and vibrations. In addition to the beneficial therapy it provided, he had fun. He had a great toy. He played on it with his brother, and he didn't have far to fall. The game had minimum "risk," but produced maximum reward. It was a small fall, but a big laugh, and Rick loved it.

While the Hoyt boys were growing, learning and consuming, Dick made equally rapid progress in the military. His dedication and ambition did not go unnoticed. He caught the attention of Captain O'Neal, an officer who realized that young Hoyt had all the qualities necessary to become a fine officer. While working on the Nike Hercules system in Lincoln, O'Neal encouraged him to apply for OCS, Officer Candidate School. Dick filed the proper paperwork and wrote a letter of application, which included a chronological synopsis of his personal history. Portions of that letter covered what meant the most to Dick. His family.

"...Richard has cerebral palsy. At 3 ½ years old, he cannot do anything for himself and it is doubtful he will ever walk. He has normal intelligence, understands everything, and tries hard. Richard is a wonderful child and I derive a great deal of pleasure from him. My wife and I are trying to start a cerebral palsy parents association in the Middlesex County. A group like this would help parents with their questions and possibly get public schools interested in starting classes for these children. We now have another son, Robert Stanley. He is 13 months old and very normal. I love him very much also. My wife and I bowl on a Sunday night couple's league. Golf, fishing, hunting and softball are my hobbies..."

Dick closed the letter by stating his primary objective: "I want to attend Officers Candidate School because I believe that an education is never wasted, and I want to take advantage of every opportunity to advance myself."

The approval committee agreed with Captain O'Neal, and Dick subsequently received the necessary training to become an officer. In a few short years, his superiors promoted the youthful Lieutenant all the way to Major. The promotions were a reward in themselves, but at this point in his life, the increase in pay was critical, because once again, he whisked his wife back to the hospital in Winchester. On October 17, 1967, Judy Hoyt gave birth to their third son, Russell Alfred Hoyt. Like his brother three years earlier, Russell entered the world with gusto, leaving no doubt about having a voice. Son number three was born healthy and normal, with a fine set of vocal cords.

With the arrival of a third child, responsibilities mounted at home. Dick worked full time in the military, part time as a mason, and additional household chores now required his attention. He had no time left for those hobbies he listed on his OCS application. What spare time he had, became family time.

"Wherever I went with the other boys, I would take Rick along." He recalled a time when Rick went with him on a moonlighting job. "One time, I even took him and his chair up on the roof and showed him how to build a chimney."

Everything on the home front progressed quite well for the Hoyt family, but away from home, they encountered new challenges. By the age of six, Rick had successfully attended kindergarten at a church school. So now, academically and socially, he could attend first grade along with his peers in the public school. Unfortunately, that was not to happen.

Angrily, Judy said, "Much to my furies, our local school refused to allow Rick entrance because he could not walk or talk or feed himself."

The school had created yet another challenge for the Hoyt family. Judy prepared her team for battle, and they began the process of trying to get Rick enrolled in the public school system in North Reading. Rick and Judy attended a hearing by the school committee, but they were soundly rejected. "I felt like they laughed me out of the room," Judy said. "I can still remember going into that room and feeling like I was standing on top of the table. I was screaming and begging and saying 'My kid is bright, take him in!'"

Peter Henderson of *Our Times* offered an insightful observation in that very regard. "Sadly," he said, "physical limitations are often misinterpreted as mental ones."

It infuriated Judy when the children Rick had grown up with attended the community school, but her son could not go because he was different. She insisted that the committees work with her and discover for themselves that Rick was bright, but she never had an opportunity to prove it. They saw a child in a wheelchair and a distressed mother who could not accept reality, or she did not have the objectivity to understand their dilemma. To Judy, it had nothing to do with objectivity, but everything to do with the fact that they excluded her son.

Judy lost that first round, but it was a temporary setback that only added fuel to the flame already burning inside her. The invisible battle lines had been drawn, and Judy was ready, willing and able to engage in war, one confrontation at a time. In the meantime, Rick would have to obtain his education, segregated, right along with other disabled children.

"It was an inferior education," Judy stated emphatically. "It was more like a sitter service than an education. It was not mainstreaming, and it was *not* inclusion."

CHAPTER 5 — THE HOPE MACHINE

All the engineers were at our house that night, and everybody was betting whether the first words Rick is ever going to say is 'Hi Mom' or 'Hi Dad.' Some of them thought it might be 'I love you' or even 'Thank you.' But we were all wrong. Rick had a mind of his own.

—Dick Hoyt

The public school system denied Rick's entry into kindergarten, but they allotted him a home-study program of four hours per week. That responsibility fell on Judy's shoulders, and trying to raise three small boys, including one with a severe disability, proved a difficult assignment. She had bad days, primarily from the frustration and challenges with Rick. The knowledge that he would never be able to speak, to feed or wash himself, or to use the toilet, gradually wore her down. Sometimes the reminders were very subtle, but there were many.

"There were times," she confessed, "that I said, 'I just can't take this child any longer!' And some days, I was so angry that I went into a closet and screamed and cried."

But Judy always got right back into the game. It helped when she could see progress with Ricky. His sense of humor was a Godsend, and whenever she said something funny, he burst into laughter. It warmed her heart every time they made that intimate connection, and when she looked into his eyes, she knew what to do. His eyes always brought her back.

"They were so bright," she repeated with passion. "When you look at a person with intellect, the eyes respond, even if they're locked inside a body."

Rick attended private kindergarten with other children in the neighborhood. He also made regular visits to the United Cerebral Palsy training facility in Lawrence, Massachusetts, where Fay Kimball, an occupational therapist, recognized the intelligence behind those "bright" eyes Judy liked to brag about. The compassionate woman devoted her time to learn Rick's sandpaper alphabet, which enabled her to understand his words and phrases. The relationship that followed proved to be a crucial turning point in Rick's life. His abilities left a positive impression on the woman, one she would not forget.

Rick related well with his younger brothers, and they reciprocated by including him in all their sports and activities. As Rob and Russ grew older, the Hoyts engaged in recreation the same as any other normal, happy family. In adhering to Doctor Fitzgerald's advice regarding taking risk and doing what normal families would do, they took up camping.

"We would take off for New Hampshire," Judy said. "When we arrived at the campsite, Dick would set up the tent and disappear without saying a word. When we heard the crash of a tree hitting the ground, I would look at the kids and say, 'That's got to be your dad, getting us firewood for the weekend.' Sure enough, out of the woods he would come, looking like Paul Bunyan, with his arms chock full of wood."

"We went mountain climbing at Mount Managnock," Rob added. "Everyone was concerned about how we would get Rick up the mountain, but not Dad. He said, 'Don't worry, I'll take care of it. It's only a mountain.'"

Judy said, "Dick just picked him up in a fireman's carry and up we went, with Russ, Rob and I trailing behind with the food."

Rob chuckled. "People stopped to look at us, and we overheard them whispering that they thought we were taking a dead child up the mountain for some sort of sacrifice."

While draped safely around his father's neck, Rick climbed to the top of many mountains, where he stopped to marvel at glorious views of the Great Northeast.

Doctor Fitzgerald also suggested that the Hoyts take Rick swimming, so whenever the brothers went to a pool, they took Rick along. They simply took him out of the wheelchair and tossed him into the water. While holding his breath, he slowly began sinking, but he trusted his brothers to rescue him, and they always did. No one could have known it at the time, but this training technique would be very valuable later in Rick's life.

Tense moments occurred on occasions when the Hoyts swam in public pools. The other swimmers were dumfounded when they saw two young boys toss a quadriplegic child into the water, then stand by and watch him sink. Anyone who witnessed the event for the first time thought they were trying to drown the poor disabled boy.

"We certainly drew attention," Rob recalled.

Rick felt less disabled in the water because it required minimal use of his legs. "After all," he would one day write on his computer, "Dad doesn't use his legs when he swims."

Swimming provided a unique source of exercise for Rick. He could wriggle around well enough that he actually felt like an athlete. Rob couldn't resist tossing a barb at his good-natured older brother. "With all that training, Rick perfected the art of *sinking.*"

The Hoyts refused to let Rick's disability preclude him from participation in things they did as a family. Russ said, "Some families might have said, 'We'll have to find somebody to watch Rick so we can do this, but that was never how we did it. If we went, Rick went.'"

Rick's first opportunity to display his swimming technique came on a day when Dick and Judy took him fishing. "We secured the hook and bait to one end of a string," Dick explained. "Then we tied the other end around Rick's finger. Whenever he caught anything, I would help him pull in the fish."

Judy wasn't a great fan of fishing, but she enjoyed going along with the guys, packing the lunch and taking a ride on the lake. She took a nap if she got bored. One day, she dozed off and took a tumble from her resting place. It caused the boat to capsize and Rick went under water. He didn't get far. "We all panicked for a moment," Dick said, "but I grabbed him and got him on the boat. It was pretty funny."

Judy disagreed. "It was *not* pretty, and it was *not* funny."

Although it may have been frightening at the time, the experience strengthened Rick's confidence in his father and lessened his fear of the water.

When the Hoyts took up cross-country skiing, Dick provided the arms and legs. He wrapped Rick in a sleeping bag, tied him to a plastic sled, harnessed himself to the sled and off they went. Once, when the sled got away from them on a hill, it went between Dick's legs and knocked him flat on top of Rick. Dick thought he had hurt him, but when the sled came to a stop, Rick only laughed. Again, Doctor Fitzgerald deserved kudos.

Since Rick loved the Boston Bruins, the letter he received from Bobby Orr was one of his most prized possessions, which explained why he had it hanging so near the television in his apartment. "Rick joined a street hockey league for the disabled," Judy recalled. "He absolutely got into it. He was the goalie, with the stick, and he was very competitive."

Hockey was one of Dick's passions as well. He played hockey with all three of his sons. Field hockey, ice hockey, lawn hockey, street hockey, or any other form of hockey, it really did not matter to the Hoyt gang. Give them a stick and a puck, and watch out, the game was on.

"We used a plastic puck," explained Dick. "Rick would be in his wheelchair, and we'd tie the stick to him. One of us would push him. He went nuts when he blocked a shot."

Of all the sports Rick played as a youngster, he recalled one game of soccer better than any single event because he still had the reminder. While at camp, his PCA got so excited over a goal, Rick slipped from her grasp and went face first into the ground. He landed hard, and the results can be seen every time he smiles because the impact knocked out his two front teeth.

"The replacements were made from silver," Dick said. "Everyone called him tinsel tooth."

Rick took another tumble, face first again, but this time he fell from the van and onto solid pavement. The tinsel teeth were knocked out the same as the originals, only they were never replaced after the second accident. Rick displays the gap like a badge of honor, but in his easy going style, he said, "I wish they were knocked out playing hockey. Nobody falls out of a van."

In 1970, at age eight, Rick still communicated primarily by smiling and nodding in response to questions. Understanding his thoughts required unimaginable patience, and even his family had to guess what he wanted to say. Without some kind of aid, it was the best they could do.

During Rick's visits to the Cerebral Palsy Training Center in Lawrence, he met some engineers from Tufts University. Fay Kimball, the same woman Rick had impressed in the past, had invited them for a visit. She had seen the engineers working with older disabled people, and she wondered if they might be able to help a young kid like Rick. She believed that a more highly advanced method of communication would allow him to become more independent.

One of the young graduate students asked Judy the same question the Hoyts had heard from the public school officials: "How do you know your son is bright?"

"Tell him a joke," came the prompt response.

Doctor William Crochetiere – a biomedical engineer from the Department of Engineering Design at Tufts – stepped forward. He paused thoughtfully, kneeled down, and shared the best joke he could think of. Since he knew the workings of a young boy's mind, he told Ricky a joke about little girls.

Judy remembered the moment fondly. "Rick absolutely cracked up," she said. "They bonded immediately. He knew Rick was bright."

The doctor returned to the lab with his crew of engineers. He told his class of five students, including Rick Foulds, that he wanted them to get involved with the project, to help the Hoyt boy speak. The doctor revealed a sense of humor of his own when he said, "A sense of humor is a terrible thing to waste."

His students accepted the challenge. They put their heads together, put pens to paper and fingers to keyboards. Rick Foulds immersed himself totally and emotionally into the effort. He was determined to develop a non-speech communication device that would help Rick and others just like him. Over the next six-week period, in addition to their regular schedule and course load, the team members devoted hundreds of hours to the challenging project.

Hope soared, and eventually the youthful engineers emerged from the lab, ready to present the results of their labor. They designed a portable unit that consisted of a display monitor with rows of letters, numbers, and symbols. In a predetermined sequence, lights flashed slowly along the panel and paused briefly on each row of alphanumeric characters. They referred to it as *scanning*. With the click of a switch, the operator could pick out a row of letters. When the lights began to sequence once again, another click selected the actual letter he chose to display. The letters then lit up on the display panel, where Rick could check for mistakes. Using that same method, he could also correct the errors and continue until all the letters had been selected and presented on a *moving sign* type of display.

Rick activated the switch by pressing his head against a narrow metal bar attached to the right side of his wheelchair. He could create complete sentences even though it took several minutes to spell each word. One of his brothers said, jokingly, "It brought new meaning to 'using your head.'"

The engineers named it the *Tufts Interactive Communicator,* or, for short, *TIC.* But, for clear and obvious reasons, the Hoyt family referred to it as *The Hope Machine.*

They had limited success initially, but the equipment was too bulky, too fragile, and far too slow. It required two briefcases to transport it. The team decided to redesign it, to create a smaller,

58

more reliable version, and they also thought a knee-activated switch would make it faster and give Rick more control. Back to the drawing board they went.

"But the newer version cost money," Judy said.

Fortunately, the prototype model cost the Hoyts nothing. The engineering students did not charge for their labor, but they had to scrounge for everything they needed. Bill Lauffer, editor of *Design News,* said they cannibalized surplus equipment to provide most of the parts, and the Burroughs Corporation donated the display unit. But they were not so fortunate with the newer version, which meant they had to raise money.

Once again, good leadership and a community effort would be required. Members of the TIC team helped Rick demonstrate the communicator before a number of church and civic groups, which generated donations. Judy held bake sales and organized a dinner dance. When the contributions reached $5,000, Foulds and his crew returned to work.

"The second version was a wire-wrapped unit," said Foulds. "It had much better PC boards, and it weighed a lot less than its predecessor. The knee-activated switch cut Ricky's response time nearly in half."

For more than a year, Ricky worked with the device on a daily basis, and the likelihood of greater success improved rapidly. A third version of the TIC allowed him to produce hard-copy output, and it eventually incorporated a synthesizer that would give him a voice.

Rick celebrated birthday number twelve the same year his TIC team reached their goal. Once the Tufts engineers had everything working properly in the lab, they packed up the equipment and called for a meeting at the Hoyts' home. Rick's therapists, neighbors and friends showed up to share in the excitement of his conversational debut.

Rick Foulds orchestrated the demonstration. He mounted the latest version of The Hope Machine on a table and prepared it for operation. Dick rolled the wheelchair into position. Foulds secured the *mouse* where Rick could reach it with his knee and announced that all systems were ready to roll. "Let's give her some juice," he said confidently.

Foulds flipped a switch and the machine came to life. All heads turned toward Rick, and his eyes lit up more brightly than the lights on the display panel. Mom, Dad and brothers squeezed closer and peered over his shoulders. With the exception of a humming sound made by the TIC machine, the room went silent.

With a smile for encouragement, Foulds said, "Okay, Rick, you're up. Talk to us."

During the ensuing excitement, everyone made their jokes and called out their wagers. Rick heard them, but he smiled and concentrated on the task at hand.

"His first words will be 'Hi, Mom,'" Judy said confidently.

Dick corrected her. "No, no. It'll be 'Hi, Dad.'"

One of the therapists also offered an opinion. "My money is on 'Thank you.'"

Someone said, "I think he will say 'I love you.'"

The brothers didn't agree with any of them.

Robbie guessed, "It'll be 'How's it going, Robbie?'"

Russ echoed, "It'll be 'How's it going, Russell?'"

The speculation and chatter did not faze Rick. He concentrated on the lights that flashed along in sequence, row by row. Suddenly, he activated the electronic mouse with a slight movement of his knee. The machine made a sound: *Click!*

Everyone hushed. Rick had paused the machine on a row of letters that contained the one he wanted. The scanning resumed, but this time it sequenced horizontally, and it momentarily stopped on each letter in the row. As each letter highlighted in sequence, the Tufts Interactive Communicator softly repeated its own name: *Tic. Tic. Tic. Tic.*

Then another *Click!*

With another subtle movement, Rick had kneed the mouse again, and the first letter was selected and displayed.

"It's a *G*," Robbie whispered.

A "*G*?" someone asked.

"Uh-huh, a *G*."

Rick kept his eyes glued on the monitor, but he kept smiling. *Tic. Tic. Tic. Click!* He selected another row. A brief pause, then, *Tic. Tic. Click!*

The second letter appeared.

"It's an *O*."

Someone offered a guess: "Go?"

Then a second guess. "God?"

Tic. Tic.

"Good? Gone?"

Tic. Tic. Click!

The tension mounted.

Tic. Tic. Tic. Tic. Click!

A space displayed next.

Someone said, "It's a space."

Then more guesses. "Go away? Go home?"

Rick laughed out loud. He called all the shots at this game, and he milked it for everything he could. The machine kept ticking. A couple more clicks and another letter displayed.

Another voice rang out, "It's a *B*!"

"*G-O-B*? Gob?"

"No, there's a space."

"Go back?"

"Go back home?" Robbie asked.

"We are home," answered Russell.

The resulting laughter broke the tension, but only until the ticking resumed. Rick repeated the routine until someone said, "*G-O-B-R-U*?"

Judy squinted curiously at the machine. "Gobra?"

Robbie again provided comic relief. "Remember, Mom, he doesn't spell very good."

Rick grinned and kept right on ticking. He had them right where he wanted. He had control of the situation for once, and he loved it.

Tic. Tic. Click!

61

The flashing lights mesmerized everyone as they watched the selected letters magically appear before their eyes. They were Rick's words, his first words, for everyone to see.

With all the excitement over a machine, an electronic device that would change their lives, even Dick had forgotten Rick's passion for sports, and that hockey was his favorite. At that particular time, the Boston Bruins and Bobby Orr were going for the Stanley Cup. But Rick had not forgotten.

Tic. Tic. Click!

Tic. Click!

"Go Brui?"

Tic. Tic. Tic. Click!

"Go Bruin--"

"Go Bruins!" Dick exclaimed.

Ricky's body tightened, nearly lifting himself out from the chair. His arms shot skyward in the victor's pose. He wailed with delight. The young man could hardly contain himself, and why should he even try? His bright eyes flashed as they darted about the room to witness the sheer delight and jubilation on the faces of the people he held most dear.

Before the exhilaration subsided, Rob moved closer to have another look at the panel. "Go Bruins? That's it, Rick?"

Rick's wry wit had shone through. On this occasion, however, no one had to guess what he was thinking. Hugs and kisses came from all sides. Tears flowed. Ricky Hoyt had spoken his first words. Only two words, but they were long overdue. With them, another hurdle had fallen, but this time it was not a small one.

Go Bruins.

With those two words, Rick demonstrated his intense interest, understanding, and love of sports. Not only did he watch and listen, but now he could also share his opinions. For Judy, it held a more profound meaning. Now she had proof of what she had been saying all along, that Rick's eyes were not deceiving her. Not only did he have a wicked sense of humor, but he was also the bright child that his family had always proclaimed him to be. Judy could no longer be accused of being a distressed and angry mother who didn't have "objectivity."

Her war was not over yet, not by a long shot. But the TIC machine certainly helped her score a victory. This was not an insignificant or Pyrrhic victory, either, but a momentous win. It gave her ammunition for battles that loomed in the future. Rick and the Tufts team had armed her with a new weapon, and that mechanical baby was loaded.

For the dedicated team of engineers, it had yet another meaning. Their success on the TIC project would lead to the establishment of the Biomedical Engineering Center at the Tufts-New England Medical Center in Boston. And there, under the auspices of its newly named Director, Rick Foulds, many other projects could be funded to help the handicapped in a variety of ways, with innovations that would have far greater reach than the TIC machine itself.

Champagne flowed long into the night. Laughter, music and regalement emanated from the little house in North Reading. The celebration lasted far into the darkness, but the repercussions from that moment would have impact for a lifetime.

Ricky smiling at his TIC machine.

CHAPTER 6 — BROTHERS

It literally broke my heart to take Ricky to the bus stop with the other children, then to see the sadness in his eyes when the school bus drove away with all his friends, but he was left alone in his wheelchair.

—Judy Hoyt

Judy wasted no time gathering evidence and returning to confront those who had concluded she was merely an angry woman who refused to accept reality. She proudly restated her case, that Rick had normal intelligence, only now she had proof.

"Look!" she demanded of a committee member. "The words came from him, not me!"

"Yes, Mrs. Hoyt," said another committee member. "We can see that. Please calm down."

"This *is* calm," Judy answered. "I want to know you're paying attention, that's all."

Judy would no longer be ignored. Whether she addressed board members, camp directors, school officials, race directors, or even members of congress, she knew how to capture and hold their attention. Until all her goals regarding disabled children had been met, she would not "calm down," and she had no problem defining her immediate goal. "Ricky *will* be included in the public school system."

When not attending classes or at the lab doing research with the Tufts design team, Rick was at his mother's side, always ready to answer questions about himself and the *Hope Machine*. He worked tirelessly to reinforce Judy's words and decisions. As the star attraction and quintessential ham, he enjoyed the attention he received, and took advantage of the opportunity to learn about other people.

Not a day passed, however, that Judy was without painful reminders of the struggle. With a pensive sigh, she said, "It broke my heart to take Ricky to the bus stop with the other children, then to see the sadness in his eyes when the school bus drove away with his friends, but he was left there all alone in his wheelchair, waiting for 'special' transportation."

Ricky's young, hyperactive brothers were far too impatient to communicate by nodding, gesturing, prompting and sometimes even guessing. That clumsy method was slow and frustrating, so Russ concluded that everything he learned in school could be applicable to Ricky. Since they were learning sentence structure at that time, which included the use of vowels, Russ came home from school each day and worked with Rick to create what they called the *Russell Method.*

Russell explained his method: "There are five blocks of letters, and each block begins with a different vowel. The first block contains the letters between *A* and *D*. The second block contains the letters between *E* and *H*. The third block is *I* thru *N*, then *O* thru *T*, and finally *U* thru *Z*. Whenever Rick had anything to say, I started by asking him, 'Is it *A*?'"

If Rick indicated it was an *A*, Russ would then ask, "Is it *A* itself?"

If Rick nodded again, it meant the sentence under construction began with the indefinite article *A*, and a singular word would soon follow. However, if Rick shook his head, that meant it was not *A* itself, therefore he wanted to construct a word that began with a letter in the block that included *A, B, C* or *D*. Russ then went from *A* through *D* until Rick acknowledged the first letter of the word. Then he would start over, back at *A,* until he found the second letter, and so on. They worked with the system until Russ was able to decipher the words and sentences before Rick had to enumerate every letter. By then, he could make an informed guess.

"For instance," Russ continued, "If the first letter was *D*, then I would say, 'Is it Dad?' If Rick nodded to confirm, I knew it had something to do with Dad and I went to the next word. If the next letter was *I* itself, meaning Rick himself, I knew it was something Dad and Rick needed to discuss. I'd go get Dad, or I would have to determine what he wanted to tell Dad."

"We'll give you an example," Russ said, and turned toward Rick while the brothers demonstrated the method.

Russ started, "*A-E-I-*"

Rick stopped him at *I*.

Russ asked, "Is it *I* itself?"

Rick nodded, which indicated he wanted the pronoun *I*. Therefore, he meant himself.

Russ went back to the beginning to search for the block containing the first letter of the second word. "*A-E-I-O-U-*"

Rick gestured it was in the *U* block; Russ moved on. "*U-V-W-*" When he said *W*, Rick nodded; Russ now had enough information to offer a guess. "You want?"

Rick confirmed he wanted something.

"You want, *A-E-I-O-*"

Rick acknowledged the desired letter was in the *O* block.

Russ said, "*O-P-Q-R-S-T-*"

Rick stopped him at *T*.

"Okay, it's a *T*. You want time? You want to?"

Rick nodded.

"You want to sleep? Eat? Drink?"

He wanted none of those. Russ continued. "*A-E-*"

Rick stopped him at the E block.

Russ went on at *E*. "*E-F-G-*"

Another nod indicated a G. "You want to go?" Russ asked.

Yes, he wanted the word *go*. "You want to go to bed? To the bathroom? Uh, let's see, you want to go outside?" That did it. Mission accomplished. Rick told him he wanted to go outside.

Although slow and tedious, the unsophisticated process worked for anyone who desired to communicate with Rick.

Russ shrugged. "We didn't think it would ever become anything. That was never the purpose. But now, even with all the technology and the advances, it's still the best and most efficient way for him to communicate. All his PCAs learn it."

Not all the communication changes were positive. Rick constructed his thoughts much faster than he could go through the alphabet using the Russell Method. It frustrated him when people became impatient. They would often be distracted, or they simply walked away before Rick completed his thought.

Another "negative" change became evident; Rick could now "talk back." Like any other child in the process of sprouting wings, he didn't always say what the listener wanted to hear, even when that person happened to be his own mother or father.

"Discovering you have a pair of wings is one thing," Dick said. "Learning to fly is another."

A reporter from a show called *I Witness Video* interviewed Rob and Russ at length. He asked them how their lives had been affected when Rick learned to communicate. Rob went for humor. He said, "Well, when Rick learned to talk, that gave him the ability to talk back to us." He looked over at Russ. "Maybe it wasn't such a good idea after all?"

"Yeah," Russ agreed, "It definitely got us in trouble a time or two."

The brothers shared an esoteric laugh.

* * *

When Dick completed advanced military training at a base in El Paso, Texas, the administrative powers reassigned him to Otis Air Force Base near Cape Cod. Since they had promised him a long-term duty assignment, Dick and Judy bought a new home in Falmouth. Robbie and Russell were involved in activities of their own at that time, activities such as hockey and Little League baseball. Rick played hockey in a league for disabled kids, and Dick still worked two jobs. Everyone stayed busy. Too busy.

"I got it from all sides," Dick said. "Rick thought I spent all my time with Rob and Russ, but they thought I spent too much time with Rick. Judy didn't think I spent enough time with any of them. Whoever said, 'Dads will always be in demand,' sure knew what he was talking about."

That door swung both ways. Judy knew that a degree in education would enhance her credibility, so while pounding on doors — and sometimes pounding on heads — she continued her education at the University of Massachusetts in Amherst. When the situation called for it, she took up her sword and slashed a path all the way to the Governor's office. Influenced by her determination and leadership, the Massachusetts congress passed a piece of legislation called Chapter 766, the first Special Education Law in the country. The new law mandated that public education be provided for all children, including the disabled. With such formidable allies as the *Hope Machine* and Chapter 766, Judy opened the doors to public schools. Because of her determination and persistence, those doors were eventually opened wide enough for the entry of a wheelchair, one with a computer attached.

Judy became more confident with each victory. She matured over time, and as she blossomed into an effective spokesperson, she learned how to use less force and more finesse.

In 1975, the government terminated the contract for the missile program at Otis Air Force Base. In the subsequent months, they gave Dick several options, including one that would mean moving to Westfield. Although another year or two in Falmouth would have been financially rewarding because of the escalating value of homes and property, the Hoyts decided to sell their new home and move to Westfield.

To limited fanfare, Rick rolled his electric wheelchair over the threshold and into fifth grade of a Westfield public school, but Judy didn't stop there. She jumped into the recruitment of parents and volunteers to feed, toilet, and assist the disabled kids who attended classes. One of her recruits was a lovely girl named Mary Conners. She worked with Rick for a while, which led to a serendipitous meeting with his younger brother, Robbie.

Enamored by Robbie's smile and charm, Mary went home and happily told her mother she had met her Prince Charming. "I will marry Robbie some day," she announced. "You'll see."

Robbie was unaware that his mother had once said the same thing about his father, so he never gave it any thought. "I met a lot of people because of Rick," Rob admitted. "He was always the center of attention."

Russ agreed with Rob, and for a very good reason.

Michael Murphy also had cerebral palsy. He lived in Medford, but his family often made trips to Children's Hospital, where he befriended Rick. Through that connection, 12-year-old Russell had the good fortune to meet Michael's friend, Lisa Donovan, and he was instantly smitten with puppy love. When Russ was asked if Lisa had also gone home and announced that she had met the Hoyt of her dreams, he said, "Probably, but she has never admitted it."

When Judy completed her undergraduate work, she enrolled in a Master's program, but obtaining further education wasn't enough to satisfy such a highly determined and motivated woman. She volunteered to work at an organization called ASHS — the Association for Human Services — where she became involved in recreation programs for the handicapped.

"I wanted to create a place where all children could go," Judy explained. "A place where families would eventually realize they can make a difference, and that they don't have to be owned by their disabilities."

To accomplish her lofty goal, Judy founded Kamp for Kids, a summer program that offered a variety of programs and activities for all children through age twenty-one, the able-bodied and disabled alike. She got involved in every aspect of the operation, from planning and promoting, to teaching and training. Dick found a campsite they could use, and with the help of the Air National Guard, he provided tents and camping equipment. To make it a family affair, the three Hoyt boys became regular visitors and volunteers at the camp. It was at that camp, in fact, where Robbie worked with an abandoned boy named Jamie Decenza. Rob said, "The respect and love I learned there helped me understand my own brother and family."

Judy also became involved with the Easter Seals Society. Through that organization, she worked with an area high school to open its swimming pool to disabled children. From her experience with Rick, Judy knew the therapeutic value in swimming, and she rounded up volunteers and scheduled classes for the children. For her efforts in that arena, she earned an award from the Massachusetts Easter Seals Society.

The swim program produced another unexpected reward. Robbie had traveled around the country with his military family most of his formative years, and he spent a great amount of time helping with Ricky, but he had not developed any lasting friendships or interests. The sessions at the pool changed all that.

"I really enjoyed swimming," Rob said. "I met other kids, and once I learned the proper swimming technique, I excelled."

No longer was he simply Ricky Hoyt's younger brother. As the more mature "Rob," he had found an activity that made him feel special, and he became a star in his own right, another Mark Spitz. Plus, he said, "I looked great in my Speedos."

They Hoyt boys all enjoyed baseball. Dick even volunteered to coach a Little League team, and eventually league officials selected him as their chief umpire. Along with that dubious assignment, however, came responsibilities. When a scheduled umpire failed to show up, Dick had to work the game himself. One weekend, Dick got the call to report for umpire duty. It was a lousy day for a game, and frequent gusts of hot wind from the outfield didn't provide any relief from the heat, but instead whipped up the dust and dumped it in Dick's tired eyes.

"Nothing went right," Dick recalled. "A woman in the stands hassled me about the calls. She finally got to me, so I stomped over to her and handed her the mask. I said, 'Here, if you think you can do any better, do it. I'll sit and watch.' I never heard another peep out of her."

It was an uncharacteristic display of emotion for Dick, but everyone has limits.

Rick realized that umpires held a position of awesome authority and control. He enjoyed control. Other people had controlled him all his life, and as an umpire, he had a unique opportunity to settle some old scores with his brothers. As an avid Red Sox fan, Rick had seen enough baseball to learn that the strike zone is subjective, and it can vary considerably from one umpire to the next — sometimes, from one hitter to the next.

In a backyard baseball game, Rick donned his gear and rolled into position behind the catcher. Rob strode confidently up to the batter's box, tapped his bat firmly on home plate and dug his cleats into the ground. He looked intimidating and strong, ready to smash a fastball into the neighbor's yard. He watched the first pitch whistle over his head, but Rick raised his right arm.

"That's not a strike!" Rob protested loudly. "Are you blind?"

Someone shouted, "You can't argue strikes and balls!"

Another player yelled, "Kick him out of the game, ump!"

Rick smiled broadly, avoided his brother's glare, and thought to himself, "Ah, yes, control. It's a beautiful thing."

Sibling rivalry was alive and well in a backyard in Westfield, Massachusetts. Rick had served notice that when anyone bullied him, he would find ways fight to back.

Rob struck out that time at bat. He shot Rick an angry glare and stomped off in disgust. That night, at the family dinner table, he confronted his older brother with the "poor eyesight." He told Rick exactly what he thought about the lousy umpiring, but big brother only laughed.

Rob ended the conversation with a subtle warning. "What goes around, comes around."

Rick refused to be intimidated. With a dead-serious scowl, he raised his right arm, and with the same emotion he used when umpiring, he emphatically gestured *You're outta here!*

That brotherly confrontation took place about a week before Rick entered the sixth grade, and with the anxiety and excitement of returning to school, his nights were restless. Although Rick had limited mobility, he could move around on the bed somewhat, and one night he tumbled over the side and onto the floor. The nasty fall left a bump on his forehead that remains to this day, but even Rick couldn't say for certain how it happened.

"That'll teach you," Rob told him, and smugly claimed responsibility for the mishap. "If you mess with me, you better sleep with your eyes open."

To punctuate his point, Rob lifted his right arm to emulate Rick's gesture when he called a *strike*! Rick didn't know if it were true or not, but he went to his first day of school thinking he could "save face" by telling curiosity seekers that he earned the discolored lump in a game of hockey. That's what he planned to say, but he couldn't bring himself to it. Instead, he stuck with the truth as he knew it. He told everyone, "I fell out of bed."

The younger brothers had ways to "even the score" with Rick. When they came home from school, Rob and Russ helped themselves to the Refrigerator. They usually started with a Coke, but without brotherly help, Rick could only watch.

"Rob and I would take out the Cokes," Russ said. "As we drank them, we would place the cans down in front of Rick, but we wouldn't give him any."

"There was nothing Rick could do about it," Rob confirmed.

Rick took a philosophical view of experiences such as the one with the unreachable Coke. To him, it was a lesson about life, about being disabled. It took a wheelchair for Judy to accept the reality that he was different, but that didn't mean anything to Rick because he had been in a wheelchair all his life. But the Coke, that was different.

"It was part of the learning process," Rick said candidly. "It taught me to accept the reality of my limitations."

Rick found other ways to one-up his brothers. "For my birthday," Russell recalled, "Rick gave me a jacket. On the birthday card, he guaranteed it would fit perfectly. Well, he was right, it did fit, because it was already my favorite jacket. He and one of his accomplices stole it from my closet and wrapped it up as a gift."

Rick laughed and said, "I gave it to Rob first, but he didn't like it."

* * *

Rick Foulds eventually redesigned the switch on the TIC machine so Rick could control it more effectively with his head. With the new mouse, Rick clicked out his responses to a series of probing questions from a television interviewer. One question referenced his desire to be included in events with able-bodied kids, even when it meant risking an injury. Risk — a word Rick had heard too often. The man asked the question in a way that implied Rick might be more content staying in his own little world, doing things specifically designed for the disabled.

Rick never wavered in that regard. He was consistent because it exemplified how he felt and what he believed. He thought of several clever, flippant answers to questions such as those, but he decided to give the interviewers a break. With the help of his computer, he said, simply, "People with disabilities should be included in daily activities just like everyone else."

Actions speak louder than words, and in Rick's case, that meant written words. When Judy involved her sons in the Kamp for Kids program, Rick spent many days at various summer camps. The director at Camp Warren, Frank "Coach" Robinson, took a special interest in Rick. They became friends.

As a teacher and a leader, Robinson related well to the handicapped kids. He recognized their strengths and the areas where they needed help. The patient man quickly learned to communicate with Rick. The first problem Coach encountered with Rick was related to drinking. Dick and Judy limited the soda consumption of their three sons, but at Camp Warren, Rick thought he could take advantage of the freedom and indulge in the more wicked and prurient side of his personality.

"Rick thought he was in charge," Robinson said. "He decided he wouldn't drink anything but Coke, and he refused to eat. Coke, that's all he wanted. I brought it to Judy's attention and he found out who was in charge, real fast."

Rick's pranks were indicative of his age. He was a typical teenager, with the testosterone screaming for attention. With Camp Warren being coed, it offered plenty of "eye candy" for a young man. When they discussed the daytime raids on the girl's cabins, Rick eagerly came to the forefront and masterminded a plan. Robinson couldn't conceal his amusement when he told the following story: "Rick was always an instigator. He would say, 'Let's raid the girls tonight!' That was his goal for the day. A raid. Then he would want to run their pants up the flagpole, like it was some sort of victory salute, or something like that. When he left the camp, I gave him the *Captain of Raids* Award."

Rick and his brothers had a special relationship, one of mutual caring and respect. They developed a bond that most siblings could never understand or equal. They knew the realities that accompanied his condition, and they offered support and assistance in everything he did. They had their differences, sure, but Rick was their brother, their big brother, and they never lost sight of that fact.

"Rick is basically helpless," Rob said. "Yet he always has a joke, and he's always ready with a smile. He can find pleasure in the simplest of things. What's not to respect about that?"

"I learned plenty from Rick," Russ acknowledged. "He taught me about honesty and trust. He brought new meaning to the word *patience*. Because of him, I'm a better person."

High praise indeed from one's siblings, especially when it came from younger brothers who once held his Coke in abeyance.

Rick always looked for the opportunity to display his keen wit and, on occasion, his caustic sense of humor. During an interview with *I Witness Video*, he explained why President Clinton jogged to McDonalds so often.

"He went there to meet hookers," Rick said.

Dick laughed. "We live in Massachusetts, Rick. It's not politically correct to criticize a Kennedy or a Clinton."

On our drive to the Sun and Surf triathlon, I noticed that the overhead road signs used the abbreviated words "Mass Pike" to inform drivers they were on the Massachusetts Turnpike.

I read it and said, "There must be some big fish ahead."

The humor was subtle, but I thought I heard Rick chuckle.

Rob and his two sons were playing baseball in the backyard when we returned from the triathlon. Jayme had played in a Little League game earlier that morning, while Rob shared the coaching duties. The boys ran over to greet Granda and Rick.

"Hi, Uncle Rick," Jayme said.

"Jayme hit a home run today," Cameron reported.

"But we lost the game," Jayme quickly added.

"Well, it must have been your coach's fault," Dick said, taking a playful shot at Rob. "You better trade that coach for a better one."

Jayme defended his father. "It wasn't his fault."

When we went inside the house, I asked Rick some questions and listened to his responses on the voice synthesizer. I knew he would be curious about me, too, and I welcomed him to interview me. The questions a person asks can be very revealing, and one of his questions offered insight.

Pointedly, Rick asked me, "Are you a man of your word?"

Rick possessed political savvy along with his wry sense of humor. So, although we were in Clinton and Kennedy country, I risked responding to his question with an irreverent reference to Clinton's infamous non-response to a prosecutor during the Lewinsky testimony. The President responded to a direct question: *It depends on what the meaning of the word is, is.*

I said, "Well, Rick, that depends on what the meaning of the word *are, is.*"

Rick rewarded me with a perfunctory laugh even though my impious answer avoided his question. At that point, a simple "yes" may have sufficed, but I offered a more detailed answer, and whether or not it satisfied his curiosity, only Rick knows. But his question served as a reminder that the young man had a mind of his own and he knew how to use it. Although terribly limited physically, Rick was astutely aware and observant, always thinking and always learning. As Judy had trumpeted since his infancy, his brain and intelligence worked fine.

Rick impressed me with something else he said. My minimal contribution to humor during the drive to Marlboro had not escaped him. On his computer, many hours after the fact, Rick wrote, "I enjoyed your joke about the Massachusetts Turnpike."

He looked at me and smiled. I said, "Thanks." Then I stole a quote from him: "Pants up the flagpole."

The Hoyts at Kamp.

Dick, Judy, Rob, Russ and Rick.

CHAPTER 7 — THE CHARITY RACE

When we crossed the finish line, Rick had the biggest smile on his face you had ever seen in your life. When we got home, he wrote on his computer, 'Dad, when I am running, it feels like I'm not even handicapped.'
—Dick Hoyt

Along with his other activities, Rick enrolled in a Challenge Curriculum at the high school. He went swimming with friends at the Cerebral Palsy classes, and often attended and supported his brothers in their sports. Dick took part as often as possible, including taking them to classes, games, or other events they were involved with at the time.

At times, however, Rick felt left out when it came to any father-son activities because they never found a sport in which he could participate with his dad. Usually, he just shrugged and excused it as another consequence of being a disabled person. That was the hard reality he had already learned to accept.

When Rick entered the seventh grade at Westfield Middle School, P.E. class consisted of the able-bodied only. After all, the *P* stood for *physical*. Therefore, without much thought, Rick's aides would take him into the library where he studied while the other kids went to Phys. Ed. When Rick's absence came to the attention of Doctor "Doc" Steve Sartori, the gym teacher, he demanded to know why the Hoyt kid avoided his class. Had he known about Rick's disability, it probably would not have made any difference; he was way ahead of the curve when it came to inclusion. Sartori looked up Rick's phone number and called his mother. After Judy told him the situation, the teacher said, "I'm sorry, Mrs. Hoyt, but a disability is not an excuse to cut my class. Either he is here, or you are here. I'll leave it up to you."

The Hoyts identified with Sartori's can-do attitude regarding the disabled, and the following morning, Rick rolled into the P.E. class. Rick's determination intrigued Sartori. He really liked the youngster, and soon had him participating in events right along with the other students.

"Steve even created new ones specifically for Rick," Judy said respectfully of the coach.

Dick and Judy were delighted when Rick would come home and share all of his stories about the P.E. class and the new gym teacher, who also coached for the Westfield State College basketball team.

"Sartori called one day," Dick said, "and asked if it would be okay to take Rick along to a college basketball game with him. By that time, we had heard so much about the man, we felt like he was a member of the family."

"Rick wanted to go," Dick said. "He wouldn't have accepted 'no' under any circumstances.

Rick made the same point, but said it differently. "I would have crawled all the way, if I had to."

Not only was Rick invited to attend the college basketball game, but it also meant he would be going along with his gym teacher, and some of his new classmates would be there. The fact that the team had outstanding cheerleaders was merely frosting on the proverbial cake. To Rick, things simply couldn't get any better than that. It was true, life begins at fifteen.

Rick and the coach arrived at the basketball game an hour before the scheduled start time. Sartori wheeled Rick through the front entrance, where they stopped briefly to chat with another member of the faculty. As they walked toward the gymnasium, a large poster on the wall caught Sartori's attention. He recognized the name at the top of the poster to be that of a Westfield State athlete.

"Wait a second, Rick." Sartori stepped over to read the poster. "I know that kid," he said, referring to the name associated with an upcoming charity event:

RUN FOR DOOGIE
USE YOUR LEGS TO HELP HIS. SHOW YOUR
FAVORITE MIDFIELDER YOUR LOVE. FUND
RAISER, 5-MILE RACE ON SATURDAY...

"What a shame," Sartori uttered sadly. With a dispirited shake of the head, he said, "He was in an automobile accident."

Sartori escorted Rick into the locker room and introduced him to several of the Westfield players. Before the game started, they took seats near the front row. Rick enjoyed the ballgame, but at halftime, a soft, pleading voice came over the PA system. The voice belonged to a student, a female friend of the midfielder injured in the automobile accident.

"I want to remind everyone about the race on Saturday," the girl said nervously. "Doogie needs your help. He is paralyzed from the waist down." She paused to regain composure. "And we are trying to raise money to help pay his medical bills. Let's remember how much fun we had watching him play on our Lacrosse team, and now we have a chance to do something nice in return. The race starts at eight o'clock on Saturday, here in front of the gymnasium, so if you can make it to a basketball game, you can make it to the race. Oh, and some of us cheerleaders will be there, too, and we want you to come out and help support Doogie. Thank you very much."

The announcement touched all of Rick's hot buttons. He could identify with the paralyzed player, no question about that. He also knew about paying medical bills, and remembered all the moonlighting hours his father had worked over the years. Rick qualified as an expert on the subject, and he felt considerable compassion for other disabled people. After all, many of his friends and acquaintances were disabled.

The aside about cheerleaders being there was a bonus, no doubt about that, but a higher priority entered his mind — he would need a partner before he would be able to run in a race. An athletic partner. Someone he could trust. But where would he find one? Coach Sartori maybe? All this information bounced around in his brain like a pinball. When the basketball players returned to the court for the second half, Rick cheered and followed the remainder of the game, but he kept thinking about Doogie, and how he might be able to help. By the time he arrived home that evening, he had formulated a plan.

"Rick went to his computer right away," Dick recalled. "And he wrote something about Doogie. Then he said he would like to run in the charity race. I thought he meant with Steve Sartori, so I told him it was fine with me. Then he went back to his computer and tapped out another message. I was wrong. He wanted *me* to push him."

Dick never thought of himself as a runner, but as a method of weight control, he did jog two or three times a week, a mile or so each time. Nothing serious. He also played on an ice hockey team whenever he found time, but none of that mattered. Although the competitive spirit stirred inside him, he found far greater meaning in Rick's request. The charity race presented a unique opportunity for him to participate in an athletic event with his son, as a teammate. Dick never gave it a second thought. He flipped a thumbs-up.

"Okay, we'll do it," he promised.

When Saturday morning arrived, the entire Hoyt family packed up the van and drove off to help Doogie. What started out as a simple, compassionate gesture by Rick, would soon change their lives more dramatically than they could ever imagine.

Wearing new running shoes and shorts, Dick rolled Rick and the Mulholland wheelchair up to the starting line with the mob of runners.

"It was a prescription chair," Dick said with a laugh. "The wheels were small, like those on a shopping cart. The thing had not been built for speed. It was hard enough just pushing it, never mind running with him in it."

The paid participants all wore their race numbers. Sartori had spoken with the race director in advance, and had asked him to give Dick and Rick the first number, a double zero.

"It matched his front teeth," Russell teased.

"It meant nothing and nothing," Robbie chimed in.

Everyone had a joke about the number double zero, but they said it in good fun. Rather than pinning the bib to his shirt, Dick secured it to a handle on the Mulholland.

Doc Sartori brought his wife and introduced her to the entire Hoyt family.

"She had a camera around her neck," Dick recalled. "She ran around taking pictures of everyone she knew."

"Are you going to run all five miles?" she asked Dick.

"Sure."

Judy laughed. "He will probably turn around at the corner and crawl back."

Dick had no intentions of turning around at the first corner. He had signed up for a five-mile race and he would run the full five miles, and anyone who knew him very well should have known better. He had no delusions that it would be an easy task, but that point was moot.

"Rick won't want to stop at the corner," Dick told her confidently. "Neither will I."

For most of the five miles, they ran on a road with a crown in the middle, which caused the chair to pull hard to the side and forced Dick to run with an abnormal stride. He had to struggle, to use every muscle in his body just to keep the chair from pulling him off the road.

"Everyone looked at us," Dick said. "Cars came to a stop when we ran by. People standing on the sidelines were gawking all over the place."

Team Hoyt did not turn around at the first corner, nor did they turn around at the second or third corner. They kept right on

83

going. Spectators pointed, slapped their hands together, and shouted encouragement; they had never seen anything like this before. To everyone's surprise, Dick and Rick survived the full distance and completed the race.

Mrs. Sartori spotted them coming in. "Here they come!"

She stood near the finish line with her camera, where she snapped a great shot of the Hoyts crossing the line. Clearly, it was a blissful moment for Rick. He beamed with delight and lifted his arms in a victory salute.

"He had the biggest smile on his face you have ever seen in your life," Dick said.

When she saw her men return, Judy leaped for joy, just as you would expect from a former high school cheerleader. She ran up to her heroes and gave them a hug.

"Look, Dad," Robbie said. "You beat that guy."

Robbie pointed to the man who finished last, close behind Dick and Rick. Dick looked at the man, then he forced a small smile of acknowledgement.

"I had a hard time walking for two weeks," he admitted. "My body hurt all over. I strained myself to the point where there was blood in my shorts, and I had blood in my urine for three days after the race."

Rick, better than anyone, understood the effort his father had made to complete the race. With sincere appreciation and love reflected in his big brown eyes, he looked up at Dick and flashed the "thank you" smile.

"Did you see that?" Dick said, and shook his son's hand. "We didn't finish last."

* * *

The Hoyts were a big, happy family when they returned home. Dick could barely walk, but he considered it a small price to pay. The race turned out to be a great success. He really had fun, but more important, Rick loved it. In fact, when he arrived back home, he went directly to his computer to tell everyone exactly how he felt.

When the *Tic, Tic, Click!* finally stopped, Dick looked over Rick's shoulder and read the following note. "Dad, when I am running, it feels like I'm not even handicapped."

The lump in Dick's throat grew too big to be swallowed. His heart swelled. With the help of Doctor Sartori, Dick had found a sport Rick could enjoy like everyone else, one they could do together. Finally. Now Dick could give his son the athletic experience that he had always admired in others. He could give Rick the joy of a person who had freed himself from the bondage of a disability.

"This has completed his life, and made him into a whole person," Dick said proudly. "Now he looks forward to the weekends, to the races, to seeing the different scenery and meeting all the fantastic people. It has brought us closer together as a family."

Rick agreed. "It solidified our relationship."

Dick's entire body hurt for two weeks. Clearly, he would have to replace the Mulholland chair and start doing some serious training. He stated his competitive philosophy: "You run for fun, but you race to win."

The search for a chair that would be more conducive to racing began immediately. Dick experimented with a number of ideas, and even called on the engineers from Tufts University for advice, but they game him no satisfaction. They tried several different chairs, but one of them wobbled and another had problems with the flimsy, unsafe tires.

"One chair had wheels like those on a grocery cart," Judy said. "When we went on vacation to New Hampshire, a wheel fell off. We tried to buy a grocery cart wheel at one of the local supermarkets, but they wouldn't sell it to us, so we waited until it got dark, then we went back to the parking lot and stole the whole cart." As an afterthought, she shrugged and said, "Well, you do what you gotta do."

During one of the family vacations to the White Mountains in New Hampshire, Dick had the good fortune to meet a man who agreed to help him come up with something that would work. After evaluating the requirements, the man molded a seat that fit Rick's body, which solved a big part of the problem. Whenever the Hoyts were near the town of Greenfield, New Hampshire, Judy visited the Crotched Mountain Rehabilitation Hospital, and on one of those visits, she met an engineer who agreed to build a frame. Dick searched around until he found some bike tires that worked with the new frame. Rick contributed his input to the project, and with all their collaborative talent, at a total cost of thirty-five dollars, they unveiled the *running chair*.

"It was like a baby jogger," Dick explained, "but we had a special insert of foam fitted to Rick's body."

They retired the Mulholland wheelchair to the basement and went to work with the new chair, unaware that it would sprout a whole new industry in baby joggers and eventually end up in the New England Sport's Museum.

"We should have put a patent on it," Dick lamented. "We'd be rich today."

True to form, Dick became a disciplined runner. He came up with a schedule and logged the miles, bought his first pair of cushioned running shoes and pounded the pavement the same as any other competitor. Rick had higher priorities, such as doing schoolwork, so Dick had to be creative. He bought a hundred-pound bag of cement to push along in the chair. Two years after the 5-mile charity race, with a new chair, new goals, a greater level of fitness, and a stronger father-son relationship, Team Hoyt set out to compete and have some fun.

"The Hope Machine had freed Ricky's mind," Peter Henderson said in an intimate interview with *OurTimes*. "Now his father had freed his body."

Dick and Rick signed up for their first serious race, one that took place in Springfield, Massachusetts. It would be an official race, a 10K held in conjunction with a community celebration called the Glendi Festival. However, another unexpected barrier promptly rose up to challenge them.

"When we first got there," Dick said, "we met a lot of negative people. The crowd, the authorities who organized the race, and even some of the other runners."

The oddball team perplexed the race directors. They did not know what to do, and were even reluctant to let the Hoyts register. To make it worse, the other runners snubbed them.

"Everyone acted like they would catch some kind of disease," Dick observed. "They wouldn't come near us." In an article titled "He ain't heavy, He's my son," published in the *Sunday Boston Herald*, Michael O'Connor reported, "The only thing many runners 'caught' was a draft as the unlikely father-and-son tandem trundled past them."

The entire family accompanied them to the race to offer support. Robbie and Russell even abandoned their regular activities to join in the festivities. It started as a beautiful day, but to steal a quote from Yogi Berra, "It was deja vu all over again." That's how the Hoyts felt when the directors tried to exclude them from the race.

Judy was livid. "The officials said they 'didn't fit' because Dick was pushing him. Dick did it 'differently' than all the other runners. The wheelchair athletes didn't want them because Rick wasn't powering his own chair, and the able-bodied runners said, 'You're just going to get in the way. Why do you want to push this kid of yours who doesn't talk and just sits in the wheelchair?'"

Dick would not be intimidated. He secured Rick in the running chair and moved to the starting line with the other runners. With nothing to support his argument, the director in charge of the race finally relented and allowed them to run as official entrants.

"You and me," Dick said to Rick. "Here we go."

The race began with a bang.

All the training and preparation paid off handsomely. The tires on the running chair held the road like Radials and worked to perfection. The chair went straight and stayed the course, and the bicycle wheels absorbed the shock and remained firm. Dick looked fit and strong. Although Rick had not slept well the night before, Dick gave him a well-deserved share of the credit.

"Rick worked hard to keep his weight down," he teased. "That helped a lot. He cut back on girls and candy."

Rick responded with humor. "Girls and candy? But isn't that redundant?"

Judy didn't expect her men to return nearly so quickly as they did. She, Robbie and Russell assumed they would finish near the end, the same as in Westfield. Like everyone else on that day, they underestimated the dynamic duo. While the other family members meandered around the game booths, Rick sailed across the finish line in 38 minutes and 30 seconds, one tick ahead of his father. They had beaten 150 of the 300 runners, placing them smack dab in the middle of the pack. A remarkable improvement from their first race.

Judy and the boys arrived with a reward of hugs and kisses.

"Way to go, Dad!"

"Nice job, Rick!"

"How did you get back so fast?" Judy asked.

After the hugging had subsided, a short, sweaty runner walked up and offered his hand to Dick. "Good race, man. You guys did great."

"Thanks."

The man then introduced himself as Pete Wisnewski. He shook hands with Dick and welcomed him to the racing scene.

"There are a lot of good races around the state," Wisnewski said to Rick. "You guys will have fun."

Pete took time to speak with Rick — one of the few runners who did — and he was the only one who treated the Hoyts just as he would treat any other runner. The friendly gesture left an impression on Dick.

Dick and Rick met a new friend, found a new sport, and every weekend for the rest of the year, they found a race somewhere. The competitive juices seeped through their pores like sweat in a sauna. At that time, Wisnewski could run faster than the Hoyts, so they targeted the slender man to measure their progress. They became best of friends and regular training partners, and at a 10K race in Worcester, Pete eased up and let Team Hoyt beat him.

"Rick didn't appreciate that at all," Dick stated flatly. "So he and Pete had a standing bet on every race. The loser had to take the winner's bib home and hang it in the bedroom, where he had to look at it every night until the next race."

Every weekend from that day on, Dick loaded the running chair into the car and off they would go. Sometimes they traveled to neighboring states, and Wisnewski often went along and competed with them. After a number of races, the other runners began to recognize them, and they discovered Rick had a good sense of humor, a great personality, and he loved life. He wanted to be out there having fun with everyone else.

"Our first official year of racing was 1980," Dick said. "On some weekends we would run three races, sometimes two in the same day. Rick had a real killer instinct, and if he saw someone he wanted to beat, he got so excited I worried about him. I told him to take it easy or he would tip over the chair."

When it came to the "killer instinct," Rick and his dad were the perfect match. In the heat of competition, Dick pushed himself to the limit, sometimes beyond. Rick listened to Dick's breathing rhythm.

"If my breathing became labored," Dick explained, "Rick would turn around and give me a smile."

Dick would back off enough to bring his heartbeat down where it belonged. They had the ability to communicate simply by looking into each other's eyes.

Regarding the three-race weekends, Dick said, "We always ran the third race fastest. It seemed that the more we raced, the stronger we got, so I thought we should go for the longer race distances. Maybe even a marathon."

Pete Wisnewski ran in marathons whenever he got the chance, and the thought of running along with his new pals intrigued him. "You should do it," he told Dick. "Rick will lead the way. He'll take care of you."

Dick thought a moment, then looked down at his son and said, "You know, I think they have a marathon in Boston every year, don't they?"

Rick's eyes widened. He blinked curiously, then realized, if his dad said it, it's a done deal. Rick answered with his eyes, and it was absolute approval.

"Go Boston!"

The Charity Race for Doogie.

The first "running chair."

CHAPTER 8 — BOSTON

I understand all things said to me. Being a non-vocal person does not make one less of a human being. I have the same feelings as anyone else. I feel sadness, joy, hunger, love, compassion and pain.

—Rick Hoyt

"Here we go again."

That's what the Hoyts must have thought after they applied to the Boston Athletic Association (BAA) for entry into the 1981 Boston Marathon. With little explanation, the rules committee rejected their application. They could not run in the race, not officially anyway, and they did not qualify for the wheelchair division. End of discussion.

Although Judy wondered if her husband and son had crossed the line of insanity for even considering a 26.2-mile race, the rejection didn't come as any big surprise. For them, rejection was a road well traveled. However, since Dick and Rick decided to run in the renowned event, she supported them.

"Do you have to be official?" she asked innocently. "I've seen runners without bibs."

Dick frowned. "Run unofficially? No way."

That option disgusted him, but after a second thought, it sounded considerably better than standing idly on the sidelines and watching the world go by without him and Rick on board. He made a mental note of Judy's comment, and diligently increased his training mileage. As far as he was concerned, official or not, Team Hoyt would be running in the Boston Marathon on Patriot's Day.

"Dick began running every day," Judy said. "He ran with a bag of cement in the wheelchair because Rick was at school and studying, unable to train with him."

Dick badgered the BAA often, but they stood firm. Just like the 10K race in Springfield, the Hoyts did not fit into any of the standard divisions because they were "different." But, as April drew near, Dick's persistence cracked their impervious shell.

"Okay," the officials finally told Dick, hoping it would get him off their backs. "You can run but you won't be official. You won't be registered and you won't have a race number, but you can line up behind the wheelchair participants and run with them."

Grudgingly, Dick accepted their terms.

"It's a start," he told Rick. "At least we'll be in the race."

To Dick, the word "unofficial" was nothing but a euphemism. The term runners used for anyone who participated in races without registering and paying the required entry fee was a little more harsh: *Bandit.*

Dick marked the date on the Team Hoyt racing calendar. Come April, after less than nine months of competing, he and Rick would run in their first marathon while millions of people watched on TV and along the route. Given that knowledge, Dick prepared well, and he began searching for any upcoming races that were longer than ten miles.

Pete Wisnewski had heard about a race called the "Chop-a-Thon," an 18-miler in Albany, New York, to be held one month before Boston. It sounded like a good test, Dick thought, and with no regard for the winter weather, he signed up for the race.

Dick said to Rick, "If we can run eighteen, we can run twenty-six."

"Works fine for me," Rick told him. "I can beat you at any distance."

The weatherman gave the Hoyts and 1,300 other runners an unfriendly welcome when they arrived in Albany. The message was clear — go back home!

Barry Nolan, a correspondent for Channel 4 in Boston, drove across the state to interview the Hoyts at the race. Nolan hosted a television show called *Evening Magazine*, which had held a contest called "Amazing Stories." At a previous race, a female competitor was so inspired by Dick and Rick that she submitted a story about them, and subsequently won an all-expenses-paid vacation for two in Honolulu, Hawaii. Nolan went to Albany to do a follow-up segment.

"Our goal is to run a 7-minute pace," Dick told Nolan the morning of the race.

"Really?" Nolan asked. "For the full 18 miles?"

"Sure."

"Pretty big challenge, isn't it?"

"We've been training," Dick answered honestly.

Eighteen miles pushing a hundred-pound boy in a wheelchair was pretty impressive stuff, thought Nolan, but the onerous weather made success that much more improbable. He observed the worried face of the young quadriplegic bundled up like a mummy, wearing sweats, a hooded sweatshirt, gloves, sunglasses, and a cap. He watched closely as the solemn, forty-year-old father stripped down to a T-shirt and running shorts and went through his perfunctory stretching and warm-up routine. Nolan admired the determination of the two men, but he had doubts about them completing the race, and he hoped they would prove him wrong. Like everyone else, Nolan could only see what was on the surface. Their motivation was internal.

As excitement mounted, Dick pushed Rick to the starting line. "It was snowing, freezing and a miserable, cold day," Judy recalled. "Rob, Russ and I followed them in the van. We drove along a parallel road, and kept stopping to jump out and cheer them on. We could see the comradeship and the energy between Rick and Dick each mile they ran. Rick's arms shot out to his sides like wings and Dick waved each time they saw us."

Nolan was standing at the finish line when Rick's patented grin and outstretched arms crossed in two hours and six minutes, which was good enough to beat nearly 900 other runners. When Nolan applied the math, it equaled a seven-minute pace.

Word had spread about the Hoyts. With each race, more runners felt comfortable in approaching them to offer good wishes and congratulations. For those who were hesitant to speak to Rick, Dick and Judy urged them to go right ahead and talk to him. "Grab his arm," Dick would tell them. "Shake his hand."

The interaction and commitment impressed Nolan. He asked, "What's next for you guys?"

"Couple more short ones," Dick answered. "Then Boston."

"Boston? The marathon?"

"Yeah. Boston."

"Really?"

"Yeah, really." Dick looked at Rick and winked.

* * *

Bostonians celebrate Patriot's Day on the third Monday in April. Most of them take the day off work, and many thousands flock to the streets to support the Boston Marathon. The race is run point-to-point, starting in the town of Hopkinton and ending near Fenway Park in downtown Boston. In an effort to complete the Patriot's Day games before the marathoners ran by, the Red Sox always scheduled the game earlier on the day of the race.

The Hoyt family arrived in Hopkinton four hours before the twelve o'clock start time, but Dick experienced an unfamiliar anxiety prior to the race. He felt tense, made frequent trips to the porta-potties, kept checking the chair and the tires, guzzled water, and queried Rick's state of mind far more often than usual.

A news reporter stuck a microphone in his face and asked for a prediction.

"Three hours," came the terse response.

The man asked a follow-up question, but Dick ignored it and went about his preparation. He was consumed with the fear that an official would approach him at the last minute and say something like, "We've decided it's not safe with you guys on the course. You can't run. Please step off to the side."

Since Dick didn't wear a watch, he kept asking about the time, and as the crowd noise intensified, so did his nervous-energy level. He felt like he and Rick could fly through the full 26-mile course. He wanted to prove it to the BAA. He heard someone announce they had one minute to start, and for the wheelchair athletes to get ready to go. They wouldn't dare pull them off the course this late in the game, he assumed. Even if they tried, too bad, they were running Boston.

"We're going, big guy!" he shouted to Rick. "Hold on."

Everything became a blur at that point. By the time Dick's head cleared, they were sprinting through Hopkinton, where mobs of cheering spectators greeted them at every turn. Whenever he and Rick came into view, the applause increased and bystanders shouted encouragement. They hammered along in high gear, soaring like a couple of eagles. What a marvelous day it was, everything Dick and Rick hoped it would be.

That quickly changed. For the first time in his brief running career, Dick learned what runners mean when they talk about "The Wall." His early pace eventually took its toll, and Mister Wall introduced himself to Mister Hoyt at mile twenty-two. He hit it hard.

Dick's legs cramped. His chest hurt. His arms ached and felt like rubber. To recover, he was forced to walk. "There goes the three-hour goal," he mumbled to Rick.

Rick never heard what he said, nor did he care about the three-hour goal. He heard frenzied cheering from the spectators and he loved it. These were his new friends and fans, and he owned them. No reason to hurry through such a good thing, he thought. Smell those Patriot roses.

Dick ran a little farther, then walked a little more. As runners went by, they reached out and patted him on the back to show their support.

"Looking good, men!"

"Three miles to go, guys!"

"Way to go, Hoyts! Hang in there!"

"That wall really hurt," Dick said. "When people patted me on the back, it felt like they were slugging me with hammers. I really felt miserable. I felt so bad, I knew I would never want to run a marathon again."

The Red Sox baseball game started at 11:00 and ended before Dick and Rick arrived at Fenway Park, but many of the fans remained in the area to watch the runners. The vocal reception reverberated through the streets as Team Hoyt passed by. Rick became so excited and animated that he nearly flipped the chair. The exhilaration slapped a charge on Dick's batteries that lasted the remaining two miles.

A thunderous ovation awaited them at the finishing chutes, where one spectator turned to Rob and asked, "Did he push that boy all the way in a wheelchair?"

"Yes, ma'am, he certainly did. All the way."

Officials at the finish line stopped to have a look when the Hoyts came in. They glanced curiously at the race clock, which displayed three hours, eleven minutes, and an unknown number of seconds. Regardless of the exact time, they knew an extraordinary performance when they saw one.

For Dick and Rick, the fun ended soon after the race. The wind picked up and it turned cold. It took two hours before Judy found them shivering in a nearby building. Fortunately, a Good Samaritan had come by and offered them a blanket, but they needed two or three more.

Not long after the Boston Marathon, Nolan and Channel 4 aired a story about the Hoyts. His broadcast was a huge success, and the accolades many. Tufts University School of Design received recognition for their contribution, which translated into additional funding for their projects. Nolan received an award for his excellent work in producing the show and publicizing the Hoyts, and Dick and Rick became overnight heroes. Everyone benefited from the event, but Dick was not satisfied. "We ran it as bandits," he said, revealing disappointment. "We weren't official runners. Next year, we will be."

"Next year?" Nolan asked.

"Yeah, only next time we'll do it in three hours."

* * *

A year passed before Dick and Rick would get a Patriot's Day rematch. During that time, they completed more than fifty races, including another marathon. But they focused on the next Boston, and Dick had it marked on his calendar before he recovered from the first one. He wrote several more letters to the committee, each time listing another accomplishment and another reason to justify an official entry.

Dick applied a little pressure. He asked them, "Isn't that what a community event like this is supposed to be all about?"

To his chagrin, even with a successful Boston notched on the team belt, the BAA remained firm on their decision. "We welcome you to the race, but you won't be official."

"I guess that's progress," Dick mused. "At least we will be 'welcome' next time."

Dick sent a personal letter to Will Cloney, the executive director for the Boston Marathon, but that only got him a terse, sympathetic rejection.

"I'm sorry," Cloney said. "There is nothing I can do."

Dick never gave up. "April is a long way off," he told Rick optimistically. "Keep training."

Along with the running they did as a team, Dick now had more responsibility in preparing his teammate for the races and caring for him after each race. He became increasingly more involved in all aspects of Rick's life, including the bathing, feeding and toileting.

With all the racing, his friends, and working with the TIC machine, Rick developed a well-rounded life. He followed the same curriculum as his classmates and maintained satisfactory grades. He fit in socially, and even had a couple upperclassmen to keep an eye on him. When he requested assistance or needed to learn a little humility, they helped out. One friend was a young man named Kevin Snowver, a tough kid, but not the bully type.

Rick had met Snowver through his brother and they become close friends. He had one other upperclassman to rely on. It was Rob Hoyt, the same kid he used to race on the Creeper.

Rick also had a friend and protectorate coming up from middle school. It was another kid named Hoyt, and he, too, was born with athleticism in his genes. When it came to sports, Russell excelled in football, wrestling and lacrosse.

Doctor Sartori, the same teacher who opened the door for Rick's birth as a marathon competitor, also coached Russell's football team. Unfortunately, a crushing tackle put young Hoyt in the hospital with a broken ankle, and his football career came to an abrupt end.

"He was a great player because of his blazing speed," Sartori stated. "The kid could really motor. We hated losing him."

Rob took a piece of the credit for his brother's speed. "He got so fast because he was always running away from me."

When it came to athletic accomplishments, Rob also took a turn at center stage. Although his mother was the one who initially forced him into a competitive swimming pool, Rob took control from that point on. With plenty of natural ability and a good dose of discipline, he climbed to the top of the ladder among New England's swimming elite. The higher he climbed, the more Dick became involved. It brought them closer.

While Judy neared completion of her college degree, Kamp for Kids continued to grow in numbers and successes, and when the year ended, the Hoyt family found many of reasons to give thanks. Rick shared his feelings in writing, with the following letter to his parents:

Dear Mom and Dad,
...I feel like I am a pain sometimes, because of my handicap. I'm glad to have you both for my parents. Mom I feel that I have the most caring mother in the world. Dad, I love very much going running with you. Thank you for taking me. Your loving son. Rick.

The Hoyts received acclaim from unexpected sources. At a local church, the pastor mentioned them in his sermon with a "family" theme. Another source was Bill Como, a member of that same congregation, who worked for Major Dick Hoyt in the National Guard. One morning, Como was stopped in traffic due to a 10K race. While he waited, the Hoyts trotted past, with their names shouted out by nearby spectators. When Como saw Dick at work, he jokingly said, "Sir, I have to see you at work every day. When I go to church, the preacher is talking about you. I take my family shopping, the road is blocked for you. I simply can't take it any longer. I want a transfer."

Dick could not generate that same level of respect and acceptance from everyone. By the time Patriot's Day came around in 1982, he had not yet convinced the committee to let them in, so once again, they would participate as *bandits*.

"If we're bandits, maybe we should wear masks," Dick quipped sarcastically.

Rick lightened the moment. He spelled out the words, "It would help your looks."

Dick may have failed in the quest for legitimacy, but he and Rick were successful in performance. They ran the marathon in two hours and fifty-nine minutes, as Dick predicted, less than three hours. The news media took notice, and members of the BAA made an effort to congratulate them. The committee members soon realized that the inspirational Hoyts had public appeal and drawing value. However, those doggone rules kept getting in the way.

A reporter asked Dick, "Why do you do this?"

"Because Rick loves to run," he replied truthfully. "And I love running with him."

"Would you ever race without him?"

"Why should I? He's what drives me."

"Well, Major Hoyt, some people say you could be a world-class runner if you ran alone."

Dick shrugged and said, "That's not my objective."

"Your objective? What? You mean, for, um—"

Dick cut him short. "We race to have fun and to promote awareness. To include the disabled. How could I do all that if I excluded my son?"

The man persisted. "I understand, sir, but—"

"I don't run without him," Dick said flatly. "I wouldn't know what to do with my arms."

The remainder of 1982 was a repeat of the previous year — a race every weekend, with the focus on Boston in 1983. The goal: run it faster and without the masks. When asked why he found it so important to be official entrants and to wear a race number, Rick said, "Dad is the one who wants the number. It's not that important to me. I'm satisfied because I have a lot of friends along the route who cheer for me."

As a follow-up, the woman asked, "How does it feel when you cross the finish line?"

Referring to a four-time winner of the event, Rick said, "I feel like Bill Rodgers."

In 1983, while a senior at Westfield High School, a teacher gave Rick an assignment to write an essay. Wisely, he chose a subject with which he was very familiar:

What It Is Like To Be A Non-Vocal Person

...At first, I felt cheated and angry. Even though my parents talked to and treated me the same as my brothers, I felt and knew I was different. I understand all things said to me. Being a non-vocal person does not make one less of a human being. I have the same feelings as anyone else. I feel sadness, joy, hunger, love, compassion and pain...

Rick aced the assignment. Judy continued to run her own race. She accelerated through school and graduated with a Master's Degree. That accomplishment gave her the additional clout she needed, and it elevated her status with ASHS. With

Judy at the helm, Kamp for Kids became a year-round facility that included programs for families.

Russell moved into high school and continued his athletic endeavors. Once he had recovered from the broken ankle, he immersed himself in wrestling, and while Rob streaked to victories in state and regional swimming events, Russ slammed older, larger kids on their backsides.

Dick always took interest in his sons' successes, but he still had obligations to the military, to his wife, and, of course, to his training. With Boston right around the corner, he had no time to rest. As public support dribbled in, Dick took another charge at the members of the BAA. This time they informed him that Rick was not a runner, nor was he pushing a wheelchair; therefore, Dick was the only athlete. "But you are welcome to participate in the race, unofficially."

As Dick found new allies in the press, pressure from the news media intensified, and finally, after it was too late for the 1983 race, the committee resorted to one final objection: "You're okayed to race, but just like everyone else, you will have to meet all the requirements."

"That meant we needed a qualifying time," Dick explained.

Dick had run fast enough to quality. For a man his age, 42, he needed a 3:10, and in 1982, he ran the course in 2:59. However, the committee decided to modify the rules for Dick and Rick. For them to qualify, it had to be in Rick's age division. To do that, they were required to run in a sanctioned marathon and complete it in two hours and fifty minutes, the same as the requirement for any other twenty-year-old runner.

Dick and Rick blazed through the 1983 race in 2:57, a new Personal Record. That left only one more hurdle — the masks must come off. They would be bandits no more, but it could only happen if they turned in a supreme effort elsewhere. When Dick opened the 1984 Team Hoyt race calendar to schedule the next Patriot's Day race, he added one word: *Officially!*

Dick's sisters cheering.

Another successful Boston Marathon.

We love Boston!

CHAPTER 9 — A FEW GOOD MEN

Society has limited expectations of the handicapped, and it hesitates to impose the discipline needed to raise a child to be independent because we feel sorry for them. You have to give them rules so they can grow and develop.

—Judy Hoyt

For one full school year, all three of the Hoyt boys rocked the halls of Westfield High School together. Rob graduated first, finishing his high school swimming career with honors. He mastered all four of the basic strokes, but his forte was the 50-meter freestyle. He closed out the season as one of the top swimmers in Massachusetts, and found himself perched near the top of the New England YMCA rankings.

After watching Rob win a local meet, Dick boasted, "He was so much better than the other swimmers, he wasn't even tired when he climbed out of the water. Everyone else was gasping for air, but Rob wasn't even working hard."

Since Rob's point of view came from water level, he had a more realistic opinion regarding the effort. "Dad only *thought* I wasn't tired," Rob said. "I worked my butt off."

The entire Hoyt family usually attended the swim meets, but, unfortunately, Dick missed the one most meaningful to Rob. In his final high school competition, one that encompassed the entire New England region, Rob knifed through the water at a record pace. He went stroke for stroke with the reigning champion, and he appeared to take a slight lead, but the timing system indicated he slapped the wall a microsecond after the winner. He came out of the water smiling, only to learn that he had not won.

There was no shame in second place, certainly not in a race at such a competitive level. After all, it was the New England Championships, and either man could have won. On any other day, Rob might have been crowned king of the New England pools, but it didn't happen on that particular day, the one that counted. Rob admitted his disappointment was not so much that he didn't win, but because his dad had missed sharing his greatest athletic moment. Though he knew in advance his parents could not be there, that was little consolation. He was well aware his father found a way to race with Rick every weekend, so right or wrong, he felt slighted.

"I had a weekend obligation with the Guard," Dick explained. "I would have been there if I could. It wasn't possible."

For the family that had been through so many struggles together, and had overcome so many obstacles as a team, this seemed like a minor misunderstanding that could easily be resolved, but family disputes are never quite as simple as they seem. Life was back to normal Monday, but the emotional wounds would take time to heal.

Rob was pleased to see his younger brother enter high school. Before Russell's arrival, he was the one who attended to most of Rick's needs. Although Kevin Snowver helped, the feeding and toileting responsibilities defaulted to Rob. However, when Russ entered the scene, sibling rivalry had more opportunity to flair. After all, Rick was five years older than Russ, and he could be very demanding. Like his father, Russell had a quiet and easy-going demeanor, but he was never the type of person you could push around, a fact readily confirmed by some of the best wrestlers in the state.

At school one day, Russ carried Rick into the rest room. They had a serious difference of opinion on some meaningless issue, but the ensuing disagreement angered Rick to the point he forgot to consider the consequences of his actions.

"He took a bite out of my arm," Russ said. "I yelped, grabbed my arm, and Rick hit the floor howling."

Both men suffered battle wounds. The commotion landed them a restriction at school and a lecture at home. It was a bad day for the brothers, but the good days were far more common. Russ became a defender for the underdog at an early age. He charged into battle more than once because some insensitive bully caused problems for a defenseless person.

Russ said, "I couldn't watch a weaker person get mistreated, not without getting involved. I suppose that was from growing up with a brother who couldn't defend himself."

Rob had a great time in high school. He graduated with honors in athletics and academics, then enrolled in college at nearby Westfield State. "But it wasn't what I wanted to do," he admitted. "That's what my parents expected."

Rob reluctantly took the path chosen by his parents, but his college days were few. When a friend helped him land a job as an apprentice machinist, he went out the door every morning with textbooks in hand, but stashed them on the floor of the car and reported to work. Rob knew the pretense couldn't last long, that his parents would find out eventually, but that was something to worry about later. After all, he was still a teenager.

"I really liked my job," Rob said. "It was totally different from anything I had ever done. It became a higher priority than going to school."

Rob made one major mistake. Since he still lived at home, he was unable to avoid the watchful eyes of brother Rick. In retrospect, he would have been wise to keep big brother in his confidence, but he got careless.

"Dad told us he would pay the bills and we could live at home if we went to college," Rick wrote with a mischievous glint in his eye. "I figured out that Rob wasn't going to school."

When a brotherly conflict erupted between Rick and Rob, the cat was out of the bag. Rick's motivation may have been to teach his younger brother an important lesson in life, or maybe he simply felt it was the right thing to do, but regardless, he decided their father needed to know the truth. While Rob prepared for work one morning, Rick lodged his electric wheelchair between the bedroom door and the bathtub. With the door securely blocked, he waited. When Rob tried in vain to open the door, Rick ignored his angry protestations.

"He was late for work," Rick admitted. "When his boss called, Dad was the one who took the call."

Dick and Judy were furious with their middle son. They sat him down for an adult-to-adult talk on responsibility, and when the lecture ended, Rob agreed to finish the semester.

"I was mad enough to toss Rick in a lake," Rob confessed with a laugh. "He didn't get any Cokes from me for a while, I'll tell you that."

Once the dust settled, Rob decided it was time to think about moving out on his own.

Rob had always been a caring brother and a compassionate young man. He loved Rick, and he had done his share of providing support. Had he chosen, Rob could have created a stellar career working with the disabled at any level. His understanding and empathy would have been a Godsend for other children like Jamie Decenza, the boy who had been abandoned at the door of an institution. Growing up with Dick, Judy, and Rick had prepared him well, but that was not what Rob wanted. Not at that time, anyway.

Dick and Judy lost that round. After the semester ended, Rob worked two jobs and had soon earned praise for his potential as a machinist. He was a young, ambitious man on the move, so that's what he did. He moved out of the house and into his own apartment.

"We wanted him to stay in college," Dick said. "But I've been in his shoes, so I understood."

"Rob had a lot to offer the disabled," Judy said, a little less forgiving. "He would have done extremely well. It was a loss of good, needed talent."

Perhaps Judy was right, but Rob had to find his own pathway to happiness just like any other adult, and that's exactly what he did. Then along came Mary Conners, the same young lady who had staked her claim to him the first time they met.

"Mary was a lot like my mom," Rob acknowledged. "She knew what she wanted, she went for it, and she usually got it. I didn't have a chance."

* * *

Following their third consecutive and successful Boston Marathon, the Rick and Dick duo were increasingly in demand. Everyone wanted to punch their ticket. Race directors invited them to races without charging an entry fee, and sponsors nibbled at their heels. They participated in every race they could find, including relays, benefits, charities, long- and short-distance runs, and even one for Judy's Kamp for Kids. It was all part of their training. They were having fun, too, but their ultimate goal was to qualify for the next Boston Marathon.

"We didn't like being called bandits," Dick repeated.

When Dick Hoyt didn't like something, he changed it. He leveled his sights on the Marine Corps Marathon in Washington, D.C. Wisnewski told him that it was a highly visible event, and since it took place late in the fall, the weather was generally good for long-distance racing.

"It's also a great race to notch a personal record," Pete said. "I'll run it with you. I'll be the rabbit."

"What do you think, Rick?" Dick asked.

Rick offered his traditional smile of approval, and he told his dad, "I can outrun you there, too."

Friends and spectators had often pointed out the fact that Rick always crossed the finish line ahead of his dad, in every race. Rick once told an interviewer, "I always beat him, but only by a second."

That trivial point became a source of humor between them. At the Boston Sheriff's Race, a fundraiser for law enforcement, Dick turned the tables on his confident, unsuspecting son.

"He loves the police-sponsored races," Dick said. "The cops always talk to him. He was having a lot of fun at the race, but he got a little too cocky." Rick had heard the story often. He acknowledged with a grin and Dick continued. "When we got to the finish line, I turned around and pulled him over the line after me. This time, I beat him by a second."

In August, Team Hoyt packed up the running chair and headed back to their former hometown. The Falmouth 7.1-mile race had become one of the most popular road races in the state, and it took place just a short jog from where the Hoyts had once lived. Since Judy's parents owned a home in Cape Cod, it gave her a chance to visit them.

"If we only did two races a year," Dick said, "they would be in Boston and Falmouth. Those are our favorites."

Falmouth loved the Hoyts, too. They were welcomed as hometown heroes, and stood equally in stature to another entrant, Alberto Salazar, a man who had set world records in the marathon. When Dick and Rick jogged side by side with Salazar prior to the race, a dutiful photographer jumped into the street and captured the moment. His photo of the threesome appeared along with the story in the newspaper the following day. That picture earned a permanent place of honor on Rick's wall.

Dave McGillivray also raced at Falmouth that day.

"You look like a good athlete," McGillivray said to Dick during the awards. "How about doing my race up in Medford?"

Dick accepted without thought. "Sure."

The friendly man was top dog at Dave McGillivray Sports Enterprises (DMSE), a prominent sports promotion agency in the Boston area. He also pioneered the sport of triathlon and other endurance events throughout New England, and had organized his own triathlon series. The publicity generated by Dick Hoyt's participation would give his operation a boost and invite greater interest, he concluded, just as they were doing for road racing.

"But it's a triathlon," McGillivray added, thinking that might change Dick's answer.

"That's okay. As long as my son can do it with me."

McGillivray never expected that response. He glanced down at Rick, then raised his brow and looked over at Dick like he was some sort of nut case. He smiled, shook Dick's hand, and walked away to recruit elsewhere.

Wisnewski was right about the Marine Corps Marathon. Being in the nation's Capital, it had national appeal. Runners from all over the country headed east, including a high percentage of first-time marathoners. It came at a perfect time of the year for a marathon, as Pete said, and because they held it in D.C., many runners scheduled their vacations around the race.

Dick and Rick arrived in Washington determined to accomplish their lofty goal. Dick stood on sacred ground near the Lincoln Monument, but his mind was on the race as he mentally visualized the clock that would be waiting at the finish line. Dick knew this would be his best opportunity to qualify for an official race number in the 1984 Boston Marathon, but he had to cut seven minutes from his previous best time.

"Running a marathon in two hours and fifty minutes is a huge task for a 42-year-old under any conditions," Pete said. "Never mind pushing a 130-pound payload in front of him."

Dick arrived in Washington well prepared, conditioned like never before, but he had no delusions about the depth of his challenge. Everything would have to work perfectly. To him, it was more than a race. Much more. It was another mountain he and Rick had to climb. Through all the serious preparation, Rick found humor.

"On race morning, I went to get him ready," Dick said affectionately. "There he was with a shaved head and wearing a Marine uniform. He saluted me."

Dick minimized the risk of foul weather storming in and derailing his plans. If it turned nasty, as often happened during east coast races that time of year, Rick had to take the brunt of it, and a sixty-second stop to adjust his clothing or warm him up might be the difference in success and failure. As a solution, to protect Rick from bugs, debris or foul weather, he had a fabrication shop mount a plastic, transparent shield to the front of the running chair. Pete couldn't make it to Washington on the day of the race, which left them without a "rabbit" to set the pace.

"Ready, Rick?" Dick asked.

Rick nodded.

The race started and the large group of wheelchair athletes bolted into action. With an adrenalin overflow, Dick pushed through the first 10 miles in barely over an hour, a pace much faster than necessary. Rick gave him "the look," so he wisely eased back on the throttle and glided smoothly and patriotically through the streets of the Capital of the United States. Team Hoyt hit on all eight cylinders that day, with Dick's body doing everything he asked it to do. He thought about *Mister Wall* at mile twenty-two, but they blasted right through it.

"At mile 25 I started looking for the clock," Dick said. "I knew it was going to be close."

As they neared the finish, Dick heard someone call out the time, but it sounded too good. He kept looking for the race clock. Rick saw it first and bellowed out his exhilaration. From the distance, however, Dick could not decipher the time, but he was confident he saw the *two* hours, and then a *four*. If correct, they were still under two hours and fifty minutes.

"I don't see a five yet!" he yelled out to Rick, then clenched his teeth and leaned into the chair. "Hold on!"

There was a *five* on the clock when he finished, but not in the ten's digit. A boisterous, appreciative crowd greeted them when they shot between the flags in two hours, forty-five and a half minutes. They covered the course with more than four minutes of breathing room. They qualified for Boston, and this time the stoical man could not hide his emotions. He hugged Rick first, and then anyone else who came around to congratulate them.

Dick told Rick, "No masks in Boston."

According to reporter William Plummer in *People Weekly*, Bill Rodgers — one of Rick's sports heroes and four-time winner of the Boston Marathon — was so impressed with the Hoyts' accomplishment that he proclaimed, "It is a world class effort. Everyone involved in the sport of marathoning is inspired by the Hoyts."

Back home, Dick prepared a letter and application for Boston. He included the certification he and Rick received from the Marine Corps Marathon, of course, and he made sure all the *I*'s were dotted and the *T*'s properly crossed. They had come too far to make any foolish mistakes. On the line next to the word *Signature*, Dick signed his name, then made another line below it for Rick. He placed the application on the *Hope Machine* and wedged a pen between Rick's clenched fingers. "Sign it."

Rick slowly scrawled two intersecting lines below his dad's signature, which created the letter *X*. Dick folded the application, slipped it into an envelope and tossed it on the table.

"You hungry?" he asked Rick.

Rick nodded. Dick peered out the window and said, "Looks like we're eating alone tonight. You want to do the cooking tonight, or should I?"

Dick and Judy had not abandoned their mutual goals for the family or for individual family members; however, she started questioning the benefits derived from racing. She expressed concern that Dick might be losing focus on the overall goal of paving new roads for disabled people in general. He drew attention to Rick, sure, but the public saw it more as an athletic accomplishment by Dick, not an awareness of Rick's abilities.

"Do you want us to quit running?" Dick asked in frustration. "How does that help anyone? How does it help Rick?"

Judy did not want them to quit, of course, because Rick truly loved racing with his dad. Judy had no desire to interfere, but all the attention Dick got on Rick's behalf perplexed her.

"I think she felt like she was being left out," Dick said. "Like she was not really a part of the racing except when people talked about Rick's disability. But it was racing that got their attention. It wasn't easy for her. I understood that."

On issues regarding the disabled, Judy clearly expressed her desires and expectations. In an interview with Marlene Cimons from *The Runner* magazine, she stated her belief that society has limited expectations of the handicapped. "It hesitates to impose the discipline needed to raise a child to be independent," she told Cimons, "because we feel sorry for them. That is the worst thing you can do. You can't let a handicapped kid own you, just like you can't let other kids own you. You have to give them rules so they can grow and develop." She went on to say, "There are so many people who are less handicapped than Rick, but they are still in the home with their parents taking care of them. It doesn't have to be that way. You have to help your handicapped child let go, and you have to be able to let go, too."

* * *

The new year started with Dick and Rick racing, meeting new friends and gaining more recognition. Rick would graduate from Westfield High in the spring, then he planned to attend college. Rob got a promotion and still dated Mary Conners. Judy found new challenges with ASHS and Kamp for Kids, and on occasion, advised the Massachusetts congress on how to deal with the disabled. Russ climbed up the wrestling rankings as rapidly as Rob did in swimming.

With all the success of Team Hoyt, greater television exposure ensued.

Barry Nolan started that ball rolling, but after Boston and the Marine Corps Marathons, a national show took notice. *Hour Magazine* did a feature on the Hoyts and beamed it across the country in late February.

On Patriot's Day, 1984, Dick and Rick proudly wore a legitimate race number to the starting line in Hopkinton. Their long-running battle with the BAA ended in another victory, which left only one more goal: to obtain another personal record for the course. In addition to their well-deserved "official" status, they also gained in support and recognition. The fame surprised them, but, like everything else, they took it in stride.

116

Amazed, Dick shook his head. "I think everyone in Boston saw us on *Hour Magazine*. It seemed like everyone on the course knew our names. Rick said he felt like a celebrity."

One of the ironies of the event occurred prior to the race. The BAA committee that had obstructed their entry for so long, now asked Dick and Rick to receive the news media and help publicize the marathon.

"So we did," Dick said candidly. "We got more attention than the overall winners."

To accentuate their success, they ran the race in two hours and fifty-seven minutes, fast enough to eclipse their previous best at Boston. They had done it again. This was inclusion at its very best, and the view from the top was mighty sweet.

"This is what we're all about," Dick said frankly. "What's not to understand?"

As the year progressed and the Hoyt fame spread, Dick was selected as a candidate for the Healthy American Fitness Leaders award (HAFL), an infant organization that originated as an outgrowth of the President's Council on Physical Fitness. Word of the Hoyts' accomplishments had reached far and wide, and that included the POTUS — President of the United States; Dick's Commander in Chief, the Honorable Ronald Reagan.

Organizations such as HAFL set their own criteria to determine the candidates and winners of its awards, and once the selection committee had scrutinized all the letters and resumes, they made their decision. Although it's hard to imagine anyone being more deserving of the title "fitness leader," they decided Dick did not top their list of requirements.

The Hoyts had moved into broader circles. Their fame began in the city of Westfield, pervaded the state of Massachusetts, and soon engulfed the entire New England region. They went on to conquer Washington, D.C., and now they had gone national. They had found their niche.

"We enjoy the challenge," Dick said with passion. "Rick and I have fun spending time together. When I push him in that chair,

I go all out. I want to pass people. I want to beat them. I don't know if I could go as fast by myself. I don't have the desire to do it without him. Maybe someday it will happen, but I'd rather do it with Rick."

In June, Rick took center stage when he graduated from Westfield High School and became one of the few non-vocal quadriplegics in America to achieve that distinction. He received a standing ovation when his attendant escorted him across the football field, where the Mayor of Westfield presented him with a diploma. Prom night was equally memorable.

Rick was accompanied to the prom by one of his female PCAs, one whose name he laughingly refused to reveal, like he was protecting the young lady's reputation. The lad with the great memory defaulted, claiming a touch of amnesia. He said she was drop-dead gorgeous and left it at that. He had met his lovely companion through Judy, during one of her weekend workshops, and Rick flipped head over heels. Unfortunately, the young lady had other plans for her future. Romance wasn't in the cards for Rick, not with her, anyway.

One of the toughest lessons we all learn is that some of the finer things in life are not available to everyone. The pretty PCA was tantalizing, but like the Coke in the refrigerator, she was out of reach. Rejection never comes easy, not for Rick, not for any of us, but it helped that he had accepted his limitations long before she waltzed innocently into his life.

Rick stated, philosophically, "The one you can't have is the one you want most."

No one could predict what might be next for Rick, but a new challenge would never be far away. That's the way he lived his life. To him, the finish line was only an illusion, a place to wave at the world while he caught his breath and considered his next move.

A diploma and a date for the Senior Prom.

119

Qualifying for Boston at the Marine Corps Marathon.

CHAPTER 10 — THE COLLEGE BOY

*What I think is important is that people take the time
and effort to realize that first and foremost I am a
person with a brain and intelligence.*

—Rick Hoyt

Selecting a college was not an easy task for Rick because there were many issues he had to consider, and a consensus on which school best fit all his needs was difficult to reach. Dick urged him to attend Westfield State and continue living at home, where he and the family would be close by. In addition to that, having him at home would be more conducive to their training and racing schedules. The big problem with Westfield State, however, was the issue of independence. Rick wanted total control of his life.

"After all," he asserted on his own behalf, "isn't that what college is all about?" He made a good argument.

Judy encouraged him to enroll at her alma mater, the University of Massachusetts, Amherst. She respected the staff and faculty, and knew they would be attentive to her son.

"They have excellent programs in special education," she said, hoping to persuade him.

But Rick wanted more freedom, more room to roam, more control over his life, and a large city farther from home appealed to him. Since Boston had been very kind to him over the years, Boston University was his first choice, but that decision brought funding to the forefront of the selection process.

"He ran into a problem," Dick said. "The welfare department denied funds for his PCAs."

At that point, it appeared that Dick had won, and that he would get to keep Rick in Westfield, but Rick remained determined.

"In order for me to go to college, I needed to have PCAs," Rick wrote on his computer. "But the Boston Center for Independent Living (BCIL) told me that since I could not speak, I could not direct a PCA."

With the aid of the TIC Machine and the Russell Method, Judy believed her son would have no trouble directing the attendants, so after a bit of saber rattling, she arranged for a face-to-face meeting with the Welfare Department. She and Rick prepared their case and went to the hearing, where they presented a very persuasive argument.

"Once a person with severe disabilities turns 18," Judy informed the committee, "Social Security allows the individual to receive Medicaid, which pays for Personal Care Attendants. The state pays PCAs an average of $14,000, which enables a disabled person to stay home. On the other hand," she continued, "it cost $160,000 to keep him in an institution. Since you are spending taxpayers' dollars, which would you rather ask them to fund, fourteen thousand or one hundred and sixty thousand?"

Even a government agency could follow that logic. The committee agreed to allot Rick nine hours of personal care every day, but he would need to hire a revolving staff of PCAs at eight bucks an hour to help him with all his daily functions. Once the funding issue was finally resolved, Rick's worried parents and brothers packed his bags and delivered him to Towers Dormitory at Boston University.

The transition from a quiet, loving home to a dorm full of noisy strangers overwhelmed Rick at first. He had not given a lot of consideration to the negative side of independence. With his security blanket lifted, a lonely, homesick feeling crept up to take its place. Rick wept. He did not cry out like a baby, or even plead to be taken back home, he simply unloaded some of his emotions through tears. The sadness didn't last long because Rick dried his eyes and did what most young men would do to survive such a traumatic experience.

Rick said, "I had a few drinks with my new roommates."

Walking away from the son who had consumed their lives for more than twenty-one years proved quite a test for Dick and Judy. The drive back to Westfield was long and lonely, and the range of emotions clashed, just as they would for any parent whose firstborn moved far away from home.

"It was another rough trip," Dick admitted, referring to the day they returned from visiting the specialist in Medford. "But he wanted control of his life, so he got it. He earned it."

Along with independence came responsibilities. Rick had to select PCAs he could trust, who could provide the services he needed. He had to do all the scheduling for his classes, homework, study time, meals, shopping, transportation and recreation, and with the help of the PCAs, maintain it with efficiency. When he selected the discipline he would study, he chose special education. It took him six hours to do the homework that other students could do in one hour, which meant he could take only two courses each semester.

"I'll graduate in nine years," he said. "Unless I get my PHD, then it will take fifteen."

Rick acted like a wild-and-crazy college kid at times, but he also took the work seriously. His objective was to win, not just go through the motions. He had set goals, the same as most other students. Rick had a mass of homework, but he got it done, and he did it himself. He sat hour after hour, patiently listening, reading or nudging the head switch with his forehead. He worked long hours. Sometimes he fell asleep at the switch, but when he awoke, he kept on punching. Rick knew better than anyone the hardships he encountered in progressing from "vegetable" status to becoming a bona fide college student. It was a long, hard struggle, not only for himself, but for everyone involved. With a sense of loyalty to himself and his family, he remained determined to succeed.

"It was like the Boston Marathon," Rick said. "After all the work getting to the starting line, I wanted to finish."

With the help of his PCAs, Rick ate his meals in the school dining hall and did his studying in the school library. He enjoyed contemporary Rock music, supported the Boston University sports teams, and learned to party with his new friends. To flaunt his independence, Rick occasionally drank too much of his favorite beverage. He still preferred Coke, but as a college man, he eventually learned to dilute it with rum.

"I slacked the first five years," Rick confessed. "I was having a good time."

When asked to expound on "good time," Rick refused to volunteer any incriminating information. However, he elaborated on the downside of living on the same floor as the hockey team, where they all shared a community bath.

"One night the hockey players stole an ice statue and hid it in the bathroom," Rick explained. "To keep it frozen, they left the bathroom windows open day and night, in the middle of winter."

Along with his PCA, Neil Danilowicz, who had become his best friend, Rick tried apartment living. But that did not work out as well as he had hoped. After one year of watching mushrooms grow in the living room because management refused to repair a leaky roof, dormitory life didn't look too bad after all, and he moved back into a dorm with a private bath.

Rick took his studies more seriously when he moved back on campus. Once, when asked what it was like to be disabled, Rick told the interrogator he had nothing to compare it to because he had always been a disabled person. "What I think is important," Rick said, "is that people take the time and effort to realize that first and foremost I am a person with a brain and intelligence."

Although Rick became more studious, he still enjoyed drinking rum and Coke, and he had plenty of anecdotes that evolved from indulging in his favorite mind-altering mix. His partner in crime was usually good friend Kevin Snowver. Rick reluctantly shared their "drunk kid" story.

"I would lie on the sidewalk outside a bar," Rick recalled. "When someone came by, Kevin told them I drank too much and I needed help standing up. Some of them tried to help me stand before they realized what we were doing."

The unsuspecting good Samaritans who came to Rick's rescue had mixed emotions when hoodwinked by the disabled kid and his accomplice, but they had no recourse but to walk away. When the rum wore off, Rick and Kevin acknowledged they were a little embarrassed by what they had done, but, for the moment, they enjoyed a good laugh.

A surprising source of opposition encountered by the Hoyts came from other disabled athletes. George Murray, for instance, was a world-class wheelchair athlete who objected to the Hoyts being allowed to start races in the wheelchair division with the other participants. In her interview, Marlene Cimons said Murray was upset because the Hoyts started with the wheelchairs, and that race officials often listed them in that division and included them in the wheelchair results. Dick tried to prevent things like that, but, as he said, "Oversights do occur."

Murray insisted that they strictly enforce the rules for wheelchair competition, especially those that define an athlete's means of propulsion. "It's not enough to define yourself as disabled and have a 'sort-of' chair," he said in protest. "The Hoyts began racing when wheelchair competition was in its early stages, and they created an area of confusion at a time when we were trying to develop and define our rules. They received a race number corresponding to the wheelchair division and they lined up with the wheelchair competitors, but the wheelchair division is not a multipurpose, mass-participation, recreational event."

Murray had no problem if the race included a "handicapped" division such as the one in New York, Marlene Cimons went on to say, and the Hoyts should be allowed to compete in that specific division if they wish. Murray said, "If he competes only against himself and participates for the fun and fitness of it, and a lot of other reasons, I don't have any problem with that."

The wheelchair athlete did not know Judy Hoyt was in attendance when he delivered a speech at an educational conference in Indiana. During the speech, he criticized the Hoyts' participation in the Boston Marathon.

"George made some remark about this guy named Hoyt pushing his son," Judy said, "and that he felt they didn't belong in the race because it was a race of champions."

Cimons said Judy had approached Murray at a cocktail party that evening, and without identifying herself, she said, "I told him I thought it was wrong that he, a handicapped person, would discriminate like that against other handicapped people. Then I told him 'that Hoyt guy' was my husband, and that Dick ran a qualifying time just like everyone else and that they were working just as hard to be a part of it as he was."

Judy had no argument with Murray's position on wheelchair competition, and later admitted she may have misunderstood his comments on that particular evening. But she also believed that handicapped athletes had a moral responsibility to support other disabled athletes and keep their criticism discreet.

That same article in the *Herald* stated that John McGrath, the publisher of *Boston Running News,* supported Judy's opinion. He believed Dick and Rick should start with other runners. In his view, the wheelchairs start early only because the speed could create safety problems for others, but "The Hoyts present no danger to anyone."

"I have the greatest respect for him," McGrath said. "I think he should line up with everyone else. I don't see any reason for him to start early when he runs the same pace as other runners. So he should be started in a seeded race with everyone else."

Dick could not have said it better himself, and that's the way they've been running Boston ever since. Extraneous distractions such as those were not a major concern to Dick. He stated, succinctly, "Some things in life we can't control."

Rick agreed totally. He would not let his education, the partying, or anything else interfere with his racing. The Boston

Marathon now had a more profound meaning for Rick because the course went past Boston University and his dormitory, where he heard fans and friends screaming his name when he and Dick shot past. Later that month, they hustled off to the heartland of Lincoln, Nebraska, where they raced in the Air National Guard Marathon. The promoters embraced Major Hoyt as "one of their own" and presented him as their featured attraction.

Every weekend, another race. In August, they returned to Falmouth. It was a family affair again, time to visit with Judy's parents and some old friends, and to run seven-point-one miles through the streets of Falmouth. They turned in another stellar performance in front of the friendly crowd, and covered the course at a sub-six-minute pace.

Dick and Rick stayed after the race to mingle with friends and fellow runners. They chatted with race officials, enjoyed the post-race amenities, and watched the awards ceremony. They received kudos and congratulations from the many fans they had inspired on television a few months earlier in the Boston Marathon. Dave McGillivray stepped up and tapped Dick on the shoulder.

"Have you given any thought to what I said about doing a triathlon?" McGillivray asked after a handshake.

After four years of making waves and turning heads, every informed, sports-minded person in Massachusetts had heard about the accomplishments of Team Hoyt. Being very astute at the promotional business, McGillivray decided he wanted the Hoyts in his race, and since he had anticipated Dick's answer this time, he was ready with a response.

"Only if I can do it with my son," Dick replied.

"Great, do it with your son. See what kind of equipment you can come up with, then let's talk about it."

"Sure," Dick said. "I'll give you a call."

In an interview with Michael O'Connor from the *Boston Sunday Herald*, McGillivray explained his initial interest in Dick Hoyt and why he wanted to convert him into a triathlete.

"My wife and I were out pushing our new baby in a baby jogger," McGillivray said. "We took turns pushing and running. After five or six miles, we looked at each other and shook our heads. We wondered how Dick could do what he does. I mean, Rick weighs a lot more than a baby. I have a tremendous amount of respect for both of them."

When McGillivray walked away, Dick looked to Rick for his input. Without any written, spoken, or spelled words, he knew what Rick was thinking. "Are you nuts?"

McGillivray, an endurance athlete himself, realized that Dick could probably do anything he set his mind to, and he would be a tremendous asset to the sport of triathlon. Confidently, he said, "I figured Dick would take care of the details."

Dick's response was typically short and non-specific, but in his mind, he had made a commitment. It was a done deal. No need to give it more thought at that moment.

Team Hoyt had just officially completed their two favorite races and achieved Personal Bests in both. Dick had other things on his mind. He had not completely adjusted to Rick living alone in Boston, which now required greater time and effort to prepare for races. He also had some new problems he needed to resolve quickly. The "mobile" Air National Guard had promoted Dick and given him a new duty assignment, one that required a transfer to Wellesley, a small city outside Boston.

"Judy was content living in Westfield," Dick said. "And she didn't want to move that far from her work."

In addition to all their other concerns, they had to consider the youngest member of the family. Russell still attended high school, where he kicked butt as Westfield's 147-pound wrestler. He had no desire to transfer to any other high school, but instead contemplated moving into an apartment with brother Rob until he graduated. His motivation was not limited to wrestling and education, however. Lisa, the young girl he met through Rick at age 12, had grown into a lovely young woman. After graduation from Medford High School, she moved to Westfield. What began as an innocuous "puppy love" had now grown into a full-blown romance, the same as the one between Rob and Mary Conners.

As winter neared, Dick kept busy training and racing, but in the back of his mind, he knew his younger sons felt that he had not been fair to them because he spent all his weekends racing with Rick. Dick also knew Rob had never completely understood or accepted the fact that he missed his championship swim meet, a time when Rob came within a stroke of winning the high school version of the Olympic gold. To atone, Dick promised himself he would never miss any of Russell's major wrestling meets. The dual matches, maybe, but not the tournaments or championships.

Russell possessed all the inherent athletic skills of his dad and brothers, and he had the same determination and dedication as his mother and father. He demonstrated all those attributes on the wrestling mat, and whenever he emerged from the locker room in his singlet and wrestling shoes, the transformation was similar to Clark Kent leaving a phone booth in blue tights with a large, red *S* on his chest.

When a wrestler is slammed on his back, with both shoulder blades momentarily "stuck" to the mat, it's called a *pin*, the boxing equivalent of a knockout. It represents dominance over the opponent. A pin is the ultimate success, and it scores six points for the team. Russell had the highest pin ratio on the Westfield squad for two years running, and one of the best in the entire state. With each hard-fought victory, Dick realized his youngest son had entered manhood and was ready to conquer the world, just as surely as his brothers before him. He swelled with pride each time he watched Russell dominate an opponent in one of the most competitive weight divisions in the sport.

The most poignant moment for Dick and Russell came in late February. With the Western Massachusetts Sectional Championship title on the line, Russell charged onto the mat. Dick canceled an event of his own in order to be there, but he did it without a second thought, and he had no regrets. This time, there would be no repeat of the stinging disappointment Rob

129

experienced three years earlier. Once the referee raised his arm in victory, Russ rushed over to his jubilant coach for a congratulatory hug. Then, to his surprise, Dick came bounding down from the stands and wrapped him in a bear hug.

"I was stunned," Russell said. "Dad was never like that."

The outburst of emotion was uncharacteristic of Dick Hoyt, apparently, and one his youngest son had never seen before.

There was another factor looming in the family decision-making process. Dick had received a promotion to Lieutenant Colonel and planned to retire in five years. Since he and Judy would soon be suffering through the "empty nest" syndrome, they decided it would be a great time to buy their retirement home. They set out to find a strategic location that would minimize the commute to their respective offices.

While they searched for a mutually convenient location, Dave McGillivray's words popped back into Dick's mind, and the challenge of a triathlon began to intrigue him. He was well aware that competing in the three-event race meant learning how to swim, so he needed a place with a pool. Or, perhaps a lake.

"You ready to do McGillivray's triathlon?" he asked Rick.

As usual, Rick was game for anything. However, he thought it necessary to remind his dad of one small detail.

He said, "Dad, you don't know how to swim."

"Yeah, you're right about that. So what?"

Dick found the retirement home he wanted – a small cottage that needed lots of work, which fit perfectly into his handyman proclivities. The property sat at the edge of a lovely lake in the rustic village of Holland. Since the location meant the commute to and from their offices would take less than an hour each, Judy approved and they made an offer.

"It's perfect," Dick insisted. "I can run and bike on the hilly roads and do my swimming in the lake."

"But, Dad," Rick reminded him again. "You can't swim."

Dick shrugged and said, "I can learn, can't I?"

Rob winning in a New England pool.

Russ scoring 6 points with another pin.

CHAPTER 11 — THE BAY STATE TRIATHLON

I'll never forget the first day I went down and jumped in the lake. I just sank. I tried doing the freestyle, dog paddle, sidestroke, floating, anything, but I couldn't breathe. I couldn't swim, but I had committed to do a triathlon in about seven months.

—Dick Hoyt

When the seller agreed to the Hoyts' offer, they bought the home on Hamilton Reservoir and moved into the tiny town of Holland. Now that Dick finally had his own swimming hole, he reviewed the 1985 racing calendar and contacted Dave McGillivray to schedule the inaugural triathlon for Team Hoyt.

"You're ready for a triathlon?" McGillivray asked. "How will you do it with your son?"

"I'll make it work."

"I'm sure you will. Which one will you do?"

"The one in Medford on June 16th," Dick told him.

"Medford?" McGillivray said with raised eyebrows. "That's a pretty tough one, Dick. It's not one I would recommend for beginners. It's not a sprint distance."

With a little study, Dick had learned that the distances for each leg of a triathlon vary. When Dave McGillivray said "sprint," he referred to the shortest distance for all the triathlons, which is where beginners usually test the waters. A sprint swim is generally one-quarter mile, sometimes a kilometer or half a mile. The race director will determine the distance, so the bike might be anywhere from eight to fifteen miles, and the run is generally three miles or five kilometers. Technically, if the winner takes longer than one hour to complete the race, it is considered an international distance rather than a sprint distance. Neither was the case in Medford. In fact, the Father's Day race qualified for a *Long* triathlon, a jump up from the International distance. The race in Medford would most likely take the overall winner more than two and a half hours to complete. As McGillivray said, it was not a race for beginners.

Dick was not concerned about the distance for each leg of the triathlon. After all, he had been running marathons and had seven months to prepare. In Medford, the specific date of the event was what impressed him most. June 16th was Father's Day, which would make it special for the entire family.

"We'll do Medford," he told the surprised McGillivray.

"Fine. You're in."

Out came the Team Hoyt calendar. Two months after their fifth consecutive Boston Marathon, they would do their first triathlon, an event that included a one-mile swim.

"I decided it was time to do some training for the swim," Dick said. "I'll never forget the first day I went down and jumped into the lake. I just sank. I tried doing the freestyle, dog paddle, sidestroke, floating, anything, but I could not breathe. Marathons were easy for me, but I couldn't swim, and I had committed to do a triathlon in about seven months."

Dick had mistakenly assumed that swimming was not any different from running. Any athlete can run in races, he thought, all you have to do is stay focused and swim farther and farther.

Wisely, Dick called on an expert. "The big difference," Rob told him, "is that when you are running, you can breathe. There is nothing to impede your oxygen supply. But when you're swimming, that's a different story. Your face is submerged, so you need to roll your body and grab some air while you are still moving forward as fast as you can go."

"Okay," Dick said impatiently. "How do I do that?"

Rob explained bilateral breathing, focusing on the lungs, reaching as far as he could, rolling his body, proper kicking, and everything else he knew about the proper swimming technique. Dick laughed. "I tried everything he told me, but it didn't help. It only confused me. I'm forty-five-years old at the time, you know. I'm an old dog and he wants to teach me a new trick. Why not just paddle?"

Dick never mastered the rules Rob explained to him, but he had that wonderful gift of determination. He struggled and splashed back and forth across the lake and in a pool, then ran and biked mile after mile on the roads around Holland.

"Dad figured out a way," Russ said. "Just like when we did mountain climbing when we were kids. He just figured out a way and then did it."

"I jumped in that water every day," Dick said. "What else could I do? I just kept going a little farther each time, then a little farther. When the water got too cold, I bought a wetsuit. When it was too cold for that, I joined the YMCA and swam all winter."

Rick expressed his concerns when he asked, "Where will we get a saddle?"

"A saddle?" Dick asked.

"If I'm riding on your back, I'll need a saddle."

Dick laughed. "What do you think I am, a horse?"

"No," Rick answered. "A mule."

Dick bought a 100-pound bag of cement, secured it in the running chair and plodded up and down every hill he could find. Everyone just scratched their heads and wondered if maybe Rick was right — a mule.

If not carrying him on his back, how would he swim with Rick? That question popped up more than once and it had to be answered long before June 16th. Dick had not really given it much thought, because first he had to make sure he could swim the course solo. One chilly morning, while he pushed his lifeless cement bag over the causeway toward home, he spotted a man leisurely paddling an inflatable raft across Hamilton Reservoir.

135

A light went on in Dick's head. "A boat!"

When Pete Wisnewski stopped by to help work on the house, Dick floated the idea past him. "Well, if anyone can do it," Pete said, "you're the man."

"Rick will be safe in a boat," Dick pointed out. "That's the important thing."

Since Dick felt confident he would be able to find a boat in the spring and still have plenty of time to use it for training, he moved along to the next phase.

"What will you do for the bike?" Pete asked.

"I don't know. I haven't been on a bike since I was seven years old."

"It's like sex," Pete said in a serious tone. "Once you learn how, you never forget."

"How would you know about sex?" Dick quipped. When the joking subsided, he told Pete about the chair design he had been considering. "It'll connect to the rear hub of the bike," Dick said confidently. "I'll pull it like a trailer. When we get back to the transition, I can disconnect it from the bike, lock the front wheel on the chair, and we're ready to roll. Using only one chair will save me time in the transition."

Pete agreed it would probably work. "In fact," he said, "I weigh about the same as Rick, so you can train by hauling my cute ass around town."

Dick located a man in Longmeadow who built racing bikes and frames. He told him what was required from the bike and the chair. The man agreed to build it, but to have the seat fitted to Rick's body, he referred Dick to two orthopedic doctors in Springfield. Once they concluded the negotiations and planning, Dick ordered the 18-speed Trek bike and the new running chair. With a little luck, the entire rig would be ready in time for him to use it for training before the race. However, he could not get a commitment on exactly when that would be.

Judy was not pleased when she learned that Dick had agreed to make monthly payments on a new bike and chair that would cost them over four thousand dollars, but with help from Rick, he eventually appeased her. And since they were already registered for a triathlon, she accepted it as a necessary investment.

Word spread about the idea of using an inflatable raft to tow Rick in the swim, and before long, Dick received a call from a friend who worked at the Falmouth Yacht Club. The club had offered to donate a new, nine-foot Boston Whaler. A dinghy.

"She'll be a good one, Dick. I'll call you when she's in."

"Great. I'll drive down there to get it."

"I really think you'll like her," the man said.

"I'm sure we will." Dick noted his friend always referred to the dinghy as *she* or *her*.

"She's a big one," the man added. "It takes a little work to pump her up."

"Wait a minute," Dick said with a laugh. "Are you talking about a raft or a woman?"

Since the chair would not be ready until after the Boston Marathon, Dick took the bike out and rode the hills alone while waiting for delivery. He also encountered a delay with the boat, and it was not until the first weekend in June before he finally went to Falmouth to pick it up. He listened to some perfunctory instructions on how to air "her" up and how to make repairs if any were necessary, then he tossed it in the van, thanked the man, and rushed back home.

On Monday, Dick visited the supply officer at the base.

"Good morning, Sergeant," he said to the man on duty. "I need some sort of harness."

"Can you be a little more specific, Sir?"

"Well, something I can use to tow a raft."

"Tow it? With what, a boat?"

"With my body," Dick answered. "When I'm swimming."

"You want to tow a raft when you go swimming?"

"Yeah, with my son in it."

The Sergeant said, "Hey, you're the officer who pushes his son in the Boston Marathon, right?"

"Yeah, but now I want to pull him."

Dick explained what he was trying to accomplish.

The young sergeant smiled and nodded. "I think we have just what you need, Sir." He led Dick to a room filled with used and broken equipment. "Here we go," the sergeant said, and marched over to a corner of the dusty room, where he found a pile of discarded parachutes. "Take this over to the maintenance shop, and they will separate it from the harness and put a metal ring on the back. Should work fine."

Dick's eyes lit up. "Yeah, sure, that'll work."

"Good, I'll tell them you're coming over."

"Thanks, Sergeant."

Dick checked out the old parachute and decided he could do the work himself. The only thing he needed now — besides more time in the water, swimming — was a tether, so he could connect the harness to the dinghy, plus a seat for Rick to sit on.

"We had planned to put a wooden floor in the boat," Dick said. "Then bolt a chair to the floor and strap Rick in the chair."

That design created a problem. With the wooden floor, it made the boat hard to handle.

"Guess that's why he called it a *her*," Dick said with a laugh.

Dick's greatest concern, however, was Murphy's Law. That is, in the event the raft ever capsized with Rick strapped to the chair, it would be too hard to get him out.

"How about a beanbag?" Judy suggested. "A large beanbag, so Rick will be down at water level where there will be less chance of the boat capsizing."

Dick liked that idea. "And I won't have to strap him down. It would be much faster getting him in and out."

"You wouldn't strap him down?" Judy asked. "Not at all?"

"Well, I'll come up with something."

"My sister can make the beanbag," Judy offered.

One week before Father's Day, two separate publications heralded Team Hoyt's incursion into the tri-sport event. Both were in favor of the plan, but neither knew what to expect. For that matter, except for Dick Hoyt, no one knew what to expect. To him, it was simply another hurdle, but at a new venue and with different equipment.

The beanbag arrived from California on time. Dick wrapped Rick in a life preserver and finally got the boat, beanbag and his son on the water one week prior to the triathlon. The lake was abuzz with weekend boaters, fishermen and skiers, but Dick had no choice but to go for a trial swim, to confirm he could make it the full one-mile distance. Judy and Dick's brother, Phillip, went along in a separate boat so they could maintain a protective vigil from all the boating activity in the area. Dick intended to make a circle around the end of the lake, approximately one mile, but he strayed all over the place.

"I couldn't keep it straight," he said. "I got lost three times. It's not like the pool at the YMCA where you can see lines on the bottom."

"Remember, Dad," Rob reminded him, "Bilateral breathing will resolve that problem."

"Remember, Son, I'm an old dog."

Helping Dick stay on course was not the only problem the Hoyt crew encountered. "We hit a rough spot," Dick said. "There was a strong current and I almost got swept away. And halfway through the loop, the rope came untied. But that's why we were out there, to iron out the problems before race day. Better that it happened here than on Spot Pond in Medford."

Strong wind gusts and the waves created by speeding boats added to the difficulty, but in a total time of one hour and one minute, Dick had splashed and ploughed a serpentine path through the mile of turbid, choppy water. Judy and Phillip assumed Dick would be disappointed, but they were wrong. When everyone returned to shore, Dick and Rick were laughing and having a great time. "You liked that, huh, Rick?"

Dick lifted his son into the wheelchair and Judy took him back to the house so they could celebrate the innovative event over an early dinner. Dick and Phillip followed behind with the deflated boat and the remaining gear. The excursion around the lake was a success. The team had safely navigated the troubled waters of Hamilton Reservoir and they were now ready for the second leg of their trial run — the bike leg. However, Dick had not been able to train with the bike-chair combo because the form-fitted seat was not ready yet. With splashdown only one week away, he didn't even know if it would work properly.

Dick was understandably frustrated by the delay. "They delivered the seat on Saturday," he said. "One day before the race. They explained how difficult the job was and apologized that it took them so long. One doctor told me not to tell anyone where we got it because he would never build another one."

Dick barely had enough time to gather up all the gear and load it onto the van, but he accepted the reality of his situation.

"We'll have to check it out tomorrow," he told Rick. "In Medford, before the race." They had forty miles of biking awaiting them. Forty miles to check out the new equipment. *Failure* was never an option to Dick, but under the circumstances, the thought crossed his mind.

"Get some sleep, Rick. We have a big day ahead of us."

Big day indeed. Dick Hoyt, king of the understatement. He pulled a sheet over Rick's frail, tired body and turned out the light.

Medford, a suburb of Boston, is the hometown of Tufts University, where ten years earlier the team of engineers designed a computer that had a direct link to the Hoyts returning to Medford on Father's Day. It was like a homecoming. And, as was the case before any of their races, Rick hardly slept at all that night. Dick hoped they would both get plenty of rest because, according to his calculation, the race would take them five hours, nearly twice the time it took them to run their fastest marathon.

A full moon illuminated Hamilton Reservoir when Dick went to Rick's room and switched on the light.

"It's time, Rick." He pulled off the sheet and lifted him from the bed. "You didn't sleep very well, right?" Rick yawned.

Judy dressed and prepared breakfast, while over in Westfield, alarm clocks roused Rob and Russell from a deep sleep. Typically, Father's Day for the Hoyts would be a family affair. The sun rose as they drove toward Medford, but clouds in the northeast threatened.

"There wasn't much talk that morning," Dick recalled. "We were all worried about how this new adventure would come off." By the time they got all the equipment unloaded, they picked up their race packets in the rain. Rob and Russ hauled the raft over to Spot Pond and aired it up while Dick hooked the chair to the bike and locked it in place. After returning from a quick test ride, Dick said, "I don't like the way the chair follows. It's all over the place."

Dick was concerned, but he could do nothing about it at this stage of the game. He pushed the bike and chair to the end of the road and leaned it against a tree near the sandy beach that surrounded Spot Pond. Judy and Rick followed him with the wheelchair. Other athletes scrambled about in preparation for the race start. Many of them stopped to stare when they saw Dick carry his son to the raft and lower him onto the beanbag.

One athlete uttered, "What the hell is that guy doing?"

"That's Dick Hoyt," said another.

While Dick squeezed his thick torso into the wetsuit, Rob fastened the life preserver around Rick's neck. When the rain began to pepper them, Rob teased his brother. "Don't worry about the lake, Rick. Looks like you'll probably drown right here in the boat."

Judy was not amused. "Rob! We don't use the *D* word."

Dave McGillivray made an announcement. "We have Rick and Dick Hoyt here today. You've all seen them in the Boston Marathon, and now they'll be competing in their very first triathlon. We don't know what's going to happen, but please give them a hand."

All eyes focused on Team Hoyt. Nothing new about that. To many of the athletes, Dick was a novelty, like a circus strongman

141

performing a stunt. Again, they wondered if he would "go down to the corner and come back." But with one look at Rick and all the expensive, burdensome equipment, it became obvious they were serious about completing this endurance event. Those who knew Dick Hoyt didn't need to wonder about it. They only had to sit back and watch the show.

Dick waded into Spot Pond and pulled Rick in behind him. One minute later, Team Hoyt dove into their first triathlon. The rain continued to fall, but the water remained calm compared to that on Hamilton Reservoir one week earlier. The swim course went straight out and back, with the buoys always on the left, on Dick's breathing side. He stayed on the outside of the pack to avoid the possibility of other swimmers charging into the boat, and they completed the one-mile swim in less than an hour, even faster than Dick had anticipated.

Once out of the wetsuit and life preserver, Dick cradled Rick in his thick arms and dashed across two hundred yards of sand to their untested rig. They got a break, finally, when the rain stopped before they took off for the 40-mile ride.

The wind was not so cooperative. It whipped the heavy chair back and forth and dragged the bike right along with it. With Rick seated six feet behind the bike, it was difficult for Dick to keep an eye on him. Being concerned about Rick's safety, as always, he pedaled only as fast as he could go without risking an accident or flipping the unruly chair.

Although they were not pleased with the operation of the bike-chair combination, they made it safely back to the transition area, where Dick disconnected the chair and attached the front wheel. Once he switched into running shoes and scampered away, they were home free. Long-distance running was their specialty, and compared to the marathon, the ten-miler would be like a Sunday walk in the park.

But Dick didn't walk, not a single step. He ran hard. "We completed the run in one hour and five minutes."

They covered the ten miles at a six-thirty pace.

142

The Hoyts were elated when Rick's outstretched arms and ear-to-ear grin once again glided across the finish line. As Dick had predicted, it took them over four hours from start to finish.

"But they ran the 10 miles faster than most of the other triathletes," Judy pointed out. "It was incredible."

"We could have been faster," Dick joked. "But Rick took a little nap out there."

"What do you think about it?" McGillivray asked.

"We felt good," Dick answered truthfully. "We could have run a few more miles, isn't that right, Rick?"

McGillivray laughed and said, "Go ahead, but we'll have to add it to your overall time."

Again, Dick was pleased to announce, "We didn't finish last. Next to last, but not last. The same as in our very first race. Our streak is still alive."

Scott Tinley won the race and set a new course record. He walked over to congratulate the Hoyts. Since they were new to the sport, they didn't realize Tinley was ranked number one in the world and a former winner of Ironman Hawaii. During the awards ceremony, McGillivray asked the first-time athletes to say a word or two about the experience. Dick and Rick got a rousing ovation when they stepped forward. The self-conscious grin frozen on Dick's face revealed his satisfaction over their hard-earned accomplishment.

First, Dick credited Rick for providing all the motivation.

"If not for Rick," he said, looking fondly at his son, "I'd probably weight 300 pounds and be in a bar somewhere." Dick ended his comments by indicating there would be other triathlons in Team Hoyt's future.

He raised Rick's hand and proclaimed, "We are now triathlon freaks."

Rick eased back in his chair and basked in the glory.

Swim, bike, run and win at Bay State.

144

CHAPTER 12 — DEATH CHANGES LIFE

I went under water and untangled him from the buoy ropes. I pulled him out of danger, then held his head out of the water until a lifeguard arrived. When I asked if he'd ever want to try it again, he said, 'Yes.'
—Dick Hoyt

The novice triathlon "freaks" competed in six more events before the summer ended. Although the chair gave them problems, they worked through it as best they could. Rick had the distinction of being the world's only non-vocal quadriplegic who was also a college dude, a party animal, and an endurance triathlete whose favorite sports drink was rum and Coke. He had the world by the tail.

One day, during some macho jostling, Russ decided to take his oldest brother down a peg or two, just to teach him a little humility. Russ knew he had no chance at beating Team Hoyt in a marathon, or even a 5K. After all, when it came to running, they consistently beat most runners regardless of their age. But Russ was a much faster swimmer than his father was, and he had a tremendous advantage on the bike. Without a second thought, little brother flexed his muscles and challenged the older warriors at their new sport — a triathlon.

"In fact," Russell boasted, "I won't even use my legs during the swim. Just like Dad."

With confidence, Rick said, "You would lose."

If Russ Hoyt could be intimidated that easily, his wrestling career would have ended long before he took his first bold stride onto a mat. "Put your money where your mouth is, pal."

145

"Pick a race," Rick fired back.

Russ studied the Team Hoyt racing schedule and compared it against his own plans for the summer. "Right here," Russ told his brother. "The one in Vermont. You're goin' down, dude."

Dick sat back and enjoyed the macho sparing between his sons. With the bets placed and the commitment sealed, the mid-summer event would pit brother against brother on a Vermont battlefield, with Dad trailing along for the entertainment. Being a tad overconfident, Russ didn't do any additional training. The exercise from his other sports kept him in shape, he believed, plus he had the advantage of being a natural sprinter both on land and in water. In addition, he had that wonderful ally called "youth."

When the race director concluded the race instructions, Dick and Rick swam off with the first wave. Russell, the upstart challenger, waded into the water along with all the other first-timers in the third wave. The adrenalin kicked in, and under the pressure of sibling rivalry, Russell's promise to "not use my legs" went right out the window. When he shot out from the pond and back on the beach, he dashed past the empty Boston Whaler.

Russ noted that the Team Hoyt bicycle and chair were already gone, but he was confident his great swim had cut into their lead. He charged into the transition area, grabbed his helmet and took off in pursuit of his primary competition. Russ hammered away at the pedals and started passing slower riders, but it took him longer than expected to catch his namesake. He heard cheering coming from up ahead, and when he rounded a curve, he saw Dick powering his brother up a hill.

"This is easier than I thought!" Russ shouted as he rode past them. "I'll see you at the finish line! I'll be the guy sitting under a shade tree and having a cold beer!"

Rick watched helplessly as Russ pulled away. With a pleading expression, he urged his partner to pick up speed.

"Relax," Dick said. "We'll get him on the run."

Russell rode for miles with a half-smile, half-grimace. He had no worries at that point, but once he was out on the run course, he glanced over his shoulder just to make sure the guys were not coming up behind him. To his relief, they were nowhere in sight. Now he would simply have to "gut it out" for the remainder of the race.

Although Russ could whip most of the triathletes in a short sprint, this footrace went on for five miles. He had never run that far before, and certainly not after an intensely exhausting bike ride. The early miles took their toll on his legs, and before long, fatigue consumed him and he started listening for footsteps.

"I've heard other runners talk about how you can always hear the Hoyts coming from behind," Russ said. "They say you can hear Dad's plodding feet. It's like a locomotive going right by you. You can almost feel the breeze."

It was not footsteps that Russ heard first. It wasn't the wheels on the running chair, either. He heard the familiar laugh of his happy-go-lucky brother. Rick was ecstatic when he rolled up beside him.

"I tried to slap him on the rear end," Rick joked.

"We were nearly five miles into the run," Russ recalled. "Then I remember hearing the *whum whum whum* of the wheels on Rick's chair as it came from behind me. As they went by, I looked over and I could see Rick going crazy."

When Dick pulled even with Russell, the two men made eye contact and Dick said, "I don't like these short races. We don't even break a sweat."

As Dick and Rick pulled away, Russell shouted, "Is there room for two in that chair?"

Russ claimed that he returned to Vermont the following year and avenged the defeat by whipping them badly. Dick confirmed the loss, but he adamantly disagreed with Russell regarding the margin of victory. "He nipped us at the finish line."

Near the end of summer, Dick and Rick returned to Medford for another triathlon, but this time it was to benefit the New England Sports Museum, where their original running chair was destined to find its final resting place.

147

Word traveled fast about the famous marathoners who had now become triathlon "freaks." The respect they received from other triathletes grew more vocal with every race, and athletes began to recognize and accept them just as they had at the road races. Even the lifeguards knew who they were. In fact, Dick shared a story about an earlier encounter with some lifeguards. It occurred before their first triathlon, and they had not yet acquired the dinghy. While perusing a racing publication, Dick came across a biathlon at Chicopee, Massachusetts, and he decided to sign up. He told Rick, "It's a three-point-five mile run with a half-mile swim."

"A swim?" Rick said, "Then I guess I'll need a saddle."

"I'll tow you like a lifeguard during a rescue," Dick explained to his partner. "I'll do the sidestroke and hold your head above water."

"Do *what*?" Rick asked in disbelief.

At Chicopee, the swim took place in a cold spring. Dick did the sidestroke exactly as he had planned, and they were crawling along fine, making good progress in the beginning, but then Murphy's Law took over.

"It was a bad time for Rick to have a spasm," Dick said. "I felt his head go down, and before I could get control, someone swam over him. He got tangled up in a buoy."

Tense moments ensued as Dick sprang into action. He went under water and untangled Rick from the buoy ropes, pulled him out of danger and held his head above water until a lifeguard arrived. They tried to lift Rick into the rescue boat, but instead, the boat went under water and it began to fill. Eventually, they flipped over a canoe and hoisted Rick on top of it.

Back on land, after a brief rest, Dick asked Rick, "You think you'll ever want to try that again?"

"Yes," Rick answered without a second thought. "But I want you to keep my head above the water next time."

Some observers called it a "near-tragedy." To the Hoyts, it was just another risk taken, one they survived and converted into

148

a source of humor. It provided one more reminder that Doctor Fitzgerald had done his job well. Dick and Judy had done well. Rick had learned to take risks like everyone else and he was willing to continue doing so. Judy had made the point long ago when she said, "That's just the way it works."

As the triathlon season neared an end, Dick and Rick found other ways to use their gifts of fitness and compassion to bring attention to the abilities of the disabled. One such occasion was a long bike ride with all the pledges earmarked to benefit Judy's Kamp for Kids. Success came in several forms.

"Rick had a great time," Dick said. "We raised about four thousand dollars for the camp, and one newspaper reporter called us a *dynamic duo* who had a very unusual way of competing. We got a lot of recognition from that ride."

In October, another unique event popped up on the multi-sport calendar. "It's a triathlon," Pete Wisnewski told him during a phone call. "But you won't have to swim in this one."

"Oh? What is it, a run, bike, pole vault?" Dick asked. "I don't think Rick would like that."

"He would if you let him land on top."

"In that case, I wouldn't like it."

"Actually," Pete said, "it's a 10K run, a 30-mile bike, and a 7-mile canoe in the Connecticut River, near Springfield. Heck, with your upper body strength, you might even win this one."

"Nah. Not with a 30-mile bike, but it sounds like fun."

Rick agreed, it sounded like fun. However, he insisted that he would be the one delegated as "Captain of the Canoe." Dick accepted the stipulation, so Rick promptly pulled rank and assigned all the rowing duties to Colonel Hoyt.

"We'll whip your skinny butt," Dick told Pete, and then solidified the bet by saying, "Our sweaty bib will odorize your bedroom for at least a week."

Pete gracefully accepted the challenge. "Only in your dreams. You might beat me in the canoe, maybe even on the run, but my skinny butt will fly past you on the bike."

Dick borrowed a canoe one week before the event. Rick, as the designated captain, ordered him to place the beanbag at the front of the boat, right where he could "crack the whip" on his subservient boatswain.

"It's too windy out on the lake today," Dick protested, after the captain told him they needed a practice session.

Rick refused to let the wind prevent them from training. He would allow no insubordination from his crew, and he certainly didn't want Wisnewski's sweaty bib hanging in his bedroom for an entire week. Besides, the wind made for better training, he theorized, and there was always the possibility of a strong wind on race day, anyway. He invoked the motto: *Be prepared.*

After Captain Rick won that argument, Dick took him out on Hamilton Reservoir for some heavy-duty training. The wind whipped the canoe around, but Dick paddled until his triceps, shoulder and pectoral muscles begged him to stop. When Rick was completely satisfied with the workout, he consented to his dad's repeated pleadings to go home and take a nap. Again, their preparation paid off. The wind on race day created major problems for most of the canoeists, but it was easy sailing for Commander Rick and his paddle-wielding partner.

"A lot of competitors had trouble," Dick said. "Their canoes were going in circles, but we scooted right past them. We had one of the fastest times in the canoe portion."

Fast, but not fast enough to satisfy Rick. Pete Wisnewski had a great bike ride and completed the course ahead of them. Rick was not pleased when he took Pete's bib home with him that night. "It should go in Dad's room," Rick told Wisnewski.

"No way, pal," Pete replied. "You were captain of the ship. Captains don't blame the crew. The bib stops here."

The problems Dick experienced with the new bike-and-chair combination worried the race directors. They wouldn't deny entry to the Hoyts, of course, but they wanted to take every precaution that no one got hurt in their races, especially such visible athletes as Rick and Dick.

"I shared my concern with Eddie one day," Dick said. His reference was to Edward "Eddie" Burke, a very close friend of the Hoyt family. Burke had a great deal of respect for Dick, Rick and Judy. He identified totally with Rick's disability, but also how it affected the family as a unit.

"Eddie served in Viet Nam," Dick said. "He was a victim of Agent Orange, and has been fighting cancer off and on for many years." Sadly, Dick added, "He also lost a child to cancer. His daughter died while he held her in his arms."

Dick usually hid his emotions very well, but it was obvious that Eddie Burke had a special place in his heart.

John McGonigle, the Middlesex County Sheriff, organized an annual road race to raise funds in support of children with cancer. Dick and Rick were regular participants in the social event. They had become good friends with the Sheriff, and in late October, McGonigle and Eddie Burke introduced Dick and Rick to a man named John Grady, President of XRE Corporation, an engineering company involved in the development and production of medical x-ray equipment.

Eddie said, "We thought Grady might be interested in what we were doing, and maybe he would provide both financial and engineering assistance to the Hoyts."

They were right. Grady was interested, and so were two of his employees — Michael Giallongo, the Director of Operations, and David Feldmanhall, the Regulatory Affairs Manager. Both men volunteered to work on the project.

"XRE made the balance of the payments on the bike," Dick said appreciatively. "And they committed two thousand dollars for miscellaneous expenses."

The generous offer from XRE came as wonderful news to Judy. The Hoyts still owed nearly thirty-five hundred dollars on the equipment that did not work properly and, in her opinion, it created excessive "risk" for Rick.

Dick and Rick now had a sponsor. "We're professionals now," Dick told Rick. "That means you have to train harder."

151

Rick answered, "It means you have to run faster."

One of the XRE representatives picked up literature on a tandem bicycle called the Counterpoint Opus. Mike Giallongo looked it over and wrote a letter to James Weaver, the President of Counterpoint Conveyance Limited in Seattle, Washington. He told Weaver about the Hoyts and the problems they were having with the bicycle and chair. He also asked if they would be willing to donate a tandem bike or a frame, steering mechanism, and some parts. Anything they could offer would be appreciated.

"Counterpoint sent a tandem frame, a fork, steering mechanism, handlebar, stem and seat pin for a thousand dollars," Dick said. "XRE paid the grand. They also found a local bicycle dealer to donate the rest of the parts and fabricate a custom seat that fit to the frame set."

With a little help from their friends, Dick and Rick safely resumed racing, only now they rode a shiny new rig. The seat was much more comfortable for Rick, but more importantly, he sat above the front wheel, right where Dick could see him and reach him.

"With the seat up front," Dick pointed out, "I could give him a drink without stopping."

XRE built the Counterpoint to last, and it did, for fifteen years and hundreds of races. The engineers also converted the plastic shield so they could use it during the bike portion. Dick revealed his competitive side when he said, "We discovered an unexpected benefit the first time we took it on the road. We were able to go a lot faster."

In January, Team Hoyt prepared their racing calendar for the upcoming year, 1986. It included Boston and Falmouth, two of their favorite races. They penciled in nearly every triathlon DMSE had scheduled. Although they still had a few open weekends, most of them would be filled as the year unfolded. With the faster, safer bike ready for the road, Dick and Rick were eager to start the new season, to challenge the highways and the hills, and to challenge themselves.

One spring morning, before the triathlon season had opened, they received a phone call that would change not only their schedule, but also their lives. "My name is Lyn von Ert," the lady told him. "We would very much like to have you and your son 'Go Iron' in Canada."

"She said she was the race director of Ironman Canada," Dick said. "She was talking about a race they did on the last day of August. I didn't believe her at first."

Up until that day, Dick had never considered a triathlon longer than the one they had done in Medford, right in their own back yard. But this race was in Canada, and he didn't even know the exact distances for each leg of an Ironman.

"The lady convinced me she was serious," Dick said, "Especially when she said, 'We will pay all your expenses.'"

Dick gathered all the information the woman had to offer, and he promised he'd get back to her after he discussed it with his teammate. That weekend, he laid it out for Rick. "The 2.4-mile swim will be tough," Dick said. "I'll have to pick up my training. But the 112 miles will be a piece of cake with our new Counterpoint. Then we finish it out with a quick marathon. We've run that distance a lot of times."

Rick listened intently. He considered it for about a second before coming to the same conclusion anyone else would have — his dad was certifiably looney.

He said, "Are you out of your mind?"

"We can put extra cushions on your seat for the long ride," Dick said convincingly. "There'll be a lot of women at this race, you know. Those Canadian women are wild, so you'll have to be careful you don't get in any trouble."

Rick thought about it a little longer. Since school wouldn't start until September, he decided a trip to Canada during the summer would pass some time and it might be fun. Those "wild" Canadian women had no influence on his decision, of course. Rick agreed to do the race under one condition. "I'll need a nap during the bike."

They had a deal. Team Hoyt would "Go Iron" in August. Dick called Von Ert to accept her offer. She explained the details, including arrangements for shipping the equipment. When the conversation ended, Dick updated the racing calendar. For the last week in August, he wrote two words: "IRONMAN CANADA."

August of 1986 was destined to be a memorable month for the Hoyt family, but this time, unfortunately, not all of it was positive. While Dick and Rick immersed themselves in training, tragedy struck. Alfred Hoyt, Dick's father, the man who had served as his role model, hero and friend, passed away.

Rob had become an adult long before his grandfather died, and he had achieved success on his own. As he witnessed the tremendous grief his stoical father suffered, Rob came to accept the fact that Dick was, in fact, a loving, caring man who simply had his own private and enigmatic way of expressing his feelings.

Rob gradually overcame the resentment he had quietly suppressed throughout the years. Right or wrong, he had felt neglected because Rick got all the attention. He shared his feelings this way: "I just felt, at an earlier age, that I had a lot of responsibility put on me. I felt like Rick's babysitter, but as I progressed with my own ability, his disability became more apparent to me."

As everyone knows, death changes life. The passing of their father and grandfather changed the lives of all the Hoyts.

When *People Magazine* eventually got word of the Hoyts' plans to compete in an Ironman, they promptly sent a reporter and a photographer to do a feature story about them. Cable Neuhaus interviewed each member of the family and Andy Levin took some great pictures.

"I have the utmost respect for who he is," Rob told them, revealing his growth. "I don't know what drives him, but he is incredible. My father is the best athlete in the world."

To that same reporter, Russ said, "When I won my match at the Western Massachusetts wresting championship, my father and

I embraced. I think it was the first time he had ever hugged me. I had to step back and absorb the moment."

"We didn't order a child with cerebral palsy," Judy told the reporter, "but we accepted it. Rick has brought a lot of insight." Regarding his future, she said, "Rick has talked about settling down, finding a mate, and starting a family of his own. But, that's going to be hard," she added. "The physically disabled scare a lot of women."

Rick concluded his interview with humor. "I would like to try being able-bodied sometime, but having cerebral palsy has its good points. I never have to wash the dishes."

Dick was profoundly aware that family members, sponsors, fans and many friends were involved in Team Hoyt's quest to compete in Ironman Canada. He refused to disappoint everyone by letting his personal grieving negatively affect the mission that awaited him, so once the funeral ended and the tears were shed, he resumed preparation for the Ironman.

Prior to the passing of the Hoyt patriarch, members of the Hoyt family had not openly expressed some of the words and the feelings they shared with the People interviewer. However, even in death, many of the changes are positive.

With only three weeks until the big event, Dick adjusted his training regimen accordingly. Every day at noon, he changed into his workout attire and ran for 10 miles, or he biked for 25 or 30 miles. He rode a minimum of 175 miles every week, and in the evenings, he jumped into the lake for a one-mile swim. Plus, he added weight training to his schedule, which meant three nights per week he went through a 30-minute session on the Nautilus machines in the weight room at the YMCA. "Preparation is the key," Dick said, and he lived by the words he spoke.

Rick found ways to prepare. He cut weight and cut back on partying. Since he would be sitting for so many hours in the chairs, he decided to toughen his lower backside. He did this with repeated applications of rubbing alcohol on his buttocks.

Judy suspected her husband and son were both nuts.

The wrestler becomes a triathlete.

CHAPTER 13 — IRONMAN CANADA

There is no way you can complete the Ironman bike course. You will not be able to bike together over the Richter Pass Summit.

—People Magazine

On August 26, 1986, five days before the Ironman, Team Hoyt and entourage landed in Penticton, British Columbia, Canada. Rick's PCA, Michelle Dawson, accompanied them, as did David Feldmanhall, the representative from XRE who had since become a family friend. Rob could not make the trip because of his job, and with his first day of college rapidly approaching, Russ had to take a pass. Dick had planned to rest for two days preceding the Ironman, the same as he did before the marathons. That left him several days to take his teammate for a couple of long swims in Lake Okanagan, and to do a little biking and running.

Dick packed all the equipment in three wooden boxes, which totaled about 350 pounds. One box contained the bike and spare bike parts. The second box contained the running chair and the Boston Whaler dinghy, leaving the third one for Rick's seat and other miscellaneous parts. The race organizers paid the $1,500 tab. Dick was accustomed to adversity, and not surprisingly, the Ironman in Canada held true to form.

"We had planned to train on Tuesday and Wednesday," he said. "But this was the first time we ever shipped our equipment anywhere by the airlines. It got held up in Vancouver until Thursday morning, three days before the race." He added, "I did manage to swim a couple of times by myself prior to the equipment arriving in Penticton, but our first training session with the equipment wasn't until late Thursday afternoon."

The crew from *People Magazine* heard scuttlebutt about the level of difficulty on the bike course, and on Saturday, they took a Jeep and went out to take a look for themselves. They invited the Hoyts along, but Dick declined, opting instead to sit by the pool and soak in the hot tub. With only one day until the race, he and Rick preferred to relax.

"We'll get to see that big hill soon enough," Dick told his teammate. "Every foot of it."

Rick agreed. To him, sitting by the pool and checking out the latest in Canadian Bikini wear sounded like a lot more fun, anyway. Judy went along with the reporters, and when she returned to the hotel, she said, "The people from the magazine say there is no way you can complete the course. You won't be able to bike together up the Richter Pass Summit."

Dick shrugged. "They're entitled to an opinion."

"We drove it," Judy added. "I agree with them."

Dick never said a word. An expression of doubt was the last thing he wanted to hear at that stage of the game, especially from his wife of twenty-five years.

At 5:00 a.m. Sunday, everyone got up, dressed, and readied for the big challenge. Dick handled all the equipment while Judy and Michelle Dawson took care of Rick's preparation.

"I noticed Rick was wearing a cap," Dick said. "I didn't say anything about it at the time because I was too busy getting everything ready."

When Dick and his crew arrived at the race, the staff from the magazine followed them around, took pictures of everyone, and asked a whole lot of questions. Dick tried to be polite, but ignored them for the most part, trying to stay focused on his preparation. He concentrated on the details, repeated many of the steps, rechecked all the tires, and made sure the dinghy was holding firm. He tested the running chair, filled the water bottles, went through a mental checklist, and aligned everything properly in the transition area.

Dick and Rick were about to attempt the most difficult race of their entire career and the pressure mounted accordingly. Dick hadn't forgotten what someone from the crew told Judy about Richter Pass, however, and when the reporter brought it up, Colonel Hoyt looked him squarely in the eye and said, "We will complete the mission we set out to do."

Until all the equipment was in place, Dick had nothing more to say to the reporters. In a race of this magnitude, he worried more than usual. Rick sensed his high anxiety level, so when Dick had everything ready to go, Rick took the opportunity to lighten the moment. He caught his dad's attention and gave him the "guilty" look.

"What's wrong, Rick? Huh? What is it?" When Rick just sat there and grinned back at him, Dick knew he had something on his mind, but he had no clue what it could be. "Okay, funny boy, what the heck is going on here?" Rick laughed even louder. Dick studied him curiously for a moment, and then the cap caught his attention once again. "What's the deal with the cap?" Dick pulled off the cap and saw that Rick was sporting a brand new haircut — a Mohawk.

Dick said, "I took one look at him and laughed. I never know what he'll do next. He even wore a diamond earring one time."

Rick explained his mischievous eccentricities. "If people are going to stare at me, I'll give them a good reason."

The Mohawk produced the desired results. Everyone had a lighthearted laugh, but more importantly, Dick finally took a deep sigh and relaxed a little.

The final stage of preparation occurred at the edge of Lake Okanagan, where Dick encased himself in the black, tight-fitting wetsuit, donned his goggles and poked his head inside a swim cap. After several triathletes came by to wish them success, he eased his body into the chilly water and pulled Rick along with him.

159

At seven o'clock sharp, the siren screeched and hundreds of arms and legs began thrashing across the lake. Dick had predicted he and Rick would be back on dry land in around one hour and thirty minutes. The adrenaline kicked in, and for three quarters of the swim, they slashed through the water at a pace that would be difficult to sustain.

"I felt strong," Dick said. With an exaggerated sigh, he added, "But then I got cramps. I had a big knot in my stomach, my throat was tight, and I couldn't breathe. I couldn't feel my arms or legs, so I had to do the sidestroke."

While still making progress, Dick listed through the water like a damaged tugboat. His floundering caught the attention of the safety crew in a nearby surveillance boat.

"You need any help?" came a voice from the boat.

The crew pulled alongside, but Dick waved them off and kept right on stroking. He knew that if he stopped for help, it would be the end of the race. And even if he only stopped to rest, they would miss the cutoff time.

Dick said, "I did the sidestroke the rest of the way. And doing the sidestroke while dragging the boat was like pulling a freight train."

"We came very close to netting him out," a crewman admitted later. "I thought he would never make it."

Dick acknowledged that he nearly dropped out of the race at that point, and had considered accepting the free ride back to shore. But, to him, "quitting" did not appear anywhere on the Team Hoyt list of options. He kept crawling through the water until one of his powerful feet finally touched the murky bottom.

"It took them nearly an hour longer than Dick wanted," Judy told an interviewer, "but they made it the entire distance."

Pale and exhausted, Dick stumbled onto shore. As the spectators cheered respectfully, he carried Rick to the emergency tent where the medical team could evaluate their condition. "The doctors took one look at me and said we wouldn't be able to continue," Dick stated. "They said my face was gray."

160

Dick's resiliency surprised everyone. It took less than ten minutes for him to recover completely. "You're not going to continue, are you?" the doctor asked.

"Why wouldn't we?" Dick answered.

The doctor shook his head. "Good luck."

Dick swept up his son and took off to find the Counterpoint. They were the last ones out on the bike course, which enabled Judy and the crew to follow closely behind them in the van.

"My legs were stiff when we started the ride," Dick said. "But I knew we had forty miles before we got to the big hills."

Forty miles of flat land would give him an opportunity to rest and recover, he believed, and no one knew his body as well as he did. Sure enough, when they reached the base of Richter Pass, Dick's legs had loosened up and he felt rejuvenated. "It was a good thing, because that mountain was everything we'd heard about it."

The uphill side of Richter seemed like it would never end, but Dick kept focused on the objective. He shifted the Counterpoint down to "granny gear" and kept on pushing. Misfortune struck again, however, when a swarm of angry bees urged him to move along. Some of the pesky intruders got inside Dick's helmet and stung him several times.

The gorgeous scenery became nothing but a blur as they streaked down the hill at speeds over forty miles an hour. Unlike an able-bodied athlete, Rick could not grip the seat or cling to the handlebars, which left him with only two options: he could watch everything fly past, or he could close his eyes. That was it. Neither offered much safety, nor could they alleviate any fear.

"How would you like to be on the front of a bike with no control and going that fast?" Dick asked rhetorically. Then he promptly put everything in perspective. "Rick has the greatest trust in the world for me."

The Counterpoint did its job well, as did Dick and Rick.

"I only had one problem," Rick mused. "I didn't get to take the nap Dad promised."

When they returned after ten hours on the bike course, word had spread about their demoralizing swim, the quick recovery, and the courage it took to continue. In addition to that, they had gone on to traverse the mighty Richter. Since the winner had already finished the race, bystanders, fans and athletes focused on the gritty performance of the two Hoyts. Although dehydrated from spending 10 hours in the heat, sun and wind, Rick beamed with delight when they arrived at the transition.

"I asked if he wanted to quit," Dick said. "He told me he didn't, that he wanted to continue."

While Judy pumped fluids into Rick, Dick switched from his biking shorts and helmet to running shorts and a cap. A little nourishment and a short break gave Dick a blast of energy. If he could conquer Richter Pass on the tandem, he could tame any hills ahead of him on the run. Music blared from the sound system when they left town, and Dick told his son, "They're playing our song, Rick. Let's go dance."

Dick remained confident that they would complete the race, but when he tried to find his normal stride, he soon discovered that 112 miles on the bike had zapped his strength and weakened his legs far more than anticipated. Pushing Rick up the hills took a toll, and for the first time since the 1981 Boston Marathon, he found himself walking through parts of the course. The man who ran marathons in less than three hours would take nearly twice that long to complete this one.

It was after midnight when the Hoyts returned to the town of Penticton. With over a mile to go, they could hear the song "Chariots of Fire" emanating from the finish line. The music evoked a surge of energy that compelled Dick to pick up speed and pass other runners. When they neared Casabell Winery, a man ran into the street and slid a bottle of champagne onto the chair, next to Rick. A tumultuous applause greeted them when they made the final turn from Main Street onto Lakeshore Drive. Runners, bikers, cars and motorcycles converged to escort them home, where hundreds of spectators waited until nearly one o'clock in the morning just to see if the Hoyts could finish the race. They stood four deep, many of them in tears, and some even stepped off the curb to try to touch them as they rumbled by. Moved by such an emotional reception, Rick swung his head back for a glance at his father. Dick responded by ordering his rubbery legs to sprint to the finish.

The clock indicated seventeen hours and fifty-three minutes had elapsed since Dick and Rick started the race on Lake Okanagan. The calendar had rolled over to Monday, the first day of September. A voice blasted over the PA system. "Isn't that the finest sight you'll ever see in your life!" the man yelled. "What a man! What a family!"

Judy, Michelle, and David ran out to join in the celebration, and as Dick kneeled down to give Rick a hug, someone splattered them with champagne.

Dick shouted to Judy, "This is like New Year's Eve!"

Lyn von Ert, the race director, worked her way through the mob and shouted for Dick's attention. "Would you please run back past the crowd and cross the finish again?" she asked. "These people really want to see you."

"Rick laughed out loud and showed his huge, trademark smile as we went back and crossed the finish line a second time," Dick said happily. "He was having such a great time."

Dick tried to be his normal, stoical self, but his emotions spilled over and he nearly cried.

"I may have shed a tear," he confessed. "I don't remember stuff like that."

Judy also cried. Although she had expressed concern over Dick's obsession with racing, the emotions totally overwhelmed her. At times, she felt guilty about all the attention and adulation she and her family received from the racing. A few days earlier, in the interview with Cable Neuhaus, she confessed, "We are not saints because we brought up this handicapped kid and made a life for him. We're not the perfect American family. We're not different from any other family. We have made what could be a

163

'poor me' experience into a positive experience, but we aren't the Brady Bunch. I have not dedicated my life to my kids."

But on that electrifying day in Canada, the contrast was chilling. Regardless of how she may have felt about the racing, Judy shared the excitement of the accomplishment right along with everyone else. Whether she liked it or not, Judy had earned her share of the adulation. She also popped the top from a bottle of champagne and toasted her men with a cool, bubbly shot of love and admiration.

Since they failed to complete the race before the seventeen-hour cutoff time, Dick assumed the rules committee would not recognize them as official finishers. But that was secondary. Although no one seriously thought they could complete such a tremendous challenge, the Hoyts proved everyone wrong, and the achievement itself was simply too great to be tainted by a legal "cutoff time."

Incredibly, the Hoyts had once again completed the mission they set out to do. Dick found no reason to mock any of those people who doubted him, but he would be the first one to point out, "We didn't finish last."

When the list of official finishers came out later in the morning, it included the names of Dick and Rick Hoyt. Members of the committee wisely concluded that they could not let a minor detail tarnish such an extraordinary accomplishment.

Because of the demanding hills, many athletes called Ironman Canada one of the most challenging courses in the world. In fact, it was later purported that the overall winner of the race, David Kirk of Canada, said he would *never* race that course again. Von Ert had apparently overlooked information such as that when she first told Dick about the race, but the degree of difficulty wouldn't have influenced his decision to participate, anyway. To Team Hoyt, a formidable challenge was not a valid excuse to stay home and warm the sofa.

One interviewer expected some heady explanation when he questioned Dick about what it was that enabled him to survive the disastrous swim, climb Mount Richter, and still push Rick 26 miles through the darkness.

"You have to be mentally prepared," Dick answered. "I just make up my mind to finish, and my body had better go along with it."

Before the Hoyts drove back to the hotel, a man named Merv Wejr, an officer in a local trucking company, approached them. Wejr had witnessed their remarkable feat, and when he learned that Dick had problems getting all the racing equipment transported to Penticton, he volunteered to ship everything back to Massachusetts for him.

"We took him up on the offer," Dick told the reporter. "At no cost to us, they delivered everything faster than the airlines."

Wherever Team Hoyt raced, dignitaries took notice and offered regards. After the race in Canada, Prime Minister Mulroney sent a letter to the Ironman officials and asked them to pass it along to the Hoyt family.

"We felt honored," Dick said. "We still have the note."

After congratulating the Ironman organization, Mulroney wrote:

> *...I would like to extend my personal greetings to Lieutenant Colonel Dick Hoyt and his son, Rick, whose efforts are a statement of courage and love. May the both of you continue to work together so we may all benefit from your special relationship.*
> —Prime Minister Brian Mulroney
> British Colombia, Canada

Rick always took the opportunity to state his objectives, and when reporters and fans asked why he would willingly subject himself to such a demanding and dangerous event, he repeated his message. "People with disabilities should be included in daily activities just like everyone else."

If any negatives resulted from the Canadian venture, other than a little pain and discomfort, Dick couldn't recall what they were. He described it as a total success, and summed it up with one sentence. "I think you could say we owned the town of Penticton that night."

Rick suffered dehydration and was treated at the medical stations several times during the long race, but a bigger problem came from a raw and nagging soreness in his buttocks. Fifteen hours of sitting in the bike seat and the running chair had worn him thin, but he had no remorse. The glory was worth the pain. Receiving praise from his father was frosting on the cake.

"Congratulations, big man," Dick told him as they soaked their sore bodies in the hotel hot tub. "You did real good out there today. Real good."

On Monday afternoon, *People Magazine* rounded up the Hoyts for an impromptu, in-studio interview. Dick and Rick arrived in casual attire. Rick left his cap at the hotel, opting instead to wear a white sweatband around his head. In recognition of his hometown of Holland, Dick wore one of his favorite T-shirt, a black one with "Where's Holland?" written in white letters across the front. Judy dressed up in a nice suit, and while she patiently waited her turn, Dick answered questions first. As expected, the interviewer asked, "How are you feeling?"

"I'm a little sore," Dick acknowledged with a shoulder shrug. "But after I go run a few miles, it'll go away."

The interviewer smiled before asking him another expected question. "Will you ever do another Ironman?"

"Sure. We'll be ready next week."

When they directed questions to Judy, she handled them like a true spokesperson. She smiled and spoke enthusiastically about Rick, his TIC machine, and his brothers, but said very little about the race itself. As would be the case with anyone else, she felt more comfortable when the conversation involved her own area of expertise.

The Team Hoyt entourage spent two more days in Penticton, and before they left, they visited the Okanagan Neurological Society's Child Development Center and received a tour of the

166

facilities. In return, Rick demonstrated his prowess on the Hope Machine. By the time they returned home to Holland, the Hoyt family indeed owned the town of Penticton.

On September 15, 1986, *People Magazine* published the story about the Hoyts in Canada. They titled it: "Father and Son: A Lesson in Love." It included great photos, insightful quotes, and even a bittersweet anecdote. Dick told the interviewer, "Once we had a bad race and Rick wrote on his machine, 'Dad's getting old. Maybe it's time for a new pusher.'"

The humor was there for everyone to see and enjoy.

As a loving and dedicated father, Dick knew the day would come when he could no longer participate in such physically demanding events as an Ironman triathlon or even the Boston Marathon. There would be no replacement "pusher" when he could not reach the starting line, even for a 5K. Rick's future and financial security concerned Dick, but at this point, he didn't know what he could do about it. He had not found any overnight solution, but instead approached the problem as he did life itself, one day at a time, and on this particular day, he and Rick had reached the top of another mountain.

As the poem on Rick's wall succinctly stated: "...today lived well makes every yesterday a dream of happiness and every tomorrow a vision of hope."

It came as no great surprise when the *People Magazine* readers responded en masse to the touching article about Dick and Rick Hoyt. One response came from Missouri:

People Magazine,
I always cry during a good film, or occasionally when reading a good book, but never while reading a good magazine article. That is until I began reading your moving article on the Hoyt family. What a story!
—Deans P. Lynch
St. Louis, Missouri

Letters of congratulations and admiration arrived in Holland from all across the country. A teacher's aide at a school for the handicapped wrote to Rick regarding a friend of hers named Mark, who was also a non-vocal quadriplegic:

> ...*I can't wait to get to school tomorrow and show Mark your article. I'm going to encourage him to write to you, Rick, but I will leave it up to him. I would enjoy hearing from you.*
>
> —Jeanie, Gilbert
> North Platte, Nebraska

Clearly, Penticton wasn't the only town the Hoyt family owned on that August day.

Russ and Rick swimming as a team.

Team Hoyt racing in Canada.

169

Rob lending a hand.

CHAPTER 14 — CHARACTER COUNTS

I told the guy, 'Don't ever ask us to do anything like that. We are not that type of people. We have never cheated or quit before and we never will.'

—Dick Hoyt

When compared to the Canadian experience, the remaining months of 1986 were relatively uneventful for Team Hoyt, the athletes. Individually, however, all the Hoyts were blazing new trails: Rick returned to Boston University; Rob honed his creative skills as a machinist and nurtured his romantic relationship with Mary; Russell graduated from Westfield High, began studies at the University of Massachusetts in Amherst, and spent his spare time courting Lisa. Rick occasionally reminded his brothers that their blossoming romances originated through him. They agreed wholeheartedly, and readily professed, "Everyone who meets Rick is well rewarded."

Judy made steady progress with her innovative programs at ASHS, and Dick fulfilled his responsibilities to the military while maintaining the Team Hoyt racing schedule. With all three sons safely out of the nest, Dick and Judy took time to convert their property into the retirement home they wanted. Life was good for the Hoyts, but the smooth sailing got a little bumpy when they received the following letter from Rick:

Dear Mom & Dad,

I have something very important I need to discuss with you. On November 3, I have a seating evaluation at

171

Children's Hospital at 4:30, which I missed in the spring.
Could we come back from D.C. for this? I would like to
have you both come. Love, Richard Eugene Hoyt, your
loving, crippled, Ironman son.

Rick had been experiencing extreme discomfort in his back, which the doctors eventually diagnosed as deterioration of the spine. He needed an operation to insert two metal rods, but the procedure carried a risk to his health and the potential end to his racing career. After a final evaluation, Rick decided to have the surgery. The operation concerned everyone, especially Rick, but he said the pain had reached his neck and he was unable to work on the computer for extended periods. He wanted the operation immediately, and with the help of his PCAs, he would try to catch up with his classes during the recovery period.

"The most important thing is that I can keep using my head to communicate," Rick said prudently. "I am willing to take the risk that I might not be able to do triathlons, but on the other hand, I cannot afford to risk my means of communicating."

After discussing it with family and doctors, Rick selected the end of April to have the surgery, which meant it would not interfere with their seventh consecutive Boston Marathon. In the meantime, news of Team Hoyt's phenomenal success at Penticton reached the ears of the HAFL committee. In early April, the announcement went out to the public.

"They nominated us for their award again," Dick said.

Air Force General John Conway took part in the nomination process, and he led the tribute. "Colonel Hoyt has influenced national attitudes about the inclusion of the disabled in activities of fitness and health by his running in marathons, pushing his son Rick in a specially designed wheelchair."

Dick had heard it all before, so he merely shrugged and went about the business of preparing for Boston.

Also in early April, *West 57th Street*, the CBS News Magazine, ran a feature story about the Hoyt family. The three Hoyt boys had a good time during the interview. When the female reporter asked Rick what mattered most when selecting a PCA, he told her, "Looks."

Russ and Rob took turns teasing Rick, and they accused him of sleeping during the races while their Dad did the work. Rick took it all in stride.

"When he raises his arms at the finish line," Russ said, "it isn't a victory pose. He's just stretching."

Other celebrities called on the Hoyts for interviews during the days surrounding the marathon. They did a television segment for the *Good Day Show* out of Boston, and followed it up with a three-minute piece on *NBC Nightly News*. The tri-boys were busy making waves and hitting the big time.

Boston Marathon number seven delivered the same glory and excitement as the previous six, but soon after it ended, Rick had to undergo surgery. As everyone had hoped, the operation successfully relieved his pain, and to make things even better, the recovery time was much shorter than anyone expected. Many friends stopped by the hospital to wish him well and to cheer him up. Eddie Burke brought him a get-well present – a bottle of Bacardi rum and a six-pack of Coke.

"The doctor said you needed something to kill the pain," Burke said, as he handed him the gift. "Try this."

One week later, Rick returned to the university to pick up where he had left off. Since he could now perform his normal routine with minimal pair, he clicked away at the computer to make up for the missed classes and immediately resumed racing with his teammate. Barring any unexpected complications, 1987 promised to be another great year.

During recovery from Rick's operation, Team Hoyt received another invitation to participate in a triathlon. This one was more meaningful than most of the others because it came from the United Cerebral Palsy organization in Milwaukee, Wisconsin.

"We wanted to accept," Dick said, "but we couldn't do it until Rick got clearance from the doctor."

While waiting to hear from the doctor, Dick learned that the Vincent Lombardi Tournament of Champions (LTC) – a national organization that provided funding to the Lombardi Cancer Research Center – had selected him for the *Honors Court.* Committee members for the LTC included such notables as Vice President George Bush, Senators Bill Bradley, and Speaker of the House, Tip O'Neill.

The LTC did not highlight the achievements of handicapped persons, but instead focused on leadership, individual character, ethics, and a positive public image. Former winners of the award included such luminaries as Bob Hope, and football greats, Paul Horning, Earl Campbell and Archie Griffith. On Father's Day, with airfare and accommodations fully paid, Dick and Rick went to Washington, D.C. to run the Lombardi 10K and receive the Lombardi award. At the induction party, Rick had his picture taken with Patrick Ewing and David Robinson, two giants, literally, of the National Basketball Association.

Dick mingled with the other inductees, committee members, previous winners, and Mike Ditka, coach of the Chicago Bears football team. On Monday, the scene switched to a local Country Club, where he played a round of golf with the VIPs and chatted with Speaker O'Neill.

"I shook hands with Bob Hope," Dick said. "Like me, he's not much of a golfer, but he has a great sense of humor."

During that same week, a publication called *The News* covered the Hoyts. In the story, Dina Gruey wrote, "If there were an award given for the Father of the Year, Dick Hoyt possesses all the qualities to be among the top nominees. The team exemplifies courage, determination, and above all, the bond of love between father and son that can overcome any handicap."

When the Hoyts returned from Washington, Dick received a call informing him that after a second nomination, he had won one of the HAFL awards. The national honor included four days at the Hyatt Regency in Long Beach, California, with all their expenses covered. With the challenges of racing, keeping up with schoolwork, and preparing for the upcoming semester, Rick declined the trip to Long Beach, leaving Dick and Judy to attend the festivities without him.

"We got to see the Queen Mary," Dick said, then injected some humor. "That's the ship, not the woman. We also saw the Spruce Goose, which is a huge airplane, not a bird. Howard Hughes made it out of plywood, and it only flew once."

At the awards banquet, silence befell the room while the eclectic audience watched a montage of videos from various races the Hoyts had completed. Dick brought them to tears when he spoke candidly of his painful experiences in dealing with the birth of a handicapped child, and the emotional rewards inherent in overcoming them.

Gary Wilkinson, one of Dick's most staunch supporters in the press, said, "Your comments inspired us all. Your speech continues to cross my mind."

Trisha Brown, the coordinator for HAFL, bared her soul when she wrote, "Out of all the people I met, I grew the most fond of you two. I guess if my husband had been as considerate as you, Dick, I would have appreciated him more, or if I would have been as understanding as you, Judy, he could have put up with me. Tell Rick we would love to meet him next year."

"Next year?" Judy asked Dick.

"She must know something I don't know."

* * *

The doctor took one final look at Rick and gave him the thumbs up. Dick grabbed the phone and called Joyce Altman, the UCP director in Milwaukee.

"We'll be at your race in July," Dick informed her.

"Wonderful!" she responded.

American Airlines picked up the sponsorship and delivered them safely to Milwaukee, where a van shuttled the Hoyts and the three boxes of equipment directly to the luxurious Astor Hotel. Unfortunately, shipping the dinghy to the race proved to be a total waste of time and resources. By race day, the conditions on Lake

Michigan turned dangerously foul, which prevented race officials from conducting the swim portion of the race. Dick agreed with their decision. "For safety reasons, they had to change it to a duathlon." With the swim preempted in favor of a 5K, the Milwaukee Half Ironman became the Milwaukee Duathlon. Team Hoyt ran the 5K in 20 minutes. Then, with very few hills and little wind, they recorded a great bike split before closing with a 13-mile dash around the city. Since the revised format favored Dick and Rick, they passed dozens of runners and were still going strong when Rick raised his arms and streaked across the finish line.

Milwaukee loved and appreciated the Hoyts, and before leaving town, they were guests at a television interview. "You and Rick have a standing invitation to visit Milwaukee anytime," the director of UCP told them. "It would be delightful to welcome you back."

The Hoyts next took a quick trip to Montreal, Canada, where they competed in another triathlon and immediately geared up for another major challenge. "We wanted to do the Ironman distance again," Dick said, "so we signed up for the Hyannis Endurance Triathlon."

Dick was determined to atone for his horrendous swim at Penticton. He knew they could complete the Ironman distance much faster than they did that day in Canada, and the race in Hyannis presented an opportunity to prove it.

"If conditions are favorable," Dick predicted confidently, "we can do it in 12 hours. Then we'll apply for Ironman Hawaii." The forty-seven-year-old rookie and his twenty-five-year-old sidekick kept raising the bar, and in triathlon circles, the bar couldn't get any higher than the one in Hawaii.

They breezed through Hyannis. "We had a good swim," Dick reported. "I didn't have any problems and we made it back in an hour and fifty minutes, half an hour faster than in Canada."

Comparing the hills in Hyannis to those in Penticton would be like comparing a swimming pool to the Atlantic. Although they faced a strong wind on the return, the teammates sped through the flat course in less than eight hours, two hours faster than they biked the course in Penticton.

"We could've done it faster," Dick claimed, "but that darn headwind really killed us."

For anyone to complete an Ironman as a tandem with his adult son strapped to the front of the bike was an amazing feat. To do it in twelve hours would be impossible. But Dick and Rick completed the Hyannis course in 13:45, which was merely incredible. They finished the race four hours and ten minutes faster than their first Ironman one year earlier.

The racing schedule for the remainder of 1987 consisted of short road races and the Marine Corps Marathon in D.C. For the year, they completed 27 events: one Ironman, a half Ironman, three Olympic-distance triathlons, four marathons, three half-marathons, and 15 road races of 10 miles or less. "After the Marine Corps Marathon, we were ready for some rest," Dick admitted. "But we got a phone call."

The call came from Carl Bayley, who invited them to run in his December race in Barbados. Dick listened to the details and told Bayley he would have to discuss it with his partner. The year had seen Team Hoyt travel all over the country, from Vermont to Nebraska, Washington, D.C. to California, and Florida to Canada. They had certainly earned a rest, and since Rick still had classes to attend, he left the decision to him.

"It's another marathon," he told Rick.

Rick patiently waited for the full story. Dick stepped over to the window and opened the blinds. The clouds looked mean and nasty, and snowflakes drifted onto the yard below.

"It sure is cold out there today," he said playfully, and waited for Rick to react.

Rick emitted some attention-getting groans. Dick paused for maximum impact, then without turning around, he said, "It might be too hot for you down there. In fact, we'd have to take our swimsuits instead of our sweatsuits."

Dick hushed and waited for a stronger reaction, which he knew would come. As a warm-weather man, Rick thought the Massachusetts winters were too long and too cold, anyway. He rattled the wheelchair to get his dad's attention. He couldn't vocalize the words, but he implored his father to turn around and elaborate. "Talk to me!" he demanded esoterically.

Dick teased him. "Don't get upset. I didn't commit. We can stay here and do a winter race if that's what you want."

That was not what Rick wanted to hear; he wailed louder.

"Okay, okay, it's somewhere in the Caribbean. It's an island they call Barbados."

Rick's eyes widened, indicating the discussion that followed was a mere formality. The Hoyts had never been to the Caribbean, and a chance to get out of the cold with all expenses paid was simply too good to pass up.

In reference to a recent escapade in Towers Dormitory, Dick said, "I think we should go. The trip would keep you out of the women's bathroom for a little while."

Towers Dormitory was coed, with males and females housed on separate floors. The ninth floor belonged to the girls. Rick shared the following story about the dormitory. "I slept in a blue sleeping bag in my long underwear. I was almost asleep when I heard the door open, then the zipper of my sleeping bag was zipped shut. Someone carried me upstairs, put me down on the floor, unzipped the bag and left me alone. I was on the ninth floor," he added. "In the women's bathroom."

"That's his side of the story," Dick teased. "He probably sneaked up there to fool around. He just got caught."

The island of Barbados extends over 20 miles in length, is 14 miles wide, and consists of nearly 200 square miles of coral limestone. The travel agent said, "It's a sportsman's paradise on the eastern end of a chain that stretches from North America to South America. They play all day and party all night. But," she added, "there is a supreme tranquility that lends itself to relaxation." To Dick, it sounded like a contradiction.

"It was a tough decision," he said, tongue in cheek. "But Rick insisted I call Bayley and accept the invitation, so I made the call."

Run Barbados, in its fifth year, had become an annual celebration that included a10K race on Saturday and a Marathon on Sunday. The races attracted participants from the United States, Canada, Europe and the Caribbean. Once he had all the pertinent information, Dick promptly committed to run in their fifth marathon of the year. To Dick's surprise, Judy informed him she couldn't get away that week. He wondered if there might be more to the story, that staying home was her way of protesting the racing. Either way, he and Rick prepared for a glorious week at one of the world's prime destinations, where they would soak up the sun and take a first-hand look at the blue seas and warm, sandy beaches.

On Friday, December 4, Team Hoyt arrived at Boston's Logan Airport, the first stop on their journey to the Islands. Dick was eager to leave. "It was snowing when we got to the airport, and the temperature was around thirty degrees. We were happy to be getting out of the state for five days, to go where we could relax at poolside and enjoy the warm beach."

Rick looked forward to the race and the warm weather, but he was more interested in the bikinis and the umbrella drinks.

"We took only summer clothes with us, which included our swimming suits," Dick said. "When the plane touched down on Friday afternoon, it was really muggy, and the temperature was over ninety degrees when we got to the hotel. Rick and his PCA had one room and I had another. We were tired, so after a late dinner, we all went to bed."

Unfortunately, the hotel did not have air conditioning and the ceiling fans provided the only source of cooling in each of the rooms. Dick complained that even though he kept the fan spinning directly overhead, and he slept in the buff, he was extremely uncomfortable and soaked the sheets with sweat. It was a restless night for all of them, literally.

179

At ten o'clock Saturday morning, the team members rubbed their tired eyes and assembled for breakfast at the resort's patio next to the Olympic-size swimming pool. After a nourishing meal, they lounged around the pool, visited with tourists and watched the sun bathers struggle to tie and untie their bikini tops while lying face down on towels. The afternoon schedule included a short nap, an early dinner and a long walk around the village after sunset.

Dick had hoped he they would be able to sleep by then. He said, "We had to get up early enough to be at the starting line for the five o'clock marathon, and we were about to go take a nap. But the owner of the resort came up, introduced himself and said a van would come by to pick us up in a couple hours. I asked him where we were going."

The man replied, "To run in the 10K race."

"No, that's not us. My son and I are here to run in the marathon tomorrow."

"Yes, sir, but you also race today," the man insisted. "We have a contract."

Dick and Rick exchanged curious glances, but after closer review, Dick discovered that the contract indeed called for them to run in *both* races. Although not pleased with the untimely revelation, Dick agreed with the man. "A contract is a contract. So much for our day of relaxation. We got busy hydrating."

The man offered an easy out. "You can start the run," he spoke quietly. "And when you get away from the crowds of people, drop out of the race or find a short cut to the finish line."

Dick bristled at the suggestion. "It really pissed me off," he said. "I told the guy, don't ever ask us to do anything like that. We are not that type of people. We have never cheated or quit a race before and we never will."

Dick glared at the man briefly, then excused himself so he and Rick could go back to their room to prepare for the race.

Someone once coined the phrase, *Sports builds character.* But upon observing the behavior of many contemporary athletes, that adage has been changed: *Sports do not build character, they reveal it.* When discussing the subject of character, Rob Hoyt may have quoted someone, or maybe he was espousing his own personal philosophy, but he certainly nailed the concept when he said, "Personality is what you do with people around; character is what you do when no one is watching."

Dick honored the contract. Had he opted to take the "shortcut," no one would have known, certainly none of the representatives from the LTC committee. Dick's disgust at the thought of "cheating" would have withstood any LTC scrutiny and provided further testimony of his worthiness for their award. Character: what you do when no one was watching.

An air-conditioned van arrived on schedule and hustled them over to the 10K race site. "It was like the first race we did in Westfield," Dick said. "No one knew who we were or what to say to us. They just looked."

Despite the heat, high humidity and lack of sleep, the Hoyts had an outstanding race. More than 600 runners participated, and with a finishing time of 37:13, only 42 crossed the line ahead of them. When the awards presentation ended, a valet shuttled them back to the resort for more hydration and a carbo-loading dinner. At midnight, they finally turned back the sheets and collapsed in bed. Although sleeping conditions were no better than the first night, Dick slept from sheer exhaustion. But he did not sleep long. The three o'clock wake-up call jarred him back to semi-consciousness. He dragged himself from the bed, stumbled into the shower, and quickly prepared himself and Rick for the one-hour drive to the marathon staging area.

"That was the first time we started a race in the dark," Dick said. "But it made sense because of the heat and humidity. Most of the runners finished before the hottest part of the day, but some didn't finish for seven hours."

Nearly 300 dedicated runners dashed away in the moonlight, but as the sun steadily rose and the race wore on, the onerous humidity and the twenty-six miles zapped their energy and melted their enthusiasm. Less than half of them made it to the welcome side of the finish line.

Rick did his part, as usual, but Dick had not totally recovered from the 10K race, and with so little sleep, they ran the slowest marathon of their careers. But even at that, they completed the race in three hours and twenty-two minutes, which earned them an award in their respective age division. It would take far greater adversity than lack of sleep and a few sore muscles to put the words *quit* or *cheat* in the Team Hoyt vocabulary.

For the remainder of the trip, the Hoyt boys acted like tourists. The only thing on their schedule was relaxation. Excluding time they spent in the pool and in the ocean, exercise was strictly prohibited. They took a tour and consumed the natural beauty of the island; they frolicked on the beach and drank chilled coconut juice directly from the coconut.

"We also discussed tropical issues," Dick confessed, and winked at his son. "We debated the health benefits of the bikini versus the two-piece bathing suit."

The Hoyts enjoyed their vacation on the balmy island, but devoted the final day to more altruistic activities. On a visit to the children's Development Center, they gave a one-hour presentation to a room filled with disabled children, parents, and members of the development staff. Dick and Rick showed slides of Team Hoyt's accomplishments, and they highlighted their progress with a video titled *Breaking Barriers*.

Dick shook his head in despair. "We talked to them about how we do things compared to how they do things. America is very far ahead of them in dealing with people with disabilities, so I hope we were helpful."

Much to their chagrin, a powerful snowstorm welcomed them back to Massachusetts. Before leaving Boston, Rick used the Russell Method to ask Dick an important question: "Does Boston University have a campus in Barbados?"

With the exception of their sauna-like room and the unexpected 10K race, Dick and Rick had a wonderful time. Both men agreed they would return if invited. "Our biggest mistake," Dick mused, "was leaving Massachusetts two days before the race. Now when we compete in hot countries, we arrive a week early so we can get adjusted."

Rick groaned to get his dad's attention. Dick looked at his teammate and said, "Oh, yeah, and now I let Rick read the fine print on all our contracts."

In January, they pulled out the racing calendar and prepared to raise the proverbial bar to another level. Dick typed a letter to the officials of Ironman Hawaii, where entry requirements were different from any other Ironman. To earn a "slot," they had to win their age division in a qualifying race sometime during the year, or they could possibly receive a special invitation from the committee. Although Dick and Rick had an incredible race at Hyannis, they did not win the age division.

Dick began the letter with a long list of their impressive credentials, which included the successful completions at Hyannis and Penticton. He explained in detail why they wanted to compete in the race, and why he and Rick would be an asset to the event. He emphasized the point that they were experienced triathletes, and the risk for them was no greater than it was for any of the other athletes. In essence, he said, "We've earned a shot. Let us in."

Based on years of experience, Dick didn't expect a prompt welcome. More likely, they would not be welcome at all. If so, they would face that hurdle just as they had all the others.

Dick placed his arm on Rick's shoulder and smiled. "I knew one thing for sure. I wouldn't have to twist Rick's arm to get him to race in Hawaii."

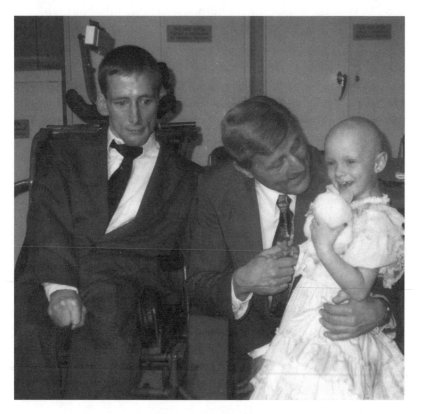

The humanitarians.

Winning the HAFL Award.

CHAPTER 15 — IRONMAN HAWAII

*If you know of someone who has made jokes about
'retards' or 'spastics,' the Hoyts still have some biking
to do. And if you know of someone who sees a
handicapped person, maybe someone who drools a bit
in a public place, and turns away in disgust, then the
Hoyts — and I suppose all of us — still have some
running to do.*

—Barry Nolan
Evening Magazine

Team Hoyt began 1988 with a mix of 5K and 10K races,
which readied them for the long season, but the first event that
merited bold letters was the Boston Marathon, their eighth
consecutive. As they prepared, word came down from the
Ironman Hawaii committee.

"Our application was rejected," Dick said. "They said the
swim would be too dangerous."

Although Dick felt the sting of disappointment over their
initial decision, he sincerely believed the setback was temporary,
and he promptly responded with another letter, politely refuting
the committee's reasons for the rejection. He then concentrated
on the Boston Marathon, where after three years of banging on
doors at the B.A.A., he and Rick had become the centerpiece for
their promotional department. People wanted to see the Hoyts,
and every year the media focused on them. One of the highlights
of Boston number eight occurred while they were still out on the

187

course. Russell waited among the spectators, and when his father and brother approached, he charged into the street and ran along with them for a short distance.

"When I couldn't keep up any longer," Russ said, "I shook Dad's hand, shouted encouragement to Rick, and disappeared back into the crowd."

During one of their many interviews, Dick revealed his intentions to ride and run across the entire United States – with Rick. Never mind the Ironman in Hawaii, an accomplishment of this magnitude required unimaginable determination and effort. His original plan had been to make it a trans-American Triathlon, but he eventually acknowledged the improbability of finding a route that started or ended each day with a suitable location for the swim.

"In that case," he conceded, "I guess we'll have to make it an ocean-to-ocean duathlon instead."

The immediate obstacle, however, had nothing to do with swimming. The problem was financial. For them to raise the funds required for such a major venture, he needed sponsors. Dick began his search by contacting the UCP, but they also rejected him, citing the same reason as the one given by the Ironman Hawaii committee — safety.

While Dick pondered the next big event for Team Hoyt, he and Rick received an invitation to run a marathon in Long Beach, California. "The race benefited the handicapped."

The invitation presented an opportunity for Team Hoyt to gain West Coast exposure, and since the sponsors covered all expenses, it was an offer they couldn't refuse. "We didn't come up with any new sponsors out there," Dick admitted, "but Rick had a good time. He got to race in California and he's ready to go back anytime."

Another negative response from Hawaii awaited the Hoyts when they returned home to Holland. The Ironman representative, Valerie Silk, politely informed Dick of all the problems inherent with wheelchair participants. She closed by offering an apology that was similar to all those he had heard before. Undaunted, Dick summoned his helpers. Judy went all the way to the United States congress, where a Hawaiian senator named Matsunaga agreed that the Hoyts would be good publicity for his state. The senator contacted Silk and expounded on the wisdom of including disabled athletes in the race. He implored them to reconsider the Hoyts' application, and to make his point, he subtly brought up the word "discrimination."

Dick called on Dave McGillivray, who had direct connections with the people in Hawaii. After reviewing the letters from Matsunaga and McGillivray, Silk reconsidered, but she felt it necessary to warn Dick of the difficulties he would encounter in Kona. Her choice of words suggested she did not know Dick Hoyt very well. As exemplified for twenty-six years, it took more than the word "difficult" to stop him. In fact, if that were all it took, Rick would still be in an institution somewhere.

Dick had the determination to make a good showing in Hawaii, but funding always presented a problem. The only solution was to find sponsors. Again, he called on his most reliable friends. Mike Giallongo and XRE stepped forward, as did the Bicycle Exchange. American Airlines volunteered to handle all the transportation for eight people.

"Dick and Rick competed in most of my races," said Dave McGillivray. "So we requested donations at each race, which contributed several thousand dollars to the coffers."

Although still short on funds, they were close enough to commit. Barry Nolan, their friend and supporter from *Evening Magazine*, decided to go along and film the momentous event. After all, who could pass up an opportunity to go to Hawaii and witness history in the making? Even the big boys entered the scene. Two years after Alfred Hoyt's death, his prediction became a reality — ABC would send a film crew from *Wide World of Sports*.

Two months before the trip to Kona, another significant event created excitement among the Hoyt clan. The family grew by one. Mary Conners, the lovely young lady who at the age of 13 promised she would one day be the wife of Robbie Hoyt, fulfilled her promise. On August 12, 1988, the Hoyts gathered at the Blessed Sacrament Church in Westfield and welcomed Mary to the family. The happy couple held the reception at Shaker Farms Country Club, and like everyone else, Rick regaled, danced along in his wheelchair, and even indulged in his favorite mixed drink. Being such a thoughtful brother, he even volunteered to help Rob if needed.

"If you can't handle the honeymoon," Rick told him. "You know where to find me."

"Your help won't be necessary," Rob assured him, then poured ice water over his head to cool him off.

The entire Hoyt family — including Rob and his new bride — arrived in Hawaii ten days early, toured the islands and adjusted to the tropical climate. Dick and Rick ran the Kailua 10K a week before the Ironman. Dick trained by swimming the Ironman course when the waves were up, and by riding his bike when the winds peaked.

"One day," Dick said, displaying fatherly pride, "Rick and I swam the entire course with Rob and Russ. A family swim."

Dick never mentioned who made it back first, but betting odds favored Rob.

The omni-present Barry Nolan rolled film. He caught the family in the hotel swimming pool, on the race course, in restaurants, and at the race orientation.

An Ironman representative addressed the athletes at the orientation. "Remember," he said emphatically, "you must hydrate while on the course." He mentioned it several times, in fact, and also told them, "Just keep doing what got you here. Don't make any last minute changes. Don't do anything different from your regular training routine."

Someone in the audience yelled out, "But this is Hawaii!"

Dick listened intently. His greatest concern about racing in Hawaii was the heat and humidity, and the repeated warnings about dehydration left a lasting impression. Since Gatorade was a sponsor of the event, representatives were on hand to distribute their products to the athletes.

Somehow, the caution about "last minute changes" did not merit the same attention as the one about hydrating. Dick drank Gatorade for dinner, all the way back to the hotel, and right up to lights out. But he failed to read the small print, which would have warned him that he was drinking Gatorade "replacement fluid." He hydrated, all right, but he also ignored the fact that he had never done it to this degree in his "regular training routine."

Pressure mounted as Dick went through his normal preparation on race morning. Cameras clicked, flashed and whirred from every direction, including one surrounded by a crew with the letters ABC emblazoned on their shirts. Rick stared helplessly at his father, pleading him to relax, but there would be no relaxing on that morning. To Dick, it seemed like the eyes of the entire world – including those of his late father – were watching every move he made.

As zero hour neared, Dick took a couple more shots of Gatorade and pulled his teammate into the water. Precisely at seven o'clock, the collection of swimmers attacked the ocean from a deep-water start. Dick avoided the mass of arms and legs by remaining on the outside of the pack. He streaked through the water confidently, while Rick stretched out on the beanbag and enjoyed the gentle, undulating ride. They had two hours and fifteen minutes to complete the swim course, but made it to the halfway turn in less than an hour.

"I felt good at the turn," Dick said. "Except my stomach was a little upset."

Soon after Team Hoyt rounded the halfway point, the joyful experience came to an abrupt halt. Unfortunately, the change Dick made in his training routine came back to haunt him; the replacement fluid struck back with a vengeance. Cramps hit him first, then a partial paralysis in the arms and legs. He switched to the same sidestroke motion that saved him in Canada, but he could not catch his breath. When the salty ocean water internally merged with Gatorade, he regurgitated a bluish-green mix and floundered like a fish succumbing to a hook.

Dick learned his lesson the hard way. "Some sports drinks are for during and after the race, not the night before."

The crew on the safety boat realized Dick needed help. They offered to pull him out of the ocean, but he refused. Only when the crew finally told him that he failed to make the cutoff time did he allow them to take him and Rick to shore. To Dick, facing his family, friends and a national film crew was more difficult than enduring the cramps. Team Hoyt had failed to complete their first race. Dick couldn't understand what went wrong, but after a good deal of mental anguish, he suspected the Gatorade. Later that day, a member of the medical staff confirmed his suspicions.

"I felt like I had let everyone down," Dick confessed. "When we got to shore, I had an urge to jump back in the ocean and swim all the way back to Massachusetts." Then he added, "Now we can't say we've finished every race we started."

Rick hurt deeply for his father. When he saw the sadness in Dick's eyes and heard the disappointment in his voice, he wanted to reach out and give him a hug, to tell him everything was okay. Throughout his life, however, Rick had never been able to do that. Not physically, anyway. But Dick knew what his son was thinking. He could read it in his eyes.

The following day, Dick and Rick met with Silk and the race director, Debbie Baker. Dick learned that the committee was disappointed *for* the Hoyts, but not *with* the Hoyts. In fact, they were extremely impressed by them, and openly appreciative of the positive contribution the family had made to the overall success of the event.

"We expect you to apply again next year," the director said. "I'm sure things will turn out differently." Dick and Rick exchanged a quick glance. The same thought came to their minds simultaneously.

Did she say *Next year?*

"Oh, sure," Dick promised the woman. "Things will be different next year. You can count on that."

After eight years of competition, that was one of the few times that Team Hoyt updated their racing calendar long before the new year started. Although it was twelve months away, October of 1989 got the bold circle, and it included a single handwritten word — *Hawaii*.

Barry Nolan returned to Massachusetts with a powerful story to report. No, it would not have the happy ending everyone wanted, but nonetheless, he had a great story to share with his viewers. Nolan referred to the event as a setback for the Hoyts, not a failure. He said, "Men like Dick and Rick don't quit because of a setback."

Nolan knew the Hoyts were extremely disappointed, but he also knew, until their mission was completed, they would never quit. He presented the story on Thanksgiving Day.

...If it still seems a bit much to you, if you still wonder why, then think about this for a moment. If you know of someone, anyone, who doesn't know what all the fuss is about concerning handicapped access to public buildings and transportation, then the Hoyts still have a few miles to swim. If you know of someone who has made jokes about 'retards' or 'spastics,' the Hoyts still have some biking to do. And if you know of someone who sees a handicapped person, maybe someone who drools a bit in a public place, and turns away in disgust, then the Hoyts — and I suppose all of us — still have some running to do.

* * *

Traveling around the country to compete in races always put Rick behind at school, so he had to work even harder to keep up with his studies. He could still graduate in the spring of 1993 if he devoted the required time and effort, and since his primary objective was to become totally independent and to work a normal, productive life, he devoted the required time.

Dick began the year like a thoroughbred out of a starting gate. He hit the pool or the lake as many as five times a week, cranked up his mileage on both the bike and the run, and sucked down the Gatorade *during* the training sessions only, never before. He wanted to run strong at Boston number nine in April, sustain the momentum through Falmouth in August, and hit his peak at Hawaii in October. Dick promised, "There will be no repeat of '88."

Rick did his share as well. He studied hard, cut a few pounds, and spent less time chasing women. "That isn't easy for a boy who likes to party," Rick said.

Before October rolled around, ABC brought their cameras to Holland. They wanted the full story about the Hoyts so they could air it during the Ironman. American Airlines again answered the sponsorial call, and the Konoloa Hotel offered rooms for the team and their entourage. XRE, the Bicycle Exchange and Dave McGillivray joined the parade.

The Hoyts – including Dick's sister and youngest brother, Barbara and Jason – arrived before Ironman week began. Dick and Rick ran the Kailua 10K, and during the Ironman Parade, they marched through the city of Kailua waving American flags. Dick trained until three days before the race, and when he and Rick attended the orientation, they heard the speakers repeat the same things they said in 1988.

"I didn't need to hear it again," Dick said seriously. "I didn't do anything different in my training. We hydrated the night before, but only with water."

All the big names came to challenge the Ironman course and each other. Dave Scott and Mark Allen took the lead overall; Paula Newby Fraser led the women. ABC cameras captured all the action, but they focused on Team Hoyt as they returned to shore in one hour and fifty-four minutes. With the swim completed, Dick made good on his promise: No repeat of 1988.

The spectators cheered when Dick lifted his smiling son from the boat and dashed into the medical tent, where a medical technician waited to help Rick relieve himself before the long bike ride. Dick looked strong at that point, and the only glitch came in the tent, when the medical staff had problems inserting the catheter.

"What's the problem?" Dick snapped at the assistant. "We don't want to be disqualified for sitting in here in too long."

With helmets strapped in place and sunblock coating their arms and faces, the duo finally got their first serious look at the Queen K Highway. As expected, the heat through the lava fields and the wind in the mountains pounded them relentlessly. While Dick powered his teammate over the sweltering course, an ABC crew pulled alongside and took footage they would telecast around the world. They filmed the moment when, without slowing, Dick pulled out a water bottle and held it for Rick to take a drink. All systems worked to perfection, and after nine hours and fifty-five minutes of swimming and biking, they returned to the transition area.

"We estimated eight hours on the bike," Dick told an interviewer. "We made it with a few minutes to spare."

Dick struggled during the marathon, but he visualized his ecstatic family waiting at the finish line, which motivated him to keep pushing forward. Then, at Rick's urging, he picked up speed, and as the cheering grew louder with every step, he sailed through the final mile in under six minutes.

ABC zoomed in closely and followed them the final hundred yards, and with the unrestrained spectators screaming wildly, the adrenaline kicked in and Dick sprinted past several runners who struggled to reach the finish line. Before the running chair came to a complete stop, the proud and tearful family, led by Judy, mobbed them with hugs and kisses. As the crowd tossed flowers and leis, Rob and Russ showered them with champagne. This wasn't the first time they were welcomed by a frenzied crowd, but nothing compared to what they experienced on that October day. Thanks to the ABC cameras and crew, people from all over the world shared an unforgettable moment.

The dedicated athlete who eventually finished last was still somewhere out on the run course when Dick and Rick crossed the line in fourteen hours, twenty-four minutes and four seconds. Again, they completed the mission they set out to do. When Barry Nolan produced a video for Team Hoyt, he selected their memorable finish at Ironman Hawaii as its cornerstone. He highlighted the moment by summarizing their life-long struggle with a quote from the ABC commentator:

...Twenty-seven years ago, the Hoyt family began the long journey that has led to this day and to this moment. Along the way, the family has faced reality squarely. Through love, they have transformed a life of deprivation into a life of possibility.

When ABC aired the Ironman, the accolades flowed and the recognition mounted. Writer Gerry Callahan understood the significance of Dick's accomplishments as well as anyone. In earlier years, he had encouraged his peers to support Dick as Athlete of the Year. However, after ten years of unparalleled success, and now the ultimate in Hawaii, Callahan upped the ante and nominated Dick for Athlete of the Decade. In his columns, he urged supporters to analyze Dick's competition for that lofty honor. He expounded on the money involved with professional athletes, and, therefore, the contrast in their motivation. He talked about drugs, crime and infidelity among the more-visible, professional athletes.

Callahan stated his opinion in the *Boston Herald:* "They are phenomenal athletes," he said of the big-name athletes. "But none can do what the Hoyts can do. Not a chance. Dick pushes Rick physically. Rick pushes Dick in every other way. Together, they swim and bike and run and inspire. Together, they were true sports heroes of the decade."

Over the following months, the Hoyts appeared on various TV shows, including *Rivera Live*, the *Good Day Show*, and *Sports Sidelines Cable*. The printed media called on them as well, with the Hoyts appearing in the *Boston Globe*, *Parade*, and the *Las Vegas Sun*. Their smiling faces illuminated the cover of *New England Runner*, a publication that anointed the Hoyts as their "Triathletes of the Year."

They received a song and a letter from acclaimed songwriter Graham Nash. President Reagan and Senator Kennedy sent them congratulatory letters, and they received invitations to speak at numerous events. Cards and letters arrived from all over the country. Everything happened at a dizzying pace, and when Judy asked him about slowing down, he told her, "No way. This is the year we will ride and run across America."

"But you're going to be 50 this year," she told him.

"I'm not getting any younger," he replied. "Neither is Rick."

Several months later, on a frigid, mid-winter day, Dick wrapped himself in sweats and a hooded sweatshirt and took a relaxing stroll down to the lake. The cold air produced a misty plume with every breath he exhaled. In serenity and solitude, he gazed out over the lake and thought about his accomplishments in the year that had just ended. He tried to put it all in perspective, and gave thought to his future, his marriage, his sons and the racing. He traced the major events that led him to that day, to that point in his life. He thought about the Ironman experience, what it meant to Rick, and how it affected their lives and objectives. Then, in a melancholy moment, he remembered the prophetic words of his late father: *You will know you are an athlete when you are on Wide World of Sports.*

Dick took a deep sigh, looked to the sky and smiled.

A family affair, Hawaiian style.

Making it look easy.

CHAPTER 16 — LOVE, WAR AND GRANDCHILDREN

To pretend there wasn't any thought given to the way Rick is, and the possibility that it could happen to a child of mine, would be a lie. But nobody can control that. We can only carry on and persevere. Some will excel despite great odds.

—Rob Hoyt

Amidst the swarm of media attention, Dick and Rick felt like rock stars. But reality soon replaced the euphoria. Dick realized all the acclaim and hoopla had its rewards, but it had done little to secure Rick's future. Although they received endless cheers and handshakes, none of it translated to long-term security.

"It's not about racing," Dick told an interviewer. "The day will come when I can't push Rick over those mountains. A day will come, in fact, when I can't push him at all, and I won't be able to help him maintain his independence."

Rick had established a successful life even without the racing, but Dick knew that the financial burdens and responsibilities were another issue altogether. Dick wanted to help other disabled people as well, but he became frustrated that everyone expected him to contribute to their issues, but offered nothing in return. When a basketball star for the Celtics asked them to support a fundraiser for the New England Sports Museum, they did it. The player didn't offer any monetary incentive, but one thing is certain, basketball stars are well rewarded for their "meaningful" contributions to society. "They seemed to think the 'little guy' should do all the giving and not expect anything in return," Dick said. "At times, I felt like we were being used."

One man had written a story about the Hoyts and entered it in a contest. His reward for winning would be substantial, so he boldly asked Dick to contribute to the story. He wanted Dick to help *him* win the award, but he never offered to share the winnings with Rick, nor did he volunteer a donation to any charitable organization on behalf of the handicapped. Dick was not a selfish person, but he had to be realistic. "I know a one-way street when I see it. I have a family to worry about, too." Then he said, "I've never met a grocer yet who stayed in business by giving away all the food."

Dick was never comfortable asking for anything, not for himself, anyway. As a military officer, his financial requirements were covered, and with the promotion to Lieutenant Colonel, he expected adequate retirement for himself and Judy. "But what about Rick?" he asked rhetorically. "We are constantly asked to speak to people, and to share our story, so I felt it was time to expect something in return for our efforts. It wasn't about racing, it was about survival."

Dick's expertise was not in the field of public relations or self-promotion. When Morton Productions contacted him about speaking engagements, he jumped at the offer.

"The maximum you can expect to receive is five thousand dollars," he was told. "You are what we call a 'fringe athlete.'"

Displaying frustration on behalf of his friend, Pete Wisnewski defined a fringe athlete this way: "One who can't hold the attention of couch potatoes for three hours every night. That puts him on the fringe."

TCBY, the yogurt giant, flew Dick and Rick to Dallas to speak at their annual corporate meeting. Dick told his story and went through the videos. He presented them with an idea for a national commercial, which included him feeding yogurt to Rick. Everyone thought it was a wonderful idea, but the prospective sponsors never followed up.

"I guess they didn't like it when Rick had trouble eating their product," Dick commented with a smile. "Maybe because most of it went down his chin. Society is a little squeamish for the realities of the disabled."

Pete Wisnewski offered a more cynical analysis. "Americans have plenty of tolerance for gratuitous violence and blood, but authentic drool? Never!"

In April, they went back to Boston for their tenth appearance and notched another Personal Record for the course. They covered the 26.2 miles in a time of two hours and forty-nine minutes, still faster than the qualifying time for a 20-year-old, and in six weeks, Dick would turn 50.

After the race, they all went to Houlihan's Restaurant in the Fanieul Hall Market Place for the celebratory dinner. It was a family affair. Russ invited Lisa, along with her mother and her stepfather. At their sunken table in the middle of the restaurant, everyone took turns toasting and saluting one another: Rob celebrated birthday number 26; Russ would soon graduate from Amherst with a degree in Psychology; and, of course, Dick and Rick scored a Boston PR.

When Russ took his turn at center stage, he toasted Dick and Rick for their excellent performance in the marathon. Next, he saluted Rob for becoming one year older. With all that taken care of, he proceeded to knock Lisa off her chair, figuratively, when he pulled an engagement ring from his pocket, dropped down on one knee and said, "Lisa Marie Donovan, will you marry me?"

Most of the other patrons overheard his proposal. The Hoyt family raised their glasses and shouted out their approval when Lisa, surprised and red-faced, accepted the ring and rewarded Russ with a tearful kiss.

"I think everyone in the restaurant cheered," Russ recalled proudly. "It was all very exhilarating."

In May, after a UCP sponsored speaking engagement in San Diego, Dick, Rick, Judy and Russ stopped in Los Angeles to rub shoulders with former President Reagan. Since Rob and Mary were back in Westfield awaiting the birth of their first child, they had to miss the memorable event.

"He saw us on Wide World of Sports," Dick said, "and asked me to call him when we were in California. We called his office and he invited us over."

"You will have to wait a few minutes," an aide told them. "Representatives from *Parade Magazine* are interviewing the President at the moment."

"We were a little concerned about Mom," Russ joked. "She's a staunch Democrat and not shy about speaking her mind."

When the secretary informed Reagan that the Hoyt family had arrived, he promptly excused the magazine people and invited the Hoyts into his office.

"He asked us questions and shared his own stories," Russ said. "He was very cordial."

Dick grinned and said, "He gave me some of his jelly beans."

Judy went into the meeting expecting to meet the man her political party had attacked as being "mean-spirited," but that was not who she met. Instead, she met the man himself, not the political enemy. The Hoyts posed for photos with the President and presented him with pictures from Ironman Hawaii. At that point, Judy impulsively stepped up and gave Reagan a hug.

Slightly embarrassed, she told him, "It's not every day you get to hug a President."

"It's better than slugging one," Reagan retorted.

After the visit, Judy informed her family of what a pleasant surprise it was to discover that President Reagan was not the evil man he had been portrayed to be. Playing Devil's Advocate, Dick needled his wife by saying, "Well, maybe some of your favorite politicians haven't been totally honest with you?" His comment quickly ended the family discussion of politics.

In June, Russ became the second Hoyt to graduate from Amherst, and the second member of his family to launch a professional career in social services. He accepted a position at the Greater Boston Association for Retarded Children and immediately took charge of a youth program called Koala — Kids of all Learning Abilities. As his mother before him, Russell helped various organizations in creating programs of "inclusion" for the disabled, a position in which he already had over twenty years of personal experience.

Dick and Rick actively and professionally supported the disabled as well, leaving only Rob on an unrelated career path.

Rob was a very sensitive man, and as a youngster, he had traveled down those difficult and painful roads with Rick, Jamie Decenza and many other handicapped children. The experiences had taken a heavy toll on his emotions, so when it came time to choose a vocation, the machinist trade suited him fine.

"I took after my dad," Rob said respectfully. "I really enjoy working with my hands. It's very rewarding to me."

Although Rob became one of those fortunate people who thoroughly enjoyed his professional calling, he had greater aspirations. "All I ever wanted to be was a dad. Having Rick for a brother, the whole idea of a family, and the thought of a child being so dependent upon me for its care and well-being was burned into my soul."

At one a.m., the thirtieth day of August, 1990, Rob rushed Mary to the Wesson Woman's Unit of Baystate Medical Center in Springfield, where emergency personnel ushered her into triage. At 5:20 that morning, the first Hoyt grandson was born — but he didn't make a sound.

"To pretend there wasn't any thought given to the way Rick is," Rob admitted somberly, "and the possibility that it could happen to a child of mine, would be a lie. But nobody can control that. We can only carry on and persevere. Some will excel despite great odds."

Mary watched anxiously as the respiratory therapist hovered over her new baby. Still, she heard nothing. The baby had not made a sound. Mary then glanced over at her motionless husband. He looked terrified.

"What's wrong!" Mary screamed hysterically.

205

To express his feelings, Rob recalled his youth. "Seeing and experiencing such courage in the people closest to me at an early age made the decision to have a child much easier. Whenever I felt down about things, the simple thought of my brother smiling would lighten my load and remind me how lucky we really are."

Mary uttered a sigh of relief. "The doctor cleared his lungs and nose, and within a few seconds, the most wonderful crying filled the room."

They named him Jaymes (Jayme) Conner Hoyt, fulfilling the promise Rob had made many years earlier. "He was very strong and alert," Mary said happily. "And very vocal."

* * *

Dick continued serious planning for the cross-country trek, but the projected expense increased rapidly. When the estimate zipped past 30-grand, he realized sponsorship was an absolute necessity. In a discussion with Dave McGillivray, he explained how he planned to resolve all the other obstacles, but asked for suggestions regarding funding. "With good publicity," Dick told him, "we should be able to raise a million dollars on the Trek."

McGillivray agreed he had a winning venture and offered to help find sponsorship. In the meantime, Dick and Rick went on speaking engagements and fundraisers, but nothing kept Team Hoyt from their racing. The circuit took them around New England and Canada. Rob, Mary and Jayme accompanied them to a race in Las Vegas, Nevada, but once again, surprisingly, Judy declined the invitation to go along, claiming that she felt contempt for the gambling and the nightlife scene.

"It's just another race," she said disdainfully. "Always another race."

Dick revealed his frustration at Judy's attitude. "She didn't think I was supporting her work, so she wouldn't support mine. We were becoming competitors rather than teammates."

In October, however, Judy went along to Orlando, Florida, where Disney held the Triathlon World Championships. During a tour of Disney World, Jose Cuevas stepped up and introduced himself as the Vice President of Taca Airlines, the national air carrier for El Salvador. "I would like you to participate in a triathlon in my country," Cuevas said. "El Salvador."

With no hesitation, Dick told the man, "I'm sure that can be arranged."

Cuevas smiled. "I'm sure our airlines will provide transportation for you and your family. And I will find others who will take good care of you."

Dick knew it would be an expensive trip. Determined to end the pro bono work, he shook the man's hand and said, "When you find those others, give me a call."

"I will do that," said Cuevas. He took Dick's phone number and walked away.

"Judy told me she wanted to go to El Salvador," Dick said. "But that was about all she said to me during the entire trip. We didn't have much fun."

Judy confronted new challenges in 1991. After serious disagreements, she felt compelled to resign as the director of Kamp for Kids. Dick, however, was not convinced she resigned of her own free will. In one of the rare times he spoke harshly of his wife, he said, "I'm not so sure she had any choice. I think they wanted a director, not a dictator."

Dissension surfaced when Dick and Rick supported the Special Olympics. Judy believed it was the antithesis of what the Team Hoyt message was all about, because the Special Olympics did not include "normal" athletes with disabled athletes. In fact, it separated them. She implied that Dick was more concerned with his own glory than with helping other disabled kids.

Dick calmly refuted her claim. "Judy is naive about some things. If the disabled had to compete against the able-bodied athletes in order to participate in the Olympics, they'd all be watching it on television just like the rest of us. When a disabled kid can dunk a basketball or run a two-ten marathon, he'll be in the Olympics against the best. Otherwise, he's excluded in every sense of the word. The regular Olympic Games are all about competition, not compassion. Why do you think we send the NBA players? Because we're nice guys?"

When it came down to "he said, she said," Diane Kopec, the former secretary at ASHS, admitted that Judy wanted to be in 'control' of every situation. On the other hand, Kopec got the impression that Dick approached things in much the same manner. Perhaps Kopec was correct to a certain degree, but there was plenty of common ground. After all, the Hoyts had accomplished incredible things together during 28 years of marriage, and there was more to come.

An upscale insurance organization known as the Million Dollar Round Table offered the Hoyts a substantial fee plus expenses to appear as their featured motivational speakers at an event in New Orleans. The entire family made the trip together. In a casual setting, with the Hoyts lined up side by side on center stage, the announcer introduced them as a family of five. He placed special emphasis on the word "family."

"But it was not always that way," the man said. "In the beginning, the Hoyts were told that one of them had no value to society."

Wearing a sheepish grin, Rick looked out at the audience as if he were saying, "Okay, guess which one of us he's talking about?"

The Master of Ceremonies asked Russell a nonsensical question relating to the struggles of a family with a disabled child. "We would change some things, sure," Russ said emphatically. "But change our family? No way."

Once the applause subsided, Rob said, "We want to change people's attitudes about people who are different, and about the fact that family is so very important for a better world."

While the younger brothers elicited the cheers, Rick moved them to the tears. After sharing his poignant story about the "unreachable Coke," he said, "With all their teasing, my brothers taught me how to accept my disability. Now that we are adults, they treat me like a friend."

Although the Round Table forum proved a tremendous success, the financial results fell short of Dick's expectations. No new sponsors stepped forward. He wondered why, but kept arriving at the same answer — reality. On the surface, everyone professed undying support for the severely disabled. They were happy to snap Rick's picture, laud his accomplishments, and occasionally toss in a contribution, but that was where it always seemed to end.

"They should support him," Dick said dejectedly. "But he is a non-vocal, spastic, quadriplegic who drools and makes indiscernible sounds. He can't give them what they want."

Dick was right. Rick was not an athlete like the ones we see on television commercials. He couldn't sell their products. But in Dick's mind, Team Hoyt was all about Rick, and when he told everyone, "Rick is the athlete," he meant it.

"Without Rick," he said sincerely, "I'm just another jogger." But what could he do about it? Barry Nolan said it best.

... If you know of someone who sees a handicapped person, maybe someone who drools a bit in a public place, and turns away in disgust, then the Hoyts —and I suppose all of us —still have some running to do.

The trip to New Orleans reminded Dick there could be only one conclusion: "I still have some running to do."

On June 16, 1991, the cover of *Sunday People* displayed a large picture of Dick pushing Rick in the running chair with an American flag secured above the front wheel. The caption below them read, *No greater love —Twenty-six miles, and running for two: A father-and-son love story.* The lengthy story by Michael O'Connor touched on all 29 years of Rick's life, from the umbilical cord to his days as a college senior. O'Connor titled the article, "He ain't heavy, He's my son," and it included a great selection of Team Hoyt racing photographs. Judy was notably missing in action; all eight photos were of Dick and Rick.

209

In the story, Dick summarized the impact racing has had on their lives. "It's unbelievable. We started out just so Rick could enjoy a sport like his other brothers did in hockey and Little League, but who could expect this?"

Rick told O'Connor, "I feel like Dad and I have gotten a lot closer. We can discuss important items, like where our next competition is, and what place we expect to come in."

Rick also said he would graduate from Boston University in two years and wanted to do other things, to expand his life beyond racing. "I am in my late twenties," he said. "I don't want to spend every weekend racing. I have a lot of friends who I want to see over the summer."

On July 20th, the Hoyt family added another branch to the family tree. Russell married Lisa Donovan. Then two weeks later, the families assembled at the Blue Wave Restaurant in Boston to see *Fathers Inc.* honor Dick with their annual Father of the Year Award.

"We didn't have any big races scheduled for the summer because we had planned to make the ocean-to-ocean Trek," Dick explained. "But when the funding didn't come through, we set it back another year. And then I got this telephone call from Jose Cuevas in San Salvador."

Since he had now found some sponsors, Cuevas invited the Hoyts to participate in the El Salvador National Triathlon. Taca Airlines, Goldenlight Beer, and the El Salvador Hotel would take care of everything, and their offer also included tickets for a few of their friends. Rick was ready for some more long-distance globe trotting, and Central America suited him fine.

"They're having a civil war down there, aren't they?" asked Phil Taylor, Rick's PCA.

Rick answered, "That's not a problem for me. They won't take a vegetable hostage."

Judy invited her friend from ASHS, Diane Kopec. The two women viewed the trip as a great opportunity to spread the word about the abilities of the disabled. And, since the sponsors were so generous, Diane brought her husband along. Still, they had room for one more.

"You want me to do a tri *where*?" Pete Wisnewski asked Dick.

"San Salvador."

"Are you serious?"

"Of course," Dick assured him. "I'm serious."

"Hoyt, you must be crazy. Count me in."

With all the negative publicity coming out of their war-ravaged country, the triathlon sponsors thought that having the Hoyts in the national event would be a well-needed feather in their collective cap. A bold headline in the Spanish-language newspaper read: *FAMILIA HOYT!*

Jose Cuevas and several members of the Santa Ana Triathlon Club met the Hoyts and their companions at the airport and hustled them off to the hotel. Although the hotel staff did not speak English, they were expecting the American guests and led them to their rooms.

"No one here speaks English," Dick joked. "It's just like San Diego."

Dick and Pete changed clothes and took off for a training run. Wherever they went, many of the friendly locals greeted them. "Hoyt! Hoyt! Hoyt!"

Before running far, Dick spotted a military tank at the side of the road. "Pete, look at that."

He pointed at the tank, where soldiers armed with machine guns were sitting on the gun turret and leaning against the tracks.

"What the hell are we getting into?" Pete asked.

A soldier waved and shouted, "Hoyt! Hoyt!"

"Wave back at him," Dick said. "But keep running."

When the soldiers waved and cheered, Dick and Pete correctly assumed that the military presence was there to protect them, not capture or harm them.

"They're just kids," Pete observed of the soldiers.

"Yeah," Dick said. "Just kids."

Before the day ended, Jose sent an interpreter named Fernando over to help Dick and his teammates prepare for the race. Fernando told them the civil war in El Salvador had turned the citizens against the federal government, and that teenage boys were taken from the streets and the fields and forced into the military.

"We saw uniformed boys as young as 14 carrying automatic weapons," Dick said. "Even McDonalds was protected by armed guards. With all this chaos and poverty around us, here we are preparing for another triathlon."

Spectators who watched the triathlon the previous year numbered only in the hundreds, but once information about the Hoyts spread throughout the villages, thousands lined the streets to see them. Children sang out "Richie! Richie!" and reached out to touch Rick when he and his family arrived. Bystanders ran up and offered to help Dick with all his preparation, including airing up the raft and placing Rick inside it. When race time approached, Cuevas handed a red flag to Judy and asked her to do the honors of starting the race. With a wave of the flag, she sent the athletes into action.

Dick had raced in hot, humid weather before, but this course held new challenges. His goggles were inadvertently pulled from his face and he had to finish the one-mile swim with blurred vision. Crosswinds blew the raft so hard he had to swim at a 30-degree angle to compensate, and when they made the turn and headed back, he had to swim hard just to stay ahead of the boat.

"The wind blew us so hard that we passed a few surprised swimmers," Dick said. "I could feel Rick gloating back there."

Dick staggered out of the water. When he removed the harness, he found blood running down his chest. Swimming at such a harsh angle had ripped the harness into his shoulders and tore open the skin.

"The transition area was unbelievable," Dick recalled. "Cars, motorcycles, a band playing, people everywhere. It was like a scene out of a movie."

The bike distance of twenty-five miles began on an incline, which made it nearly impossible for Dick to start his heavy rig rolling in the right direction. He had more success when he tacked like a sailor on a sailboat, but the rear wheel kept slipping on the rocks and loose dirt. He pushed his son and bike up a hill for nearly two miles, but they were not alone. Other bikers also had problems with the unstable terrain, and some of them pushed or carried their bikes almost as far as he did. Once the Hoyts were back on solid ground, strong winds hit them head on; gusts on the curves nearly forced them off the roads. While soldiers in a pickup trailed behind the Hoyts the entire twenty-five miles, people cheered them all along the route, start to finish.

"I was astounded at the reception they gave us," Dick said. "They're so destitute, and they have so little to cheer about."

When they returned to the transition area for the bike-to-run exchange, several spectators ran over to offer assistance. One young man even tried to help push the chair.

"No!" Judy shouted at the man. "Get back! Get away!"

The 10K run started with an uphill on rocky turf. When they descended the hill, they encountered potholes, soft dirt and more rocks. They dodged traffic around the city, and Dick said, "The exhaust from all the cars and trucks made my eyes water."

An accumulation of bicycles, mopeds, motorcycles, runners and wheelchairs merged behind them when they re-entered the city. One man carried a small boy on his shoulders while he jogged along with the convoy. A large banner proclaiming *Viva Familia Hoyt!* welcomed them to the finish line, where six men stood side by side and locked their arms together to bring the Hoyt Express to a stop.

When asked what that was all about, Dick said, "Guess they didn't trust our brakes. It's a good thing they weren't armed."

The entire village showed up for the closing ceremony. Most of the adults had children at their sides, in their arms, or sitting on their shoulders so they could get a closer look at the American heroes. In the town square, Jose Cuevas and members of the

Santa Ana Triathlon Club crowded around a self-standing microphone to make the presentations.

"The crowd was so noisy I couldn't hear him," Rick would say later. "It was real cool."

A representative for one of the sponsors said a few words in Spanish before he presented the Hoyts with gold medals. To commemorate the event, Cuevas presented Dick with an authentic Salvadorian machete imbedded in a wooden frame.

"It's my first machete," Dick chuckled.

"A man can never have too many machetes," Pete replied.

Dick joked about the unique gift, but when he returned to Holland, it went directly to his living room wall. When the formalities concluded, the admiring townsfolk swarmed around the Hoyts. Dick felt like a politician before an election as he walked among them. They shook his hands, slapped his shoulders, and begged him to touch their children. The adulation humbled him, but when his feet returned to the ground, he realized his entourage and equipment had been ushered away to a reception at the hotel, leaving him without transportation.

"It wasn't a problem. I just hitched a ride on the back seat of a motorcycle."

The Hoyts awoke the following morning and found themselves on the front page of the local newspaper, including a great photo of Team Hoyt dashing toward the finish line. In addition to the racing story and highlights, it also carried their message of hope for the disabled. The Hoyts' contribution to the Salvadorians did not end at the finish line. They loaded up the van and went for a tour of the local schools. Then they concluded with a visit to the Salvador Rehabilitation Center, a dreadfully overcrowded facility that provided care for physically and mentally disabled children, where the grim results of poverty, lack of education, and a heinous civil war greeted them.

"We were devastated by what we saw," Dick said. "The facility was short of help, short of room, short of money, short of everything except children in desperate need."

Judy was despondent over what she saw and learned. "There were so many people in wheelchairs."

"Both children and adults," Diane added.

When asked to deliver one of her inspirational speeches, Judy angrily replied, "How can I talk about inclusion when there are so many people without arms or legs! What they need here is medical attention, and they need it right now!"

What Judy witnessed at the Center touched her conscience and tested her resolve, and once again she questioned the wisdom and motivation for pushing, carrying, and towing Rick through races. Dick steadfastly disagreed. "These people see us as hope," he told her. "We show them what can happen if you don't give up. If we can't give them hope, what can we give them?"

On this issue, unfortunately, Dick and Judy were on opposite sides of the invisible battle line, and with no compromise in sight, there could be only one winner, or no winner at all. Their ideologies, objectives and solutions were no longer mutual. For nearly thirty years, the indomitable team had combined their dreams and talents to overcome insurmountable odds, but they finally met a dragon they could not slay.

When the time came, Dick included video from the San Salvador experience in the Team Hoyt motivational presentations. He told the story truthfully, exactly as he saw it. He didn't have the power or the delusions that he could change the realities facing the poor and disabled people in foreign countries, nor could he undo the deadly politics of a nation when even the powerful politicos in America could not agree on a solution to help them.

"I did the best I could do," Dick said sadly. "That's all I can do."

With Rick at his side, they had done the best they could do, and for their effort, the people of San Salvador loved and admired Team Hoyt.

When it came to his convictions, Dick never wavered. He simply considered the overall picture, back where it all began, when the doctors referred to Rick simply as a vegetable, someone who had no value. With that single thought, he had no problem justifying his actions or his motivation.

Regarding his decision to race in San Salvador, Dick said pointedly, "Rick, the 'vegetable,' is a hero in that country."

Scenes from San Salvador.

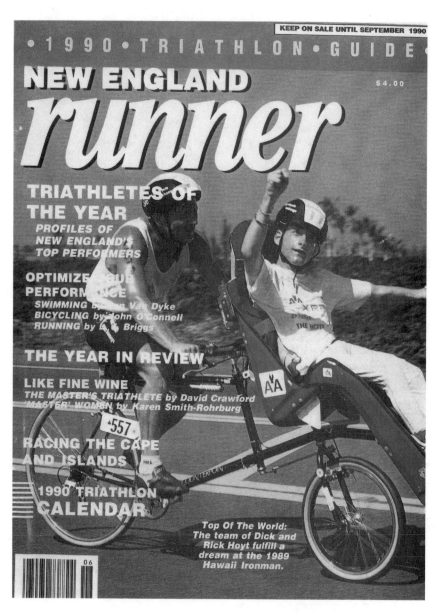

Triathletes of the year, gracing the cover.

218

CHAPTER 17 — TREK ACROSS AMERICA

It was just like, wow! And then saying, 'Guys, guys, look what you have accomplished!' 'They got to the top of the Rockies on their own power. That's pretty awesome.

—Judy Hoyt

In 1992, with the assistance of Eddie Burke and Mike Giallongo, Dick had established the *Hoyt Fund*, a charitable and benevolent organization to benefit all disabled people. The primary objective of the Hoyt's Trek across America was to raise one million dollars for the fund, and ultimately to help make every building in America accessible to the handicapped.

"I didn't necessarily want to ride across the country," Rick said in an interview with Deborah Gusin of *I Witness Video*. "But I wanted to do something that people with disabilities had not done before. I saw it as an opportunity to call attention to the Hoyt Fund and what it is all about. I felt very frightened that I would not get enough fluids to make it through the desert, but my greatest fear was how long my *bottom* would last."

As the projected cost mounted, the opportunity for Rick to accomplish his goal diminished rapidly. Before the Trek could even begin, they would need airfare to Los Angeles and a recreational vehicle. Accommodations and meals for six people on the road for 47 days required a substantial budget and meticulous planning. But Dick eventually convinced everyone that he and Rick were going, with or without them.

When asked for his reaction to news about the Trek, Russ said, "Dad came home and said, 'Okay, we're going to bike and run from California to Boston,' I thought, Oh no, here he goes again. I didn't think he could do it, but I wanted to be part of it."

Executives from Equitable Life of Iowa agreed to back the venture. If it were promoted properly, they believed thousands of dollars could be raised for the company and for the Hoyt Fund. DMSE, Etonic, American Airlines, XRE, and National Strategies for Financial Resources (NSFR) agreed to the terms and they all joined the team. The timing was perfect for Russell. He accepted a promotion with his employer, which included two months off before moving him into the new job.

Judy worried about Rick enduring the long trip, and although skeptical about the Trek from the very beginning, she knew they needed her support.

"She gave up her job," Dick said, "She planned the routing, safety, clothing, supplies. She secured an RV in California."

Rick gave up rum and Coke and began drinking juices. He asked Phil Taylor if he were ready for another trip.

Taylor asked, "Where to this time?"

"Los Angeles to Boston," Rick told him. "On the bike."

When he realized Rick was serious, Taylor joined the crew.

Rob stayed home with his wife and young son, but he helped with the planning, preparation, monitoring, and the reception upon return. Dick found a support van and signed up a masseuse named Linda Reichert. Everything went along as planned until two weeks before the scheduled departure, when Equitable Life of Iowa bailed out of the deal.

"They pulled the rug out and we landed on our butts," Russ said. "But my parents decided to refinance their house. They were willing to put it all on the line to finance the trek. It was that important to them, and that's what they did, to the tune of seventy thousand dollars."

Team Hoyt sprang into action and prepared for the road once again. Dick asked McGillivray and Michael Gehrig, an executive with NSFR, to oversee the logistics of the operation from the home base in Massachusetts. Since both men had already invested in the project, they took over the public relations details and solicited donations.

Dick said, "I knew I needed to be in the best shape of my life, so I added extra training at the Auburn Health Club. I had been mentally preparing myself for three years for this thing."

Judy was greatly concerned about safety. "People who had crossed the country before said we would have to be very careful because there are crazy people out there. You might be robbed, and all kinds of horror stories. We talked to people who had biked across America before, and they said we would run into all kinds of weather. We were prepared for the heat of summer, in the desert," Judy confessed, "but we didn't prepare for the cold."

Russ said, "One of the guys who had done a run across the country had been mugged. He also witnessed a murder. We were warned that people would try to steal from us, and we worried about the course, about being on the right roads, and about not seeing any police if we needed help."

"Nobody thought we'd be able to finish," Dick said. "Friends told me it would be too hard on my body to go 90 miles every day without taking a day off for 47 straight days. They thought I would go 20 days and that would be it, the Trek would be over."

The negativity brought back memories of the charity race 14 years earlier, when everyone thought he would be satisfied just running down to the corner. But this race went on for nearly 4,000 miles, and the Continental Divide stood in their way. Dick, apparently, was the only one who truly expected to complete the full distance. In fact, he even staked his home and his reputation on it. Since Dick and Rick would spend their days on the bicycle, someone else had to be in charge of the two support vehicles that slowly carried the other team members behind them.

"I was the Trek Coordinator," Russ told the interviewer from *I Witness Video*. "I was in charge of making sure we had a motel room to stay in if we were near one. I took care of the groceries and the bottled water, and made sure we had enough money to get to the next city. I was also the one responsible for any disagreements within the crew."

"Disagreements?" she asked.

221

Judy felt that she should be the one in charge and giving the orders, not her son. But Dick, the military officer, stood firmly on his decision. Forty-seven days on the highway would be a very long time, and he believed Russ would be a great arbitrator whenever necessary. If Judy, Dick or anyone else had complaints, they should go directly to him.

"Actually, it was my wrestling background," Russ joked.

Once Judy completed her responsibilities in Massachusetts, she told Dick she would meet the family at the pier in Santa Monica on the eighth of June, then she took off alone. "I went to a Human Services conference in Ohio," she explained. "I flew to California after the conference."

From an American Airliner seven miles above the ground, Rick marveled at the awesome emptiness of Death Valley. "I thought we were crazy when we flew over the desert," he admitted. "I said to Phil, 'Are we really doing this?'"

"Look at all that desert we have to cross," Dick teased. "Lots of buzzards down there."

Rick retorted, "One up here, too."

On June 8, ABC arrived in Santa Monica to film the event. They would record the Hoyts at various points along the way and air their progress on future broadcasts. With all the excitement, Dick forgot to eat breakfast and Phil Taylor forgot to fill a champagne bottle with Pacific Ocean water, which they would pout into the Atlantic when they arrived at Boston Harbor. At 12:00 o'clock sharp, Dick strapped his teammate into the running chair and Taylor made a last-minute dash across the beach to fill the champagne bottle. When Taylor returned to the van with Russ and Linda, Dick looked around for Judy one last time.

"Ready Rick?" Dick asked. With an affirmative nod from his son, the two men trotted off toward Massachusetts, the first steps into the world's longest duathlon.

In an interview, Dick explained: "I told Judy if she was not there by noon, we would have to leave without her. Well, she was not there by noon."

222

As planned, they switched over to the bike after several miles of running. Each day would consist of a five-mile run and 80 or 90 miles of biking. If time or timing presented any problems, they would do less running and more biking.

Before they had gone very far, they pedaled past remnants of the burned-out buildings from the riots earlier in the year. "Wow, take a look at this, Rick. The LA riots." A few short miles later, in sharp contrast, they rode past President Reagan's downtown office, the same location they had visited only a year earlier. "We've been here before," Dick told Rick.

When Russ and his van crew went back to locate Judy, he lost contact with Dick because one of the radios didn't work properly. To complicate matters, Dick made a wrong turn and had to backtrack into the wind. It was an inauspicious beginning, but it got worse. Dick and Rick came to a slight hill with an unmarked fork in the road. Since they didn't know which way to go, Dick stopped to ask for directions.

"I saw a man coming across the street," Dick recalled. "Then I passed out. Rick and the bike landed right on top of me. When I woke up, I thought, 'Here we are, only 35 miles into the Trek, and I'm on my ass and I feel awful.'"

Several people came over to help and offered to contact the police. Although confused, Dick knew that neither he nor Rick had sustained injuries, so he asked the bystanders if they would please help him over to the shade. As they did, the support van went flying past them. Fortunately, Russ glanced into the rearview mirror and saw Dick waving at him.

"By that time, I realized what had happened to me," Dick said with a grin. "With all the excitement that morning, I had forgotten to eat breakfast."

Dick spotted an ice cream stand nearby and rejuvenated himself on several scoops of ice cream. Since they were already behind schedule, Dick assured everyone he was okay and rode off into the foothills. Again, they didn't get very far. Like a scene out of an adventure movie, they came to an avalanche that had

223

blocked the road. Dick found a way around it, but as the day wore on, he became increasingly concerned about Judy and the RV.

"We didn't know where they were," Judy explained. "We came upon a bicyclist and I told him what was going on."

The man smirked and said, "Lady, there is no way a man can ride up here with his son on the front and be here in five hours."

"Yes, it's the Hoyts," Judy insisted. "They did the Hawaii Ironman together."

"The Hoyts? Yeah, you're right, they could be there by now."

Judy caught up with Dick and Rick about 6:00 that evening, halfway up a mountain. "We were 20 miles short of our goal," Dick said. "But we decided to call it a day."

In her interview, Deborah Gusin asked Dick, "Did you wonder what you were really in for now? After all those problems on the first day, did you still have confidence?"

"Well, we had gotten that far," Dick answered with a matter-of-fact shrug. "I just felt like, hey, tomorrow's another day. We'll see what happens the second day."

Russ expressed a little more uncertainty. "It didn't make us real confident, getting lost right there on the first day."

Dick had enough confidence for everyone on the team. And why wouldn't he? After all, they had already chipped away sixty miles. That left them with a mere 3,660 miles left to go.

"I am not a morning person," Rick told an interviewer. "We had to wake up at 4:30 every day. That was the worst part."

After a massage, nourishment, and a good night's sleep, Dick woke up refreshed and eager to move on and make up for lost time. He and Judy hardly spoke a word, mainly because Dick still smoldered over the fact that she had failed to show up at the starting gate on schedule. It was lunchtime when the bike and trailing vehicles made it to the desert, where they were warmly greeted with a temperature already over 110 degrees. The heat was reminiscent of the lava fields in Hawaii, but Dick hydrated often and handled it well. Rick was the most vulnerable because he sat up front, totally exposed to the heat and wind. For

224

protection, they wrapped him in white sheets, white panty hose, and used loads of sunscreen and lip balm.

Dick said, "We got lost again on day two, and we spent a good part of the day riding up hills into a head wind, which made it very tough biking."

The temperature soared. By the time they rolled into Nevada, it had hit 120 degrees. Their lips blistered and bled from the heat and the searing sun. Rick perspired and rubbed against the seat until he became sore, even raw in places. Next came the unexpected. They had neglected to bring any warm clothes along, and when morning came to the upper desert, the temperature dropped to 30 degrees.

"I had told everybody not to worry about the cold," Dick said with a self-conscious laugh. "I told them it would be hot all the way across the country. I sure missed that call."

"It was so cold in the morning," Judy recalled, "that Rick would be very tight and very spastic. It was difficult for him to take food because his body would be so tight. We wrapped him up in many layers of clothes and put him in a sleeping bag so he wouldn't get hypothermia. He looked like a mummy."

For eight hours that day, Rick sat up in the freezing cold without moving. He got so cold they stopped a dozen times to warm him inside the van. Dick ducked inside the van four times himself, and he wrapped tape around his shoes and legs to maintain the body heat. When they entered Utah, the weatherman predicted snow.

Rick shared some humor from the journey. "Once, when we were taking a break, a person asked, 'What's on the bike? A dummy?' And another time, we passed a man on the street and he asked my brother what was on the front of the bike. Russ told him it was me, but the guy didn't believe I was a real person."

The demands on Dick were tremendous, but perhaps even greater on Rick. The frigid air made his body stiff, and he felt every bump in the road, and every exposed area of skin felt like a bee sting. The muscle relaxers made him sick, but he refused to quit, and he even maintained his sense of humor. In the past, he had shaved his head, tried a Mohawk, and changed the color of his hair. But for the Trek, he had an outline of the United States etched into his short crop of hair. When they crossed each state line, Russ or Phil took out the clippers and extended the line across the state they had just completed. The "head map" depicted their progress.

"That's one thing about Rick," Russ said. "He's always using his head."

Judy had made a difficult decision when she committed to supporting her son and husband on the Trek. Her father had been very ill for some time, and he had reluctantly decided to end his dialysis treatment. The family knew he would not live long, so Judy bid her tearful goodbyes before leaving Massachusetts. As they approached the Rocky Mountains, Judy received the words she dreaded most — her father had passed away.

"It was an extremely emotional time for me," Judy said tearfully. "I wanted to be back home, support my mom and say goodbye to my dad, but I committed to be on the Trek. You just can't be in two places at once."

Judy could not abandon three members of her immediate family just as they were going through the most challenging part of the journey. They needed her. She thought about the times Dick and Rick conquered Hawaii and Canada, and how they all stuck together and brought Rick from a "vegetable" to an Ironman. As difficult as it was, she knew she would be more helpful to her son than to her mother.

"They would have difficulties in breathing," Judy pointed out correctly. "Dick was going up heights that were unbelievable and he needed to know the whole support team was there. You couldn't have someone else come in and take your place. It just doesn't work that way."

Upon viewing the massive obstacle that blocked his path, Dick said, "With each revolution of the pedals, the Rocky Mountains inched closer and closer and grew more intimidating."

Russ was equally impressed. "We hit Rabbit Ears Pass, then seven miles of straight climbing without a break. We passed through the Rocky Mountain National park. We knew there was still a lot of work ahead, but when we looked down from the Continental Divide, it was simply incredible. You had to be in awe of where you were and what my father and brother were accomplishing."

At 13,000 feet, the temperature hit 45 degrees. Russ ran up and gave Rick a jacket. He also offered one to his father, who was wearing only a tank top. "No, I'm fine," Dick said. "We're almost to the top. Just get away and let me do what I have to do."

Dick gasped in the oxygen-thin air, but he kept focused on the objective, and everyone uttered a sigh of relief when they reached the summit. After such a momentous accomplishment, they stopped to inhale the beauty and savor the moment before descending the other side. As the happy family engaged in a playful snowball fight, ABC swooped in to take pictures and ask more questions.

The descent of any mountain worried Dick. The brakes could fail, and there was always a tendency to go too fast and lose control of the bike. In the Rockies, there were hairpin turns without guardrails and snow piled as high as eight feet in places along the road. They faced strong, changing winds, and vehicles flew past them only three feet away. Since the downhills required less work, Dick got chilled and his hands became numb from the cold wind. He said, "I wore socks on my hands for protection, and in that altitude, I had trouble breathing."

"I was surprised at how high up we were," Rick said. "There was less oxygen at that altitude so we got tired more easily." He smiled sheepishly. "But I slept on the way down."

They made it safely to the bottom of the mountainous range, where everyone stopped to gaze in amazement at what they saw behind them. They had traversed the majestic Rocky Mountains in only one day. Eight hours up, two hours down. Dick and Rick then completed the daily duathlon by going out for a brisk run.

"It was totally overwhelming," Judy exclaimed. "It was just like, wow! And then saying, 'Guys, guys, look what you have accomplished!' They got to the top of the Rockies on their own power. That's pretty awesome."

In spite of the magnificent mountains that divide our continent, Team Hoyt covered 120 miles that day. Then, in contrast, the third week found them trekking over flat, empty highways and along the endless wheat fields of Nebraska. The boredom affected Rick. "I got a song in my head by Bob Seger," he said. "It wouldn't end. It felt like I was never going to stop riding."

But Nebraska had a unique way of dealing with the bored travelers. The native Cornhuskers bragged that their vast plains foment the most stupendous lightning and thunderstorms in the world. As Dick plodded methodically along, one such storm swept into his path. Lightning flashed, sheets of rain pelted them, and thunder nearly knocked the windows out of the RV. Dick pushed forward as though he hadn't even noticed.

"What the hell is wrong with him?" Judy asked Phil Taylor.

Taylor shook his head in disbelief. "Stopping for a silly little storm isn't in his game plan."

When the fiery bolts of electricity exploded too close, Russ pulled to the front and hit the horn. Dick heeded the demands of his hand-picked field marshal. He took Rick inside the RV, and by the time they switched into dry clothes, the storm had moved on to assault Colorado.

Whenever they passed through a state Capital, a welcoming committee presented them with a state flag. A large group of military personnel and disabled people met them at the Capitol building in Lincoln, Nebraska. Because of the Hoyts' participation in the ANG Marathon a few years earlier, citizens of this prairie city remembered them well. Many of the local runners and bikers joined in the celebration. A Colonel from the National Guard gave a speech, thanked them for all they had done, and presented Rick with an honorary commission to Full Colonel.

With that respectful gesture, Rick became the second colonel in the Hoyt family.

"It took me thirty years to make colonel," Dick said proudly. "Rick did it in one day."

The Hawkeye state appeared next on the Opus glide slope. Gehrig, from Trek headquarters back in Massachusetts, had committed the team to a stop in Red Oak, Iowa, where Dick would address the ANG and the Family Assistance Center. However, due to timing conflicts, Dick decided to skip the event rather than ride 50 miles off course. When the reception committee and the Mayor got word of the missed appointment, they hopped on a military helicopter and buzzed off to the cornfields in pursuit of Team Hoyt.

"If they can't come to us," said the Mayor, "we'll go to them."

In an impromptu ceremony at a remote airpark, surrounded by never-ending miles of corn and wheat fields, Dick and Rick received another flag, and along with it, sincere appreciation from the Governor of Iowa.

"I made a big mistake in Iowa," Rick said with a twinge of embarrassment. "I addressed a Lieutenant Colonel as a General. He thanked me for the field promotion. I felt very small."

ABC caught up with the Trekkers on Independence Day, in Peru, Illinois. The crew took footage of the Hoyts' progress and broadcast it during a major sporting event. Rick welcomed the break, and said he enjoyed the stop more than any they had taken so far. The Red Door Inn rolled out the red carpet, served a buffet lunch, and put the Trek team up on a grandstand next to a banner stating, "Peru Loves the Hoyts."

When an interviewer asked Rick about the highlights of his trip, he said, "When we were in Peru, Illinois." When asked why, he told them, "Because it was on the Fourth of July and we were live on Wide World on Sports."

Another military contingent greeted them when they went through Columbus, Ohio. Dick rolled Rick up to the front of the group, where a General shook their hands and said to Rick, "I understand the Guard somewhere back in Nebraska made you a Colonel?" Rick grinned and nodded. "Well, Ohio can top that, General Hoyt." The General then removed the stars from his own uniform and pinned them on Rick's shoulders.

Judy expressed delight over her son's reaction. "Rick was as excited as he was on that first race. You could sense he wanted to jump right out of his chair."

Rick now outranked his father, and with greater authority, he elected to remain in the seat and delegated Dick to do all the strenuous work. In fact, when the ceremony ended and they were ready to roll on, he had one command for his paternal subordinate. "Keep pedaling, Colonel."

Additional news outlets picked up the story about the Trek as it progressed eastward. The media showed up to interview them, and in many cities along the way, they visited schools and facilities for the disabled. To prove they accomplished their mission, they videoed all the state signs to show the states they entered and states they were leaving. As Dick had promised, the Trek was delivering the message of "awareness" to the conscience of America.

Heavy rain awaited them on the border of Maryland and Virginia, and along with it, wet roads created new hazards. At a slippery intersection, Dick lost control and the bike went down hard. Rick tumbled headfirst onto the pavement, and with a thud, his helmet cracked open like a ripe watermelon. Dick jumped up and rushed to his aid.

"Rick just laughed," Dick said. "He wasn't hurt at all."

Rick explained why. "My head is harder than the helmet."

While the Hoyts blazed trails across America for the betterment of the country, tension mounted between the two dynamic people most responsible for this incredible tale of love, courage and determination. On some days, Dick and Judy did not speak to each other. Dick was totally consumed with the awesome task of physically escorting his son safely across the country on the front of a bicycle. However, while driving at a monotonous ten miles an hour, Judy had too much time to entertain thoughts that went unheard.

For someone who wanted to be in control, Judy had very little during the Trek, and she put it in perspective much as her friend Diane Kopec had done earlier. "For me," Judy told the media, "the hardest part of the Trek was not being in charge. Just being a person who did the wash and cooking, and helping Russell beg for hotels and motels, and things like that. That was the most difficult because I'm the kind of person who likes to tell people what to do, and it wasn't my role to do that. I had to go through Russell. It was very hard for me, and very humbling."

In Dick's mind, Judy's own words, "...I like to tell people what to do," were more than a simple confession or statement of fact. They went directly to the root of the problem.

"We race or we don't," Dick said flatly. "That decision belongs to Rick."

Judy told Gusin, "Dick's love for his son is what drives him. It's what finally bonded them. That was the bonding point. What drives Dick to continue running and racing is his love for Rick and what they can accomplish together."

When it came to the racing, a reasonable family compromise seemed attainable. But, sadly, it wasn't.

Still, the Trek team held together for all the right reasons. They arrived in Washington, D.C. on schedule, where they rode directly into an enthusiastic reception from media, military and bystanders. With cameras ready, the ubiquitous ABC crew captured all the action when the Trekkers rolled in. To Rick, the stop in D.C. was another highlight of the journey.

"Because of the cameras," Dick said. "He's such a ham."

Their schedule allotted some time for sightseeing around the monuments before making the final leg of the trip. Russ noted the lack of accessibility to many of the attractions. When they went to the Lincoln Memorial, for example, he couldn't locate the wheelchair access. In frustration, he said, "You're in the nation's Capital, and there are three huge flights of stairs. What can somebody alone in a wheelchair do at the bottom of that? It really drove home the point that we still have a long way to go."

Russ turned to his brother and asked if he wanted to go up the steps to have a look at the enduring statue of President Lincoln. "Yes!" Rick nodded excitedly. Russ promptly snatched him from the wheelchair and took him up to meet the 16th president of the United States.

Russ said, "I figured if my father can bike him across the country, the least I can do is carry him up the stairs." He poignantly added, "Not everyone has a brother who will carry him up the stairs."

"It was really great to see Russell carrying his brother up to the memorial," Dick remarked, revealing fatherly pride. "It brought back memories of them as children, when they would be playing outside together."

"I don't know the singer's name," Russ said, "but there's a song with the lyrics, 'He ain't heavy, he's my brother.' That's how I felt at that moment. It meant more to me personally than any other point on the Trek."

The President's Director of Physical Fitness presided over a short ceremony for the Hoyts and they were back on the road, heading north to Boston. Phil Taylor pulled out the clippers and extended the Trek line farther across Rick's fuzzy head.

Forty-three days and twenty flags later, the inspirational teammates rolled into the state of Massachusetts. As they rode through the small towns, well-wishers ran to the street to chat with them and offer coffee. With Westfield directly on their route, they were welcomed to the city by old friends and dignitaries, and they even made a stop at a ballpark where Mary and Jayme were watching Rob play in a softball game. The next day ended in the town of Auburn, twenty miles from Holland. Police cruisers with flashing lights and blaring sirens escorted the caravan to the Auburn Health Club, where club members had charted the Trek progress on a huge U.S. map that was hanging on an interior wall of the club. Photographers snapped pictures of the Hoyts, including one that would appear on the front of the local newspapers.

On the morning of July 23, Team Hoyt and support crew gathered at the green "HT" symbol for the final time. Russell said the symbol stood for "Hoyt Team," and he explained the purpose. "At the end of each day, we marked our stopping point with green, fluorescent paint. We would come back to that point each morning and actually put the bike tire right on it so we would continue the Trek from exactly the same spot."

The green markings, therefore, were traceable all the way to California. Most were approximately 90 miles apart, but they varied between 60 and 120. With great fanfare, Team Hoyt left the final HT and set out to complete the Trek. As they arrived in Boston, spectators appeared from everywhere and other bicycle riders rode up to follow along behind them. Vocal fans lined the streets, and as they approached City Hall, the ABC crew filmed the final leg of their incredible journey.

The reception overwhelmed Judy. While trying to suppress the tears, she said, "It was a very proud moment to see all those people honoring and welcoming my son. People who said he 'didn't matter.' He came riding into City Hall Plaza, past the Boston Marathon committee, who had a BAA ribbon for Rick to break through. It was an incredible thrill for him to do that, because he loves the Boston Marathon. It was a feeling of love, and care, and admiration from the people who live in the same community we live in."

A banner reading "WELCOME TO BOSTON" stretched across the finish line. When Rick saw it, his eyes lit up and his arms went skyward. He threw back his head and hit the ribbon chest high, and for the first time in his racing career, he had the privilege of breaking the ribbon at the finish line in Boston.

Amidst the celebratory music and cheering, Russ lifted Rick from the bike and placed him in the running chair. He then removed Rick's helmet, revealing the map with the progress line clipped in his hair, which now connected Santa Monica and

Boston. The Mayor and Lieutenant Governor made speeches and declared it "Dick and Rick Hoyt Day." Adjutant General Wayne Wagner of the Massachusetts Air National Guard congratulated them and presented Rick with the Massachusetts state flag. The Trek would not officially end, however, until Dick and Rick made it down to the harbor.

Judy explained the champagne bottle filled with water. "The theme of the Trek was Ocean to Ocean," she said. "The symbolism was to collect water from the Pacific and carry it across the country, then pour it into the Atlantic at Boston Harbor. It was a message of awareness for people with disabilities, having the two oceans meet and bringing all of that together."

When the ceremony on stage ended, Dick took Rick to the harbor and emptied the Pacific water into the Atlantic. With the throng of friends, family, spectators and dignitaries looking on, he pulled a second champagne bottle from behind the chair and doused Rick and himself with the bubbly contents. However, while caught up in all the excitement, Dick overlooked one small detail. Judy had gotten tangled in the crowd and never made it to the harbor in time to see the climactic merging of the oceans. She was late again. Either that, or she simply decided to register one final protest. Regardless, the unforgettable experience came to an unfitting end.

Dick praised each member of the Trek crew. "Phil Taylor took care of all Rick's needs, and he did a great job driving both the van and the RV." About Linda Reichert, he said, "Rick and I wouldn't have been able to go 47 straight days without the one-hour massage she gave us every night. She iced us down so we weren't stiff each morning." He went on to say, "Judy was very crucial because she drove the motor home. She was also responsible for buying all the groceries, and doing the cooking and laundry. More importantly, she gathered all the signatures for the ballot measure regarding families with disabilities, and presented them to Senator Kennedy."

When asked about Russell, Dick quickly added, "He did one heck of a job. Russell kept us on course and on schedule. He helped with the cooking and found the motels. He contacted the newspaper, TV and radio people. And Rob took care of everything back here in Massachusetts. He helped a lot. It was truly a family accomplishment."

Russ joked about the Trek, saying, "Although I love my family, I wouldn't want to spend another 47 days locked in a 29-foot RV. There is not enough space to be with your family. Just a little too much quality time."

The Hoyts and crew all shared one major disappointment. That came later, when Michael Gehrig informed them that the Trek only generated a fraction of the million dollars they had hoped to raise for the Hoyt Fund. The total contributions covered the new mortgage, but not everyone recouped their expenses and investments. Unfortunately, every financial venture has a certain degree of risk. As Judy often said, That's just the way it works.

Team Hoyt had demonstrated profoundly what people with disabilities can do once they set goals and persevere. With the Trek across America, they accomplished their primary objective, and nothing could ever change that.

Rick had very little to say throughout the memorable journey. Instead, he chose to wait until they were back home, back where he could relax, take his time and put everything in perspective before offering his comments. When that time came, he thoughtfully tapped it out on his computer:

"I am amazed by the beauty of America, and I am amazed by the beauty of the people we met as we crossed the country. I now understand what the song 'America the Beautiful' is all about. I have a lot more respect for the people who first crossed this country to begin a new life."

Riding the Rockies.

General Hoyt takes Ohio.

The Team takes a break in Colorado.

CHAPTER 18 — THE HOYT FUND

Imagine yourself being trapped inside a body with lifeless limbs. Unable to walk, unable to talk, unable to feed yourself. But in your heart and soul, you are an athlete. You can feel the burn in your legs as they pump. You can feel the burn in your windpipe as you breathe. Because in your mind's eye, you are an athlete — sleek, strong, swift. Invincible. But in reality, you are helpless.

—Mary Ann Drabavoy
ABC Wide World of Sports

The excitement at Boston Harbor faded into the evening but it did not end there. The Hoyts still had one more celebration to attend. Dave McGillivray put his promotional talents into persuading the owner of the Boston Red Sox to give them a welcome in Fenway Park. Rick nearly leaped from his chair when he learned he and Dick would take a victory lap around the bases prior to the start of the Red Sox-Twins game, and then watch the game from a luxury box behind home plate. To Rick, it could only get better if some Hooters' girls parachuted into the park and served him rum and Coke.

Russ finagled some rooms at the Marriott Long Wharf and the Four Seasons Hotel, leaving the Trek team with comfortable accommodations and a short trip to the ballpark on Saturday morning. Although Judy was extremely upset over being ignored at the Harbor, and angry that Dick would next be parading Rick around the ballpark, she put on a happy face and stayed for the family reception at the hotel. But she adamantly refused to make

239

an appearance at Fenway Park. After the reception, she and her mother took the RV back to Holland and then drove to the Cape the following morning.

"That was the end of the Trek for me," Judy spoke wistfully, omitting the details. "It was over in the downtown area, when we reached Boston. But for Rick and his love of sports and his love of the Red Sox, it was not over until he took his victory lap around Fenway Park."

Saturday morning found Dick and Rick right where they left off the previous day, following behind a police cruiser. But for this short jaunt, Rick's chariot was the running chair and they were singing "Take me out to the ball game."

Over thirty thousand rambunctious baseball fans hushed when they heard a voice from the PA system announce the imminent arrival of Boston's latest heroes, while simultaneously, a video system on the scoreboard displayed highlights from their cross-country Trek.

Red Sox representatives welcomed Dick and Rick to Fenway Park, where they positioned them to made a dramatic entry from behind the infamous Green Monster — a pitcher-friendly, 40-foot wall that transformed home runs into doubles.

To describe his feelings at that moment, Dick said, "When we went out that door and onto the field, I had such an adrenalin rush I could have carried Rick and the chair right over the top of the Green Monster, or even busted right through it."

As they sprinted across the outfield, the fans slapped their hands together and rose to their feet. By the time they made it to the chalk on the right field line, Rick's heart pounded so hard and fast he thought it might burst through the Velcro straps that secured him to the chair.

"Rick was thrilled," Dick said, unable to contain his own excitement. "I mean, he went really spastic when we got out there. I felt like giving high-fives to everyone in the stadium."

"The game was on national TV," Rob pointed out. "We wanted exposure and we got it."

Dick and Rick trotted down the right field line toward home plate. Dick said, "Halfway between home and first base, we were greeted by the Red Sox Manager, catcher Tony Pena, and second baseman Mike Andrews. They even let me give a speech for a minute and a half."

Dick talked about the Trek, but he also commended the Red Sox organization for their handicap awareness and for their modernized facilities that provided handicapped access. To another blood-pumping ovation, he and Rick completed the victory lap by running across home plate and up the left-field line. They disappeared inside the Green Monster, but since Lew Gorman, the Sox General Manger, had given his box seats to the Hoyt family for the day, they returned to relax in luxury while the Twins and Red Sox entertained them on the field below.

"I sat back and watched my family have a day they will never forget," Dick said. "Lew Gorman came to our box seats and introduced himself and talked to each one of us."

A member of the TV crew stopped by the luxury box and said, "The best part of the game was when you and Rick ran around the field. You guys have my respect."

"Returning to Boston was like coming home," Rick said from his patio in Holland. "When we ran around the park before the Red Sox game, the crowd cheered like crazy. That was the highlight of my trip."

Rick had earned all those highlights, because he was the one who had to endure the hardships. He rose at 4:30 every morning for 47 straight days, and he admitted being physically drained when they finally got home. "I died on the couch. On Sunday morning, I slept very late."

When it came to Hoyt dedication, Rick exemplified it. No one had earned a day of rest more than he had, and when asked if he would ever consider taking another Trek across the country, he said, "Yes, if we did not have to put in so many miles each day. I would like to take the whole summer and give speeches along the way."

Rick acknowledged that the bond he shared with his father had become much stronger after being on the road for so long. And with that thought in mind, he humbly tapped the following statement on his computer: "I think how lucky I am to have a chance to do the things I do."

If anyone assumed Dick and Rick had completed their final mission, or that they would now simply park the running chair, store the Counterpoint Opus and dock the dinghy, they grossly underestimated the Hoyts and did not understand what motivated them. Although they successfully completed the Trek, their overall mission had no end in sight. After a quiet and relaxing day at home, Dick went right back to work. "I did a lot of swimming that week," he recalled, "because we had a triathlon scheduled for the weekend."

Since the physically demanding Trek had gotten Dick into the best shape of his life, he and Rick had a great race in the Farlee Triathlon. In the 7.1 miles at Falmouth, they were among the leaders with an incredible 40:27 – better than a six-minute pace – and notched another personal best. Even Dick was satisfied with that one. After several more races and triathlons, they closed out the season by running in the Marine Corps Marathon. In doing so, they hit the tape in an incredible two hours, forty minutes and forty-seven seconds, lowering their marathon PR by nearly five minutes.

"We really trained hard for that one," Dick admitted. He explained why. "We still wanted to lower our personal record in an Ironman somewhere."

* * *

With the help of the entire family, Dick and Rick had achieved unimaginable goals over the years, but 1992 proved to be extra special. Their dream of trekking across America had finally come to fruition. Wide World of Sports had covered them a second time, intensely, and on this occasion, they were the main event, not merely part of a greater event. In addition to those lofty accomplishments, they established the Hoyt Fund.

"The goal of the Hoyt Fund is to integrate the physically challenged into everyday life," Dick explained. "One way to accomplish this is to educate the able-bodied, making them more aware of the issues that the disabled face every day."

For one other goal of the Hoyt Fund, Dick had no equal: "To actively help the disabled participate in activities that would otherwise be inaccessible to them."

Dick published an informative brochure that stated the Hoyt Fund was set up as a 501 charitable organization to enhance the lives and the mobility of people with disabilities.

HOYT FUND: *We promote integration, inclusion and acceptance of people with all types of disabilities and their families into every aspect of society. By contributing to the Hoyt Fund, you make it possible for us to engage in a wide variety of projects that enhance the lives of people with disabilities. Here are some examples: The Hoyt Fund underwrote the development of a curriculum at Boston Children's Museum, which teaches children what it is like to have a disability; provided consultation to manufacturers on the development and construction of better equipment for people with disabilities; sponsored workshops and seminars to support the vision of mobility and life enhancement of people with disabilities; paid summer camp tuition for children with disabilities whose parents could not afford to pay; sponsored a horseback riding program for challenged individuals, several of whom have competed in equestrian events in the Special Olympics; offered inspirational speaking engagements by Dick and Rick.*

The Hoyt Fund relies heavily on two annual events to generate income for all the programs provided: the annual Hoyt 5K Road Race in Waltham, and an evening of laughs at the Comedy Connection in Boston.

The brochure chronicles the fact that Team Hoyt is a father-son team who began competing in road races in 1977, and soon ran marathons, triathlons, and completed the 3,735-mile bike and run across America. What makes them so special, it stated, is that Dick and Rick competed as a tandem: teammates.

By the time Team Hoyt returned home from the Trek across America, they were squarely in the media spotlight. ABC Sports had focused the eyes of the country directly at them. Since the Hoyt Fund was now in existence, Dick decided they needed a way to support it. The timing was good to produce a promotional video. For assistance, he recruited a Boston production team and asked Barry Nolan to do the narration. After Nolan introduced himself, he invited viewers to participate as a sponsor of Team Hoyt. Then he began their story by stating that the father-son team had participated in over five-hundred and fifty athletic events. He enumerated the number of marathons and triathlons they had completed. He went on to emphasize the distances in an Ironman, and with a backdrop of motivational music and lyrics by the rock group U2, Nolan narrated over a montage of scenes from Team Hoyt races.

"The Hoyts began racing in the fall of 1979 and completed their first Boston Marathon in 1981. They started competing in triathlons in 1985. In the swimming portions of the triathlon, Dick pulls Rick in an inflatable boat, in lakes, rivers, and through the rough ocean. After the swim, Dick carries Ricky in his arms to where the bike is stationed in the transition area."

While Dick carried Rick away from the boat, Nolan talked about the bike, how it was specially built, and how much it weighed with and without its riders. As Dick and Rick pedaled up one of the many hills, Nolan bumped up the volume on the music. While the viewers watched Dick transfer Rick to the running chair, Nolan said, "Dick then transports Rick to their custom running chair, where they go on the running portion of the triathlon, where they usually beat better than fifty percent of all the other triathletes."

As the music hit its crescendo, Nolan ran footage from the dramatic scene at the finishing chute of the 1989 Hawaii Ironman, the one where Judy tearfully peered out from between Rob and Russ as Dick and Rick sprinted across the finish line.

Nolan raised his voice. "Twenty-seven years ago, the Hoyt family began the long journey that has led to this day and to this moment. Along the way, this family faced reality squarely. Through love, they have transformed a life of deprivation into a life of possibility."

As the music faded, Nolan focused on the Trek across America and ran excerpts of the ABC coverage. Jim McKay, broadcaster extraordinaire, broke in and said, "On the fourth of July on Wide World, we brought you the first part of the extraordinary story of Dick and Rick Hoyt, the father and son crossing America on bike and foot. They've competed in more than 90 triathlons and marathons, but this undertaking was the greatest challenge in their athletic careers."

They cut to the interview where Dick emotionally claimed that Rick was really the athlete, not him. Nolan followed it with clips of Team Hoyt receiving an inspirational Award.

"Sponsors will benefit with the message of being associated with Team Hoyt. The messages you send are that with determination and perseverance, there are no boundaries. That we are committed to being the best, by outworking everyone else. Give us a challenge, and we will overcome it. We are driven also by compassion. The achievements of Team Hoyt are directly related to their commitment to excellence, and their dedication. Any corporate sponsor employing Team Hoyt to market their company sends a distinct message to the potential clients, that we are committed to be the best. We have the dedication necessary to achieve lofty goals."

When Nolan emphasized the family aspect of Team Hoyt, he presented a montage of family video from outside their world of racing. He concluded by saying, "One important element that has fueled the engine of Team Hoyt all these years is the love of father and son, and of the Hoyt family. The compassion of these remarkable people. A corporate sponsor of Team Hoyt says to all its customers, and to the audience at large, that it is not simply a corporation existing only to reap profit, but rather a collection of caring individuals — a member of Team Hoyt."

In the video, Jim McKay told his national audience that Wide World of Sports had featured the Hoyts' Trek across America. McKay then brought in his stunningly attractive associate to add some of the details. "Here's Mary Ann Drabavoy with their courageous story."

"Stop for a moment," Drabavoy began, "and imagine yourself being trapped inside a body with lifeless limbs. Unable to walk, unable to talk, unable to feed yourself. But in your heart and soul, you are an athlete. You can feel the burn in your legs as they pump. You can feel the burn in your windpipe as you breath. Because in your mind's eye, you are an athlete: sleek, strong, swift, invincible." In stunning contrast, the scene switched to Rick, lying face down in his bed. Then Drabavoy pointedly said, "But in reality, you are helpless."

"Rick Hoyt is a 30-years-old senior at Boston University," Drabavoy continued. "He has a quick, agile mind, but a quadriplegic body over which he has no control. Born with cerebral palsy, he first communicated with the world via a special computer when he was twelve years old. Painstakingly tapping out each letter, he told the world what he loved."

Dick appeared on the video next, and he shared with the audience the story about Rick's first words on the computer, the "Go Bruins!" story. "We knew right then that Rick loved sports," he asserted passionately. "But yet he couldn't participate in sports."

"Or so they thought," Drabavoy interjected. "On June 8th, the father and son set out from the Santa Monica pier in California. Biking and running, they hoped to cross America and make people aware that the physically disabled should be included in all aspects of society."

Drabavoy conveyed the story about the Hoyts refinancing their home for seventy thousand dollars. She detailed portions of the Trek and some of the hardships the riders faced. The video showed Dick wearing only a tank-top and Rick peering out from a sleeping bag when they crested the Rocky Mountains with snow covering both sides of the road.

They cut to an interview with Judy. "Rick is on the front of the bicycle. What his body goes through when he's sitting up there, he feels every bump as he goes along the road. And he sits there for hours on end, and he gets wet, gets bugs in his face, gets cold, gets hot, gets sweaty. He feels all of those things." Judy then explained how she felt, and of the emotions she went through in accepting the reality of her situation. "I finally got angry enough to begin that process," she said candidly, "of admitting to myself that this baby is different. He's a guy with a heart and a soul and guts like no one has ever seen and I'm proud to be his mom."

In the next sequence, the Trek team rolled through the hills of West Virginia in a rainstorm.

Dick said, "I don't know what happened, but we tipped over. And we went down. As a matter of fact, we went down pretty hard, and Rick split his helmet open. I just bruised my arm and leg a little bit, but we picked ourselves up and went on."

The touching scene of Russell carrying Rick up the steps of the Lincoln Memorial came next. "When I feel like I'm running low on energy, or whatever," Russ said, "all I gotta do is think about my brother. Everything comes right back, and I'm ready to go again. I think that's where my father draws a lot of his strength."

Finally, they arrived in Boston. As he pedaled Rick into the city, Dick said, "We always knew there was a bond between us that was inseparable, but that bond goes beyond that now. We're gonna do it, we don't care if there's a freight train in front of us. We're gonna go over it, through it, around it somehow. We're gonna accomplish the mission we set out to do."

"Dick and Rick Hoyt," Drabavoy said with passion, in her closing comments: "A father and son; A lesson in love; A lesson in humanity." The presentation ended with a pre-dawn shot in a rural setting. And with the quiet serenity of trees and a blue sky in the background, Rick's words scrolled down the screen:

I am amazed by the beauty of America, and I am amazed by the beauty of the people we met as we crossed the country. I now understand what the song 'America the Beautiful' is all about. I have a lot more respect for the people who first crossed this country to begin a new life.

Fenway Park in Boston.

He's my brother: The Lincoln Memorial.

Washington welcomes Team Hoyt.

CHAPTER 19 — THE GRADUATE

*His capacity to transcend the limitations of his body is
an inspiration to every member of this class, and you
will have the pleasure of saying you graduated with
Rick Hoyt.*

—John Silber
President, Boston University

The third annual ARETE awards took place on Monday,
December 7, 1992, Pearl Harbor Day, at the luxurious Fairmont
Hotel in Chicago, Illinois. Arete is the Greek term meaning *The
pinnacle of human performance in its purest form; the pursuit of
excellence through perseverance, goodness, valor, nobility and
virtue.* The originators of these esteemed awards professed that
their winners were "the embodiment of Arete, and honored not for
their victories alone, but for the quality of their effort and the
manner of their striving."

Pete Wisnewski agreed. "With that definition, how could
anyone dispute the selection of Dick and Rick Hoyt?"

The committee had considered the Hoyts the previous year,
but, apparently, they decided the duo needed to enhance their
resume by including a tandem Trek across the country in order to
earn one of their awards. It was very similar to the HAFL award,
when the Hoyts were passed over the first time, but then they won
it after completing Ironman Canada. So again, the second time
around, with completion of the Trek added to their team resume,
the Hoyts won the coveted Arete award.

251

A plush limousine escorted Dick and Rick to the Fairmont Hotel, where ESPN and WLS-TV covered the prestigious event that featured a Who's Who of famous athletes, presenters, previous award winners and current winners. The nominees themselves were selected from candidates submitted by sports editors from all the major newspapers throughout the country. The selection committee for 1992 consisted of Ken Venturi, Arthur Ashe, Mary Lou Retton, Terry Bradshaw, Rocky Bleier and Joe Theisman: a golfer, a tennis player, a gymnast, and three football players.

Winners of the Arete awards included boxer Muhammad Ali, baseball player Dave Winfield, and Fred Lebow, creator of the New York Marathon, who was battling brain cancer at the time. Gail Devers, a track star who overcame Graves disease, received one of the awards, and the junior Arete award went to Sarah Billmeier, a 15-year-old skiing sensation who lost a leg and hip to cancer. Evander Holyfield, Jim Valvano, Bleier and Retton made the presentations. Ken Venturi, the man who inspired the awards after his miraculous effort in the 1964 U.S. Open, served as Chairman. Venturi had suffered a heat stroke during the final round of the Open, but he ignored advice of doctors, continued to play, and eventually won the tournament. Jack Whitaker, the esteemed ABC sports announcer, hosted the awards.

When it came time for the "Superlative Performance Award," Whitaker turned the show over to Venturi. Wearing a black tux and bow tie, the trim, gray-haired golfing great stepped up to the crystal podium. "We are gathered here together to honor the spirit of the Arete awards," Venturi began. "Each year I find it more unbelievable to be in the presence of such greatness. Success is a spiritual quality. It's a power which inspires others. That's what this night is all about. Superlative performances. Year in and year out, history will record those single accomplishments that transcend sports itself."

Venturi directed everyone's attention to a huge screen on the wall behind him as Whitaker's voice consumed the ballroom.

"Heralded as the world's greatest female athlete, Jackie Joyner Kersee earned her second consecutive Olympic gold..."

Shots of Kersee's Olympic efforts splashed across the screen while Whitaker highlighted her career. Once it ended and the audience applauded, Venturi turned back toward the camera and continued. "Equally remarkable, was the performance of this unforgettable team, a father and his son."

Again, Venturi looked to the screen and Whitaker took over the commentary. "As they emerge from the distance, it's apparent that Rick and Dick Hoyt are not average athletes. What is also visible is their determination and courage."

The film clips started with Dick and Rick running up a hill, heading east, away from the pier in Santa Monica, California. They had just begun the Trek across America. The second clip showed them on the bike, leaving Los Angeles.

"Dick Hoyt is a Lieutenant Colonel in the Air National Guard," Whitaker reported. "His eldest son Rick is currently studying for an education degree. Rick is wheelchair bound because he was born with cerebral palsy, and he cannot walk, talk, or feed himself. As he watched his eldest son grow, Dick saw a competitive spirit of burning desire in Rick."

After videos of Team Hoyt running and biking, they showed Rick as an infant, lying on a blanket next to Judy, then one of Dick teaching him how to swim at about age three. With a hockey stick tied to his wheelchair, an older Rick participated in a game of hockey with his two brothers. The montage switched to Rick working with the Hope Machine, and then it progressed chronologically to the early days of the running chair.

Whitaker resumed his narration. "It was many years later that he found a way for his son to experience his feelings — in competitive racing. Since 1979, this wonderful joyride of love and courage has included more than..."

Whitaker mentioned how many marathons and triathlons the Hoyts had completed, while at the same time they displayed footage from all three legs of the Hawaii Ironman. Several more clips from the Trek illuminated the screen, and after some shots from atop the Rocky Mountains, they ended with Dick and Rick breaking through the welcome banner at Boston Harbor.

"This summer marked their greatest triumph," Whitaker said while the video rolled. "The Hoyts across America Trek, a 3,700-mile, 47-day journey from Los Angeles to Boston. The goal was to raise one million dollars and to make every building in America accessible to the handicapped. And on the 47th day, as they returned to their hometown of Boston, Rick and Dick Hoyt proved once again that desire, fortitude and courage come from the heart."

The audience stood and cheered when the film ended and Venturi took over the microphone. "I am proud—" He waited until the applause subsided. "I am proud and I am pleased to present the Arete Superlative Performance award to Rick and Dick Hoyt!"

Wearing his military-dress uniform, replete with medals and epaulets, Dick pushed his ecstatic, bright-eyed teammate up to the stage. Rick looked resplendent in his black suit, and his left arm waved about excitedly as Venturi marched across the stage to greet each of them with a handshake. The moment truly belonged to the Hoyts.

The woman in charge of the production said, "The Hoyts were my favorites. They even had Muhammad Ali crying."

The award gave them national exposure once again. However, being a national celebrity and award winner did not make the situation any better at home. The Arete committee gave no recognition for Judy's efforts. And when Dick designed Christmas cards that referenced racing and included a plea for contributions to the Hoyt Fund, Judy was furious. Dick argued that anything involving the Hoyt Fund would help all of them accomplish their goals for the disabled and that it made sense to promote the Fund on a Christmas card.

In early 1993, Judy took off to Florida for a vacation with her mother and sister.

"When she came home, things were different," Dick recalled sadly. "They only got worse."

In early April, prior to the Boston Marathon, Judy announced to selected family members, in writing, that she could no longer remain married to Dick. In the letter, she admitted much of the fault was hers, because she paid more attention to her own growth and changes than she did to being a good wife. She apologized and expressed hope that the divorce would be amicable.

The Boston Marathon came and went, successfully, with even greater fanfare. But for the first time in 13 years, the post-race dinner did not include the entire family.

* * *

A picture of Rick Hoyt filled the cover of the May 1, 1993, issue of *The News,* a Worcester County Newspaper. With his hair cut in a buzz and a studious look on his face, Rick posed for the picture while Neil Danilowicz, his PCA, wheeled him across the Boston University campus to meet with his professor. The title of the article written by reporter Tim Kane revealed the subject of the story within: "Graduating to Success."

The picture on the following page showed the real Rick, sitting in his dormitory with a poster of a lovely swimsuit model emblazoned on the wall behind him. Kane titled the caption: "Rick Hoyt handles dorm life quite well at Boston University."

Like most articles about the Hoyts, the story began with Rick's most recent athletic achievement, where, in this case, he and Dick finished in the top 400 at the Boston Marathon, their thirteenth consecutive race in Beantown. The first quote came from Dick, when he told Kane, "Success is really failure turned inside out."

The article stated that Rick was a quadriplegic who communicated by manipulating a head switch connected to a computer. It went on to say that Rick would soon receive a degree in special education, but in the beginning, he did not take college seriously.

"I pretty much had a good time the first few years at Boston University," Rick confessed. "But by the fifth year, I got serious and moved into a quiet dorm."

Rick shared the story about the hockey team stealing an ice statue and freezing everyone in the dorm, and also the one about the leaky roof at the apartment where he and his two buddies lived when they moved off campus. *The News* article briefly covered his progress in both education and athletics right up to a short blurb about the national exposure from the Trek. In his closing comment, Kane wrote that Rick foresees his sporting activities revolving around talks and speeches he hopes to deliver to the rest of the world.

Rick had compiled many *firsts* in his 31 years, but now he was poised to become one of the few non-vocal quadriplegics to graduate from a university. More interviews and television appearances followed, and the weeks leading to his graduation were hectic. Rick decided to sleep late and skip the senior breakfast, but that quickly changed when Neil Danilowicz roused him from bed with the news that he was one of the graduates to be honored by University President, John Silber.

Rick and Danilowicz rushed over to the Student Union Building where Silber addressed the graduating class. The bespectacled professor strode to the podium in a dark, tailored suit. He delivered his erudite comments, elicited a few laughs, and even belted out a song. His attention then turned to his most famous graduate, Rick Hoyt. He began by telling the audience how many years Rick had been a student, and added, "Rick always tells me, when the university loses the support of his tuition, I will have to take a cut in pay."

Silber instructed his assistants to project pictures from Rick's racing career onto a large screen. When the soft-spoken professor finished enumerating Rick's various racing accomplishments, he turned to the students and said, "More remarkable, however, is Rick's achievement of graduating from Boston University with a degree in Special Education."

Rick's classmates cheered and applauded. Silber then pointed out that Rick had inspired many other people with disabilities, and that his example compelled them to question their own capabilities. With pride, the professor said, "His capacity to transcend the limitation of his body is an inspiration to every member of this class."

Silber told them that Rick's advisor, Donna Lehr, said Rick wanted no special treatment while at BU. He requested minimal accommodations because he preferred to show what he could do with his abilities. Silber turned in Rick's direction. "Yours is a remarkable athletic accomplishment, Rick Hoyt. But more than that, it is a triumph of the human spirit — one of many such triumphs to your credit, individually and jointly."

The applause grew louder and longer each time the man spoke. He then turned back toward the graduating students and told them what an important event this was, and that they were very fortunate because, "You will have the pleasure of saying you graduated with Rick Hoyt."

The university president then joined the students in another ovation. When the dapper man brought his hands up from the podium and slapped them together, he revealed a disfigured right hand and arm, and it appeared there was no movement in his fingers. Clearly, he was a kindred spirit who had hurdled some barriers of his own.

Danilowicz wheeled Rick up to the podium. When the room fell silent, he read Rick's brief, unprepared speech. "I would like to address President Silber," Danilowicz said, speaking for Rick. "I called the Governor to see if you could get some financial assistance now that you will have to take a pay cut." Danilowicz paused for the laughter. "Fellow seniors, I wish you all good luck and I am looking forward to being out of this university." More laughter ensued. "And I'd like to thank the fine School of Education for giving me this opportunity."

Danilowicz took Rick back to his table while the students gave them an ovation.

On May 16, 1993, Boston University celebrated its 120th commencement ceremony at the university's football stadium. Over 5,000 students in caps and gowns listened intently while Silber stood on the speaker's platform and offered an eloquent tribute to their success. Rick, seated amidst his classmates, wore a white, long-sleeved shirt under his red gown. When the ceremony concluded, and the graduates were exhorted to go into the world and make BU proud, Rick shed a few tears. Then, along with everyone else in the graduating class, he howled deliriously and pumped his fist into the air with the same passion he displayed when he crossed the Boston finish line.

The *Boston Herald* covered Rick's graduation with articles on May 17 and May 19. The earlier issue devoted the entire front page to Rick Hoyt, with the photographer capturing the blissful moment when his arm shot skyward. The bold headline screamed Rick's sentiments: "My greatest triumph!" The subtitle read: "Special BU student goes this marathon alone — and wins." Jules Crittenden wrote the story and included quotes from Rick. When asked to contrast racing success to the college degree, Rick said, "I can't compare the marathons to my graduation. I feel just great. Overall, great. Euphoric."

"Today beats them all," Dick told the journalist. "Today is Rick's day."

Rick told the interviewer he planned to spend the summer working at the Children's Museum, where he would be an adviser on an educational device to teach children about people with disabilities. In response to a question about his future, Rick said, "I hope to get a consulting job and travel and speak around the world." On the lighter side, Rick said, "The hardest lesson was learning how to work and not party too much."

Danilowicz told Crittenden, "Rick wants to spread the message to the disabled and to substance abusers, that if there is hope for him, then there is hope for them."

For the story on May 19, the headline read: "Tenacity's his way of life." The quarter-page photo showed Rick relaxing in

Holland, wearing a Boston Marathon sweatshirt, blue sweat pants, and sporting a grin that had not changed since his graduation four days earlier.

According to the author, Samson Mulugeta, the back of Rick's wheelchair sported an Air National Guard bumper sticker that read: "My other car is a jet." The article devoted an aptly titled column to the *Russell Method* of spelling: "He speaks his own language."

Mulugeta wrote that Rick "Bopped to AC/DC and Queen, lived for the Boston Bruins to win another Stanley Cup, and hung out at bars imbibing his favorite drink, rum and Coke. He lived at Shelton House, attended classes, ate in the dining hall and studied in the library." The story outlined the responsibilities of Rick's PCAs, how much they were paid and where he acquired the funding. He covered Rick's course load at BU, his homework, the computer and the head switch.

He quoted Dick saying, "His patience is unbelievable. He sits there for hours on end doing his school work." Dick also told them, "We fought hard to keep him in the mainstream, but once he got in, he worked hard to stay in."

Danilowicz took over the conversation and began explaining how Rick felt about the commencement ceremony and the speeches, but he did not control the dialogue for long. Rick interrupted by banging on the wheelchair until Danilowicz translated what he had to say. Rick told him, "You forgot one very important person — me."

After ten years of following the careers of Team Hoyt, Barry Nolan returned for another story. Appropriately, and to Judy's delight, he downplayed the racing and dedicated the piece to Rick's education. Affiliates from three of the major networks swept in to talk to the "Hero from Holland." CNN aired a segment. The reporters gushed with praise, claiming it was one of the most inspirational accomplishments they had ever seen.

Rick held his graduation party at the Waltham VFW Hall. They charged ten bucks a person to attend the gala event, with all proceeds earmarked for the Hoyt Fund. As guests gathered in the ballroom, music by an Irish bagpipe team filled the air and serenaded the guest of honor. Mike Giallongo stepped to the microphone for a few laudatory comments about the past, present and future of Rick Hoyt. Coach Robinson shared stories about Rick at Camp Warren, and he got big laughs when he told everyone about his "Captain of Raids" award. Rick also received an award from the Massachusetts Congress, signed by the Speaker of the House.

Because of a conflicting engagement, Barry Nolan could not make it to the party, but he sent his crew over to roll film. His stand-in took the microphone and explained Nolan's absence, then heaped adulation on Rick in his own behalf. The tone changed, however, when Eddie Burke stepped up to the microphone. He told several crude jokes, but his macho words and tough exterior could not conceal the feeling he held for Rick.

Dick said, "Eddie would do anything for Rick. There's a strong emotional attachment, I think from what he's been through with Agent Orange, cancer, and his daughter's death."

Then Burke got serious. "I've busted Rick's cookies over the last fifteen years. But did you ever think what it would be like to spend an hour in his shoes? Any law enforcement officer who treated a prisoner for one hour the way Ricky Hoyt lives his life, would go directly to jail." Burke announced an upcoming race to benefit the Hoyt Fund and closed by saying, "Everybody loves Rick. Including me." The man marched off the stage with tears in his eyes.

Danilowicz wheeled the guest of honor to the front of the room and hooked up the synthesizer. Rick took over the show.

"For ten long years I have been a student at Boston University. I have not been a great student. I did my share of partying, but I believe that partying was a valuable part of my college experience." That comment got plenty of laughter.

"Mom knew I had the brains to go," Rick continued. "And she pushed for me to get into public school. Thank you, Mom. I also have to thank Miss Brown for taking the time to give me a lot of support so I could go to third grade math class... I know you are all saying, 'When is he going to finish thanking people?' Well, I'll quit thanking you when someone buys me a drink."

The college grad had his fans right where he wanted them, and after another round of laughter, he said, "I would like to thank someone who has bad typing. She was a classmate of mine way back in elementary school. She has made me an uncle. I would like to say happy birthday to her. Mary, have a happy birthday. Now you have to buy me a drink."

In typically selfless style, Rick pleaded for kids to stay in school. "If there is hope for me, there is hope for you." He thanked everyone and headed for the dance floor. The party began in earnest when Mary delivered the rum and Coke in a mug inscribed to commemorate the event.

During the ensuing regalement, little brothers Rob and Russ stepped up to the microphone wearing sunglasses, then three-year-old Jayme ran up and held tightly to his father's leg. They introduced themselves as the *Rick Hoyt Rappers,* and with that said, the contemporary musical presentation began. Russ held the microphone and Rob broke into song: "If you think crypt is hip, cut that crap. We're coming at you with the Rick Hoyt Rap."

As the band picked up the beat, Rick howled with delight. The Hoyt Rappers swayed back and forth and alternated delivery of their lyrics.

Russ: "See him sittin' in his chair."

Rob: "When he was born, he was so darn bare."

Russ: "Brain got damaged, as you know."

Rob: "But he's just as smart as the average Joe."

Russ: "His arms don't work."

Rob: "His legs don't walk."

Russ: "But that doesn't mean."

Rob: "The boy can't talk."

Russ: "Types each word."

Rob: "Letter for letter."

Russ: "But he still can't spell."

Rob: "Any better."

Russ and Rob together: "Any *Beh — Baa — Bee — Boo —* better!"

When the laughter finally ended, the rappers concluded their presentation. Rob lifted Jayme up in his arms and the brothers leaned into the microphone and chanted, "Graduation Day, so we will give you your due. We'll end by saying, we love you!"

Rob, Russ and Jayme walked over and gave Rick a hug.

After the emotional rap routine, a lovely, scantily dressed redhead wiggled onto the floor, sashayed up to Rick's face and sang Patsy Cline's "Crazy." Rick got so excited he could barely stay in the chair.

No one in the Familia Hoyt would ever forget that joyous day. The tiny baby — the one who doctors called a "vegetable" and should be thrown away — had earned a college degree. He had a ton of friends and admirers and brought tears and hope to people all over the world.

Unfortunately, all days and nights must end, including the good ones. Russ and Lisa left the party together, as did Rob, Mary and Jayme. Judy kissed her oldest son goodnight and quietly went home alone. Before long, Dick did the same. It saddened Rick to see the evening end as it did. He understood the empty feeling that comes with being alone, and had once told an interviewer: "Nothing compensates for loneliness."

Graduating from Boston University.

Superlative Performance award.

CHAPTER 20 — LAND OF THE RISING SUN

I set Rick and the bike against a tree, and I ran into a
sugar cane field. The TV crew shouted 'No, no, no!'
but I said 'Yes, yes, yes!' They thought I was quitting
the race and dumping Rick on the roadside.

—Dick Hoyt

Two weeks after Rick graduated, Team Hoyt returned to the media spotlight. The Boston Press Photographers Association honored them with their *Sports Personality Award*, and then in November, they received the *George Washington Honor Medal* from the Freedoms Foundation at Valley Forge. But they also had some bad days. Before the year had ended, Dick and Judy reluctantly admitted failure. Judy filed for divorce and moved out of the house. After taking time to recover from the traumatic changes, she started her own consulting business. Rick lived independently, continued racing with his dad, and eventually went to work for Boston College, where he developed computers for people with all types of disabilities. Dick remained in the house on the lake and considered retirement.

Team Hoyt started 1994 with a marathon, when on January 16, they flew to Orlando, Florida, and they blazed through Disney World in two hours and fifty-two minutes. Dick was in top form for the new season. "It was three months before Boston. We were after another PR, so we were getting an early start."

On March 26, they ran the Westfield Half Marathon in one hour and twenty-six minutes, and on the next day, they zipped over to Needham and completed a 10K in thirty-eight minutes. Three weeks later, they scored another PR on Patriot's Day.

265

On April 29, the President of Western New England College in Springfield presented Dick with an Honorary Law Degree and Rick with a Lifetime Achievement Award. Two weeks later, Dick and Rick were crowned Honorary Champions in the St. Jude 60-mile bike ride, a benefit for needy children. On the second of June, the Sports Museum of New England presented them with the Living Legends Sports Award. Team Hoyt hosted their own race, the Hoyt 5K, on May 26, and three days later, they ran the Johnny Kelly Half Marathon in one hour twenty-seven minutes.

Over a nine-year period, the Team Hoyt globetrotters had raced twice in Hawaii, three times in Canada, and once each in Barbados and El Salvador. They were ready for something just a little bit different.

"I had always wanted to go to Japan," Dick said. "Ever since I was a little boy, studying history."

He didn't say what it was that intrigued him about that Asian country, but it left a lasting impression. He had told friends about his desire to race in Japan, and the word eventually spread to David Yates, President of the World Triathlon Corporation. In September of 1992, Yates sent a fax to Yoram Ofer, the director of Ironman Japan. He told Ofer about the accomplishments of Team Hoyt, and about the positive contributions they had made to the sport of triathlon. In closing, he suggested that the committee invite the Hoyts to compete in Ironman Japan.

Seven years had passed since Penticton, and three years since their astonishing success in Hawaii. By now, nearly everyone involved with the Ironman had heard of the Hoyt family. Ofer agreed with Yates and returned a fax nine days later. He wanted the Hoyts to compete in Japan, but his committee did not have the final say regarding their participation. That decision deferred to the Shiga Prefecture Police.

With sarcasm, Dick said, "I understand they were concerned about safety, but people seem to think Rick and I have never even thought about safety. Like I would read their letter and say, 'Oh, darn, I hadn't thought about that. I'm glad you brought it up.'"

To compete in Japan, Dick had to present his case to the police. They requested a video of the Hoyts competing in other races, plus photos of them during each leg of the race. Dick sent photos, newspaper stories, magazine articles, and even a video of the Ironman Triathlon World Championships in Hawaii. In January, Yates received a fax from Hiro Irada, the Ironman Japan representative. He said they were "sorry," but the committee could not invite the Hoyts to the 1993 race because another entity of government now controlled the race. "To me," Dick joked, "it sounded like he was just 'passing the yen.'"

Ultimately, the association told Dick that they did not want to introduce anything "revolutionary" during the first year of the race. Therefore, they were not invited.

"He asked us to cooperate with them," Dick added with a smirk. "Whatever that was suppose to mean."

Dick immediately composed another letter, one with a very positive, optimistic tone. He told Irada that an apology was not necessary, then thanked him for the explanation and said he fully understood that it takes time to resolve complicated matters such as these. Behind the scenes, however, a promoter named Saku Takahata had seen the Hoyts in Hawaii, and he believed the committee should take every step necessary to bring them to the Japanese people.

"His influence made the difference," Dick said. "He convinced them to invite us and he even provided sponsorship."

Takahata told his friend – Whit Raymond, a promoter with W-Hit Productions in Napa, California – what he wanted to do, and he asked Raymond to be a translator in the negotiations. In early 1994, after some internal negotiations, Raymond made the call to Dick Hoyt.

"We received an invitation to race in Japan in June," Dick said, sporting a Rick Hoyt-style victory grin. "It wasn't an Ironman, but we were going to Japan."

Along with a PCA and a masseuse, Dick and Rick took the long flight westward, to the mystical East.

The Tokunoshima Triathlon consisted of a 2K swim, 90K bike and a 21K run. The bike leg covered endless hills and varying landscapes, including overhanging cliffs the locals called *Inu no Jo Futa*. Dick said the translation was "teeth of the dog," or something equally endearing. Regardless of what you called them, the intimidating cliffs offered a breathtaking sight for tourists and an added challenge to the triathletes. To Dick, it fulfilled a boyhood dream, so it didn't matter if they rode along cliffs, through rice paddies, or across downtown Tokyo.

The 18-hour flight left Boston early on June 7th and ended in Osaka late on June 8th. Saku met the Hoyts at the airport and ushered them over to the Grand Hotel, and after a night of rest, they hopped a flight to Tokunoshima Island. Lush, colorful vegetation surrounded the small, remote island southwest of Osaka, and the hilly countryside was dotted with ancient Japanese architecture and fields of rice and sugar cane.

What Dick saw surprised him. "The water was deep blue and crystal clear. It reminded me of Kona."

The Mayor, his staff, the race director, and representatives from newspapers, television stations and *Japanese Triathlon* magazine greeted the Hoyts in Tokunoshima. Huge banners and painted signs welcomed them to the village. Curious and playful children offered flowers, while the older and bolder children carried marking pens and asked for autographs.

"Sign! Sign!" the kids demanded respectfully.

"They gave us flowers everywhere we went," Dick said.

Rick put it another way. "By the end of the week, we could have opened up a flower shop."

In the stifling heat, a medium-sized bus waited with the engine running and the rear door wide open. With the help of a wheelchair lift, they hoisted Rick inside the van and hustled Team Hoyt off to their quarters.

When they arrived at the hotel, the diminutive proprietor trotted over to greet them with a customary bow. "Kon nichi wa, Hoyt san. Onegaimasu. Eirashaimasu."

A member of the Mayor's contingent returned the man's greeting and translated for the Hoyts. "He said 'Good day,' and he welcomes you to his home."

"Tell him thank you," Dick responded.

When the proprietor bowed a second time, Dick politely reciprocated and Rick laughed. The sight of his father bowing to someone in a flowered "robe" tickled his funny bone. Once the greetings and introductions concluded, several women in kimonos took their luggage and led them to rooms at the top of a hill, where they enjoyed a great, panoramic view of the ocean.

Dick described the accommodations. "We had a one-room cottage with a bathroom on the side. There were four beds lined up next to each other, which reminded me of basic training in the Army. The cottages didn't have real beds, just mattresses on the floor. The rooms didn't even have toilets. They had troughs you had to stand over with your legs spread. And they were coed, so it was a real challenge trying to take Rick to the bathroom."

The team ate most of their meals at a restaurant adjacent to the cottages. The family who owned the resort provided entertainment for the Hoyts, and even invited them over for dinner while a Japanese TV crew caught it all on film.

"Everyone was very friendly," Dick said of his hosts. "Rick and I enjoyed every aspect of the experience. Well, almost." He didn't elaborate on the "almost" at that time.

As usual, they encountered problems. The crates for their equipment were too large to load on the small airplanes and had to be transported from Osaka by boat. Not surprisingly, they didn't make it to the island until the day before the race, which meant Dick had to prepare without the benefit of a bicycle. As he had done many times in the past, he trained by swimming and running alone. Rick told his dad he would stay at the cottage and save his energy for the race.

"He stayed behind to look for Geisha girls," Dick teased.

On Thursday, Dick, Rick, and several other triathletes visited two schools. Again, the children presented them with flowers. A member of the Japanese triathlon team interpreted for Dick as he spoke to the students and answered their questions.

"I gave the same presentation as I did in the states," Dick said. "But at the second school, we took along some picture postcards of us, and I started signing them and handing them out to the children. That nearly started a riot. They came charging toward me, knocking down other students and almost knocked me down. I was worried about Rick. Some of the children even fell under our bus, so we got on the bus and let the teachers hand out the rest of the postcards."

On Thursday evening, the Hoyts were guests at a traditional, Japanese-style dinner. Dick checked his shoes outside the door and took Rick inside. With the entrees spread out on tables barely above floor level, Dick was forced to sit on the floor with his legs crossed and his back erect.

"The room wasn't handicapped accessible," Dick quipped. "I couldn't talk Rick into sitting on the floor with his legs crossed, so they covered the floor with newspaper and let us bring the wheelchair in."

The meal consisted mostly of seafood, and when she realized the fish was too tough for Rick to eat, she went to the kitchen and prepared a plate of spaghetti. Dick teased Rick about it. "What the heck is this? We came here for a traditional Japanese dinner and you're eating spaghetti?"

During dinner, Dick's back became tired and stiff from sitting with his legs crossed. He considered getting relief by leaning back against the delicate bamboo-and-gossamer door, but he was afraid he might tumble right through the flimsy frame. Thanks to his son, he found a simple solution. He spent most of the meal standing up so he could help Rick eat spaghetti. Except for stabbing Rick with the chopsticks a time or two, they managed to survive the ordeal, and despite all the tribulation, they admitted having a great time.

On Friday night, the Mayor, his council and the race director invited all the athletes to another special dinner that included short speeches by local dignitaries. Rick recalled the experience from the night before and offered a suggestion to his dad. "Use a spoon tonight. I don't like being stabbed with those sticks."

Saturday they ate a Japanese specialty that Dick called "raw fish." He enjoyed the meal and ate plenty. After lunch, they were hustled off to a bull fight. "Their biggest event of the year is the triathlon," Dick noted curiously. "The second biggest event is bull fighting."

As gracious guests, they accepted the invitation. Unlike the Spanish version, where a defenseless bull battles to the death with a well-armed human, Japanese bulls get a little break. When those big guys go into battle, they go head to head with another bull, not a human bullfighter.

"It wasn't bloody at all," Dick explained. "Neither bull used a sword." Then he described the action in detail. "They have the handlers bring two bulls into the ring and force them to lock horns. Once the animals locked their horns, the handlers get out of the way and see which bull escapes first. That bull is the winner. It was okay, but seeing it once was enough for me."

The night before the triathlon, the Hoyts attended a carbo-loading dinner for the race participants. Members of the race committee took turns speaking about each portion of the triathlon, describing the course and explaining the rules. They invited triathletes to step up to the microphone and say a few words of encouragement. A Japanese rock band performed on stage, and while the athletes danced and had a great time, they brought Rick up on stage to sing along with them.

"We hated to see the evening end," Dick said. "We've never had so much fun at a race."

They stayed late at the party because the race started at nine o'clock, two hours later than most triathlons. When the evening finally ended, Dick thought he would try out a new word he had learned. "Sayonara," he said, and bowed to the host. His intent was to say *Good night*, but instead he said *Goodbye*.

The man replied, "Oyasu minasai."

271

Everyone returned to their small rooms and slept well.

* * *

On race day, it looked at times like a monsoon had descended over the island and the triathlon might become one long swim. Dick and his foursome popped out of bed at 6:30, washed, dressed, and headed out to the restaurant for a meal that consisted of coffee, fruit and toast. Rick ingested some juice along with all of his tasty muscle relaxers.

Referring to the downpour, Dick said, "Our room was less than a quarter mile from the swim start and transition area. We took all the equipment and walked over, but we could have inflated the boat and floated over."

Fans of all ages arrived to watch Team Hoyt in action. Some attempted to get Rick's autograph, but he only smiled. Dick chatted playfully with the kids, but as race time neared, he focused on preparing the equipment. A volunteer attached a bracelet to Dick's arm and marked his body with a grease pencil.

"The bracelet had a magnet that triggered the computer at the start and finish," Dick explained. "It was a prototype of the Champion Chip, and they used it to time the race."

The triathlon course had two transition areas, one after the swim and another after the bike. Dick set up the bike and dinghy near the start, then loaded the running chair on a van and took it to the bike-to-run transition. Everything checked out to Dick's satisfaction, but when the horn sounded at nine a.m., the rain came down in buckets. The storm churned up the sea, the waves slapped the dinghy sideways, and the strong current pulled them far off course.

Although it created a major challenge, they survived. "It was the toughest swim we had ever encountered in a triathlon. When we finished, there was at least two inches of water in the boat. I couldn't lift Rick's beanbag because it was soaked."

To make the transfer from the ocean to the bike, Dick had to carry Rick along a concrete pathway and up a series of uneven steps. Once on the bike, they hit a steep hill and the rain pounded

272

them so hard they could barely see the road ahead. Rick thought they needed the plastic shield on that ride. "One with windshield wipers."

With such adverse weather conditions, speed was a non-issue. The goal became one of survival, to keep the wheels on the ground, and to finish the bike without an accident. Dick told his hosts it was one of the toughest courses they had ever raced, which was high "praise" from the man who had pedaled 112 miles in Kona and Penticton.

The run course started flat and easy, but after two miles, they reached the hills. Or, as Dick called them, "major" hills. But neither hills nor downpour stopped the spectators from running onto the course with more flowers for the Hoyts.

The driving rain still blurred the course two and a half miles from the finish. At that point, the handles on the running chair broke, which forced Dick to bend over and hold onto the sides of the chair the rest of the way. With all the rain and dirt, it created one final challenge. Mud. Lots of mud. The wheels sank more than an inch in some places.

Dick said, "I had never trained for anything like that. But I'd love to race that course on a sunny day."

Banners welcomed them at the finish line, where they were showered with more flowers. Under a sea of umbrellas, the spectators yelled encouragement, and like in so many races before, the children ran out to touch them.

Dick had again survived an angry ocean, conquered defiant hills, and now he had won a wrestling match with a broken chair in sticky mud. The course had presented new challenges, but to Dick, it only sharpened his triathlon teeth and honed his skills. His effort greatly embodied the adage: "What does not kill me only makes me stronger."

Although the race ended successfully, Dick met his match in an unexpected way. He traced the problem back to the seafood lunch he ate the day before the race. "I thought I had learned in Hawaii that you don't do anything differently before a race, but I

273

forgot." With a sheepish grin, he reluctantly admitted, "The raw fish made me cramp up with diarrhea two miles into the bike ride. I got off the bike, set Rick and the bike against a tree, and I ran off the road and into a sugar cane field. The TV crew shouted 'No, no, no!' but I said 'Yes, yes, yes!' They thought I was quitting the race and dumping Rick on the roadside."

Dick parked the Counterpoint and streaked into the cane fields five or six times during the bike ride. He became weak and dehydrated, and felt so miserable that he doubted if they'd be able to make it through the run. Rick enjoyed a good laugh the first time he saw his dad dash into the cane field, but after the third or fourth visit, he knew it was serious.

"It's a good thing I didn't eat sushi," Rick noted. "It would have been a lot harder if he had to carry me into the cane field six times."

At the first water stop on the run course, volunteers offered food and beverage to the athletes. Dick ate two bananas, guzzled water and pushed himself right back into the race. "I was still hurting a little at the finish," he said. "But I recovered very fast."

Even with all the obstacles and mishaps, they finished the race in seven hours and thirty-nine minutes. And despite half a dozen stops to fertilize the sugar cane, the teammates did not finish last. Their fifteen-year streak continued.

When the race ended, Dick and Rick took part in another type of celebration. Saku Takahata and his girlfriend also completed the triathlon, and at the finish line, they switched into wedding attire and exchanged rainy-day vows in front of all the triathletes and spectators. Always a gentleman, Rick celebrated the occasion by sharing his flowers with the newlyweds.

On Monday, they packed up the racing equipment and flew back to Osaka, where the Mayor, his council, and a group of representatives from a disability organization gave them a final farewell. The ever-smiling Mayor presented them with awards that would soon find a place of honor on the walls back in Holland and Boston.

"They served that raw fish again," Dick said with a straight face. "This time, we declined."

* * *

The Dick-and-Rick duo did a triathlon or a road race every weekend for the remainder of the summer, and true to form, the year ended as it began, with another marathon. In November, they once again headed back to the nation's Capital for a repeat of the Marine Corps Marathon.

They were up to the challenge. "We got another PR."

On the first day of February 1995, Rob and Mary presented the Hoyt family with their second healthy grandson. And just like his brother and father, Cameron Robert Hoyt had a very strong voice and a body fit for athletic battle.

"Although Cameron was two weeks early," Mary recalled happily, "he was a perfect pregnancy. We arrived at the Woman's Hospital at 8:45, and he was born at 11:20."

"I thought I might have to handle the delivery myself," Rob said. "When we got there, the doctors were in the middle of a shift change. They hooked Mary up to a monitor, said 'push,' then they left us alone in a room."

"It seemed like we waited forever," Mary said. "But a resident physician finally came in and took over. He let Rob off the hook. Cam came into the world strong and alert, and he weighed nearly eight pounds."

As young Cameron grew, it appeared that he had inherited Granda's fleetness of foot. Rick Hoyt took note of little details like that, of course. "When I'm recruiting for a new pusher," Rick said. "He's the one I'm looking at."

Two months later, Dick and Rick completed Boston number fifteen. Accompanied by intensified hoopla and media attention, they zipped through the course in high gear. Rick's groupies from BU crowded into the streets and shouted his name when he zoomed by with a huge grin and one arm raised.

As the triathlon season heated up, Dick got an unexpected telephone call. "The Japanese people want you to come back."

275

Dick said, "When they offered to pay our expenses, I told him, 'Okay, we'll be there.'"

Returning to the Land of the Rising Sun was, once again, the highlight of the Team Hoyt racing season. But the summer also provided a milestone of another sort. On July 28, 1995, Dick retired from the military as a Lieutenant Colonel, ending 37 years of distinguished service to the Air National Guard.

The 1996 Summer Olympic Games were hosted by Atlanta, Georgia. For delivery of the Olympic Torch, the committee organizers selected a route through Boston, and it included portions of the Marathon course. "Who better than Dick and Rick to carry it?" Pete Wisnewski asked. "They own that course."

When the Torch appeared on Commonwealth Avenue, Dick Hoyt held it high with one hand while he pushed his smiling son with the other. It was a proud moment for the city of Boston, and an exhilarating day for Team Hoyt. While a TV camera filmed the patriotic convoy passing by, Dick reached out and handed the Torch to Rick. An Olympic moment if there ever was one.

In early August, 1997, the third Hoyt grandson made his dramatic entrance.

"It was 11 a.m. when I got the call," Russ said. "I was at a client's home, working with three autistic children. Lisa was at work when her water broke. It was twenty miles away, but it only took me about twelve minutes to get to her doctor's office."

Although the expected birth date was six weeks away, Russ and Lisa sped off to Winchester Hospital. Regardless of what his parents expected, Troy Donovan Hoyt decided to make his debut sooner rather than later. "Lisa went into labor at eight p.m.," Russ said. "Troy was delivered at 3:56 a.m. on August eighth. He weighed only five pounds and needed medication for his lungs."

The doctors at the Winchester Neonatal Intensive Care Unit gave the infant a dose of *surfactant* to help him breathe, but told the first-time parents their son needed to go directly to Children's Hospital for a second application. Since Lisa had not recovered from the difficult delivery, she stayed at Winchester while Russell rushed the baby to Boston without her. Lisa, Russell and baby Troy were finally reunited at Winchester Hospital two days later. For the next two weeks, they visited their tiny son daily, where they helped him learn to eat and gain weight so he could go home and check out his new family.

"To look at him now," Russ said fondly, "you'd never know what a rough start he had."

With Dick retired from the military and living alone, he now spent more time racing, promoting handicapped awareness, and conducting speaking engagements. He also found more time for swimming and lifting weights at the Auburn Health Club. "That's where I met Heather," he said. "She worked out on the weights and Stairmaster. And now she's a runner."

Dick eventually invited Heather to dinner, and since the companionship and the relaxing change of pace pleased him, he invited her a second time. Before long, she became a regular member of the support team.

"I've never been to Hawaii," Heather told him. "But, like everyone else, I've always wanted to go."

"I'd like to go back," Dick said truthfully. "It's been ten years. The World Championships are in October."

Heather volunteered her services. "Well, if you need any help, just ask."

The following weekend, when Dick and Rick competed in another race, Dick popped the question to his son. "What do you think, Rick? Ready for Hawaii again?"

Rick thought about it second and asked, "Does that mean I have to cut weight again?"

Tokunoshima, Japan. Swim to transition.

The Japanese people love Team Hoyt.

Team Hoyt carrying the torch through Boston.

280

CHAPTER 21 — THE SOUL

*Have you ever wondered about your soul? That
spiritual or moral force that somehow animates you
differently than anyone else? Some believe a truly
fulfilling life can only come when you understand
this immaterial essence of you. What you are all
about — why you do what you do.*

— Al Trautwig, NBC Sports

The Ironman committee responded enthusiastically. "Please
come back to Kona."

To prepare for their third trip to Hawaii, Dick filled the
summer schedule with triathlons and long-distance races. For one
of the longer events, they drove to Narragansett, on the southern
end of Rhode Island, for the Firmman Half Ironman. A hurricane
had passed through the area one day before the race, but the wind
and waves had not completely subsided.

"It was very rough that day," Dick recalled. "I wanted to
know how hard it would be to pull and control the boat, so I took
Rick out to test the waves before the race started."

Dick launched and they made it safely over the first wave,
but the next wave jerked him backward and flipped the boat over
on Rick. Dick took off faster than he had ever moved in water.

"Rob should have seen how fast I swam," he said with a
smile. "He would have been proud, I used my legs."

Dick reached his son in a heartbeat. Several other triathletes
saw the mishap and ran in to help, but Dick got to him first.

"I jumped in to see if I could help," one athlete said. "I knew
who they were, and I knew Rick couldn't swim."

"I picked him up and carried him to shore," Dick said. "We recovered the boat and beanbag and got ready for the race. I knew what to expect after that."

Team Hoyt made it through the waves and over the windy bike course without further incident. They completed the half Ironman right on schedule. Referring to the capsized boat, Dick told Rick, "Glad we got that out of the way. We don't want it to happen in Hawaii."

Rick took a different view. "I don't want it to happen *anywhere!*"

In October 1999, Team Hoyt arrived on the Big Island for their third attempt at Ironman Hawaii. NBC filmed the event. In advance of the race, the network had prudently sent a film crew to Massachusetts to get video of the Hoyts for airing during the broadcast. Their intent, of course, was to keep the viewers glued to their TV sets during the advertising breaks. Everyone would be interested in the inspirational story about Dick and Rick, they theorized, so they planned to chronicle the Hoyt history while the race progressed. Once the crew canned all the footage they needed in Holland, they packed up their equipment and headed to Kailua, Kona, Hawaii to film the actual event.

NBC hired the strong, dulcet voice of Al Trautwig to narrate the race, and when the event ended, they edited the film and aired it on selected weekends. Trautwig was the perfect impresario, and if the network didn't win any awards for the production, they were slighted.

"We didn't know what to expect," Dick admitted. "They sure took a lot of video."

NBC Sports Desk, a program to update fans on everything of importance in the world of sports, preceded the two-hour Ironman broadcast. Jimmy Roberts, another strong voice for NBC, told the viewers, "Coming up next, a presentation of the Ironman World Championships, which took place in Hawaii."

Silence from a television set is a great way to get the attention of viewers, but only for a moment or two. That's what

NBC did. They opened with a dimly lit scene from the Hoyts' home in Holland, where a close shot on Rick's face filled the frame. With his brown eyes wide open, he peered down at the blue screen of his Hope Machine. The next sound the viewers heard came from Rick's computer: *tic, tic, tic.* When the capital letter *C* popped up and filled the TV screen, Rick tapped the head switch and continued his search for the next letter.

The editors next inserted a scene from outside the house, in the early morning darkness, with the camera focused on Dick standing in the kitchen near the lighted window. At that point, Dick's voice ended the silence. In his thick New England accent, he said, "My strength comes from Rick. He gives me the desire, and the power, to be able to perform."

As Dick spoke, the camera slowly panned along the house and stopped at a window in the den, where Rick was shown from behind, sitting alone at his computer. Dick's voiceover continued. "It's just something that builds up in me. It comes from his body into mine. I'm just out there loaning him my arms and my legs so he is able to compete."

From inside the house, the camera zoomed in on Rick's face while he struggled to type out the message that began with *C.* They cut back and forth, first on Rick's determined look, then to the computer screen, where the letter *A* next appeared.

After another *tic, tic, tic,* the screen door creaked open and banged closed, then the shrill chirping of crickets filled the air as Dick wheeled Rick across the patio for a pre-dawn training run. Clad in windbreakers and sweatpants, the two men descended the wheelchair ramp while Dick's voiceover came back up.

"I'm trying to include my son in everything, so he can live a life like everybody else. I don't see why any other father wouldn't do the same thing for his son or daughter."

Dick pushed Rick down a lonely, deserted road, while the morning clouds drifted slowly along the moonlit sky and the tip of the rising sun glinted through the spokes of the running chair. Then the action cut back to Rick sitting at his computer, and after a *click*, he added the final letter to the word *CAN*. Another angle revealed Rick's broad smile and sparkling brown eyes. NBC concluded the eye-popping scenes with a shot of distant clouds blotting out the moon and the booming sound of a choir vocalizing mystical lyrics. It was a brilliant opening to the broadcast, making it unlikely that any viewers reached for their remote controls.

As the ethereal music faded, a black-and-white montage of triathletes in various forms of meditation began. With each athlete clearly concerned about the overwhelming task that lie ahead, the commentator asked a compelling question: "Have you ever wondered about your soul? That spiritual or moral force that animates you differently than anyone else? Some believe a truly fulfilling life can only come when you begin to try to understand this immaterial essence of you. What you are all about — why you do what you do."

While Trautwig delivered his powerful commentary, the sounds grew louder and the images changed. It started with an underwater angle on swimmers churning through the ocean, then several shots of athletes perspiring profusely as they pumped their bicycles over the Queen K Highway. Exhausted runners pushed forward in the darkness, suppressing the nagging desire to quit.

"The secret of reaching your capabilities," Trautwig said, "is an unbreakable belief in yourself that can only be found deep in the central core of wherever it is that you find your soul. Most people don't give it much thought. That's because they have never been tested or pushed to find out what it is exactly that they are made of — spiritually, physically, mentally."

The camera cut to a solitary man standing at the edge of a jagged cliff and staring defiantly into the Pacific Ocean, while in the distance, the imminent arrival of the morning sun cast fiery beams into the underbelly of a massive cloud. "Nearly 1,500 triathletes participate in the Hawaii Ironman every October," said Trautwig, "and some were very good athletes. Most of them had no chance of winning — except in a larger sense."

When NBC returned to the Hoyt story, they ran footage of Dick and Rick competing in Hawaii ten years earlier, back in 1989. As the younger Rick sat nervously in his wheelchair, the commentator picked up the tempo. He informed the viewers that Rick was born a spastic quadriplegic with cerebral palsy, and the doctors told Dick and Judy to send him to an institution, that he would be a vegetable for life. "They chose a different path." Trautwig paused for impact while the viewers watched Dick and Rick make their famous sprint to the finish line, when they zipped past other runners and ran the final mile in under six minutes. "But that was ten years ago. Everyone is ten years older now." They went to another montage of anxious athletes preparing for the current event, and ended with the focus on Dick. He looked solemn, eager to get under way. "But Ricky's dad is a military man. And today the mission is to prove we can still do it. But how will they do it? It's a hell of a question. And while we're asking, *would* every parent do it?"

The commentator profiled other athletes, of course. He introduced previous champions, like Mark Allen, six-time winner of the event. When interviewed, Allen articulated his feeling about the Ironman. "From the outside, the Ironman can look like a day of pure torture. But it's not all blood and guts. In fact, there are points in the race when it's absolute freedom." The former champion referred only to the swim when he talked about freedom, because he went on to say, "Suddenly it hits you. This is a lot more than a swim. You are going to leave the protection of the ocean, ride 112 miles, then come up with enough reasons to run a marathon. You uncover your first layer of soul. You realize, *I can't hide.*"

Other featured athletes included the defending champion, Peter Reid, and his lovely wife Lori Bowden, the first husband and wife combination to win an Ironman, a feat they accomplished in Australia. Reid, a Canadian, had the lead in a previous Ironman in Hawaii as well, but he lost it when the hills on the Queen K knocked him out of the competition. Reid told the interviewer, "Every time you come to this race, you're faced with that 'wall,' and you've got to push yourself over it. You focus on yourself and hope the island is going to support you. It can work in your favor, but if you think you're going to conquer it, it will conquer you."

Luc Van Lierde of Belgium won Hawaii as a rookie in 1996. In 1998, he returned to finish second behind Reid. "Nature and the wind are stronger than you," Lierde said knowingly. "I cannot beat nature. It will always beat me."

As the start time neared and excitement filled the air, NBC found Dick and Rick making final preparations. Referring to all the athletes, Trautwig said, "This day will slowly peel away their layers in an unforgiving way. Until at some moment, we will see the essence of their being, and a huge bay window of light opens to reveal their soul."

While the athletes boldly waded into the ocean, the narrator detailed the distances of an Ironman swim, bike and run. Wearing black Speedos and the harness made from parachute straps, Dick stood in water to his knees and held onto the boat. Rick waited anxiously on the beanbag, his life vest snugly secured around his neck. A woman in a black bathing suit gave Dick a hug, squeezed Rick's hand, and wished them both a safe race.

"Seven percent will not even finish the race," Trautwig asserted. "They await the cannon."

When the cannon roared, 1,500 hundred swimmers filled their lungs with ocean air and began the frantic 2.4-mile swim, the first step of their 140-mile journey. The mass of flailing arms looked like the flapping wings of panicked flamingos trying hopelessly to lift themselves from the salty ocean. A helicopter filmed the action from overhead as they gradually formed a huge *V*, with the fastest swimmer all alone at the point.

A cameraman kneeling in a small boat captured the action as swimmers passed by only a few feet from his lens. Dick swam slowly across the television screen, and when Rick came into view, the commentary continued. "Ricky Hoyt has gotten the message, too. He is truly loved — and it is going to be a very long day."

While lying peacefully on the beanbag, wearing a white T-shirt with logos of the Team Hoyt sponsors, Rick looked up at the clear blue sky and smiled. Perfect timing for a commercial. Dick felt confident they could complete the course faster than they did ten years earlier, but with higher waves, stronger winds and hotter temperatures, the weather was not favorable for a personal record. And, of course, his next birthday would be number sixty. Finishing the swim before the cutoff time of two hours and twenty minutes did not concern him, and even though the Counterpoint was now fifteen years old, the ten-hour bike limit was easily attainable. To be official finishers, which was their primary goal, they had seventeen hours to complete the race.

Race coverage continued as the mass of swimmers passed a blue catamaran that marked the halfway point of the swim. When Team Hoyt reappeared, Trautwig said, "And then there's Dick and Ricky Hoyt. Dad wearing a harness, attached to a raft that gives his son *life*."

NBC cut to the Hoyt archives and showed video of Rick at a birthday party, swimming at an early age, mastering the computer and sitting in the running chair. Dick told about the TIC machine and the charity race, and he quoted Rick saying, "Dad, when I'm running, it feels like I'm not even handicapped." Regarding the charity race, Dick said, "We knew right then and there we found an event that Rick could enjoy just like everybody else."

After profiling other triathletes, they returned to the Hoyts. In one video, Rick worked diligently at his computer, and through his voice synthesizer said, "You may be wondering how I feel about being disabled. To tell you the truth, I don't know what it is like to not be disabled. I was born with cerebral palsy and it is all I know. What I think is important is that people take the time and effort to realize that first and foremost I am a person with a brain and intelligence."

In a contrasting video, Dick lifted his son from the dinghy and hustled off to a transition area. Once strapped into their helmets and smeared with sun block, they gulped water and rode out onto a bike course. As the action took place, we heard Dick quoting the doctor who said he and Judy should "put Rick in an institution and forget about him."

Referring to the video of Rick keying the word "can" on his computer, Trautwig said, "The letters *C-A-N* are *never* followed with an apostrophe *T*. That's the easiest way to summarize Team Hoyt. It took Ricky nine years, but he graduated with a degree in special education at Boston University." As Dick pedaled along the Queen K, the commentator recounted their accomplishments in marathons, triathlons, and the Trek across America, and then he said, "Not once in any of those miles did Rick ever ask his dad, 'Why me?'"

NBC left the Hoyts still out on the lava fields to catch the celebration of Luc Van Lierde winning the race. But, according to Trautwig, Van Lierde was lucky. Because by the time he finished the race, the winds on the bike course had really picked up. He said, "As for the wind, Rick Hoyt perched on the handlebars of that 15-year-old bicycle presented a huge target. It knocks them back. Dick grinds it out, but at times he's barely moving." While contrasting a 59-year-old man struggling to get his son up the hill to that of a youthful Van Lierde leaping for joy, he said, "But they had the same drive as Van Lierde, the same type of soul as him. Here is the absolute commitment of a father to his son, to try to get him to that line just as he did ten years ago."

A black pickup came into view, and on the tailgate a white placard said: "Last Biker." Dick and Rick were last, but still pushing up the highest mountain on the course. Trautwig said that they had never finished last, but the wind, the weight, and the old bike had worn Dick down, and that they would never make the transition area before the cutoff time.

He then paused and said, "But dealing with adversity is in their soul. They will try to find a way. Have you ever wondered about *your* soul? That spiritual force that somehow animates you, and makes you what you are?"

An eerie creaking sound interrupted the commentary. When Dick stopped and dismounted from the bike, a race official and his female assistant parked the black pickup and ran over to evaluate the situation. While Dick checked the brakes, the official observed, "It looks like your brake is rubbing."

The assistant asked, "You want me to call tech support?"

"Yes," the official said, and offered to hold the bike while Dick attended to Rick.

The assistant returned and said, "Here's some Gatorade."

Dick took the bottle, thanked the woman, and shared a drink with his son.

With a sigh of disbelief, Trautwig said, "A broken bicycle part? Is that how this ends? Sometimes the Ironman is like that."

Team Hoyt, the two men who scaled the Rockies in freezing weather, now found themselves stranded on top of a mountain, forced to wait in the smoldering heat until the maintenance team delivered a part. It provided another great opportunity for a commercial, and when they returned to the broadcast, the support team had already fixed the brakes.

"You want to go on?" Dick asked his son. Rick nodded.

"He wants to go on?" the surprised official asked.

Dick confirmed they would continue. He wiped drool from Rick's face, picked some debris from his cheek, and patted him on the helmet.

"Just like that," Trautwig interjected. "No hesitation. The decision is made. Care, respect, love. And it goes both ways."

When the Hoyts pedaled away, NBC cut to a touching, black-and-white shot of Dick and Rick relaxing at the edge of Hamilton Reservoir. In another voiceover, Dick said, "Rick is the competitor. He really wants to win. He's a fighter, and he's never going to give up. It's something that gets inside of me, and when I'm pushing him, I can go faster, and I can do all these things. I don't know exactly what it is."

With a closeup of Rick sitting in the wheelchair, his voice synthesizer repeated the emotion-evoking words from a previous interview. "I have thought long and hard about what I would do if I wasn't in a wheelchair. I love sports, so maybe I would play hockey, basketball or baseball. But then I thought about it some more, and what I would probably do first is tell my dad to sit down in the wheelchair and now I would push him."

The editors cut to a shot of Dick sitting next to Rick in the den. As emotions welled, Dick said, "Rick and I are out there competing together, and it's really helped me because I feel like I'm in the best shape of my life. I'm 59-years old, and I feel like I have the body of a 22-year-old." Rick's laughter pushed him over the edge. Dick looked over at his son, and for the first time in an interview, he sobbed. "...And it's all Rick's fault."

"That's when Dick cried," said the solemn commentator. "When he talked about what Ricky gave him."

Nightfall covered Kona before Dick and Rick made it back from the 112-mile ride. Although they didn't make the bike cutoff time, officials allowed them to continue because of the long wait for brake parts. Therefore, if they could complete the marathon before midnight, they were still officially in the race. Russell held the bike while Dick removed Rick's helmet and lifted him into the running chair. "Are you all set Rick? Want to go catch some people?"

Team Hoyt took off for a 26-mile dash into the darkness and NBC took a commercial break. When the cameras next found them, Dick was struggling to push Rick up a hill. "For the Hoyts," Trautwig went on, "the uphills of the marathon are agony. Dick's body is bathed in sweat, and the energy to catch some runners, has not come. The Ironman continues to peel away the layers until we see the core."

Back at the finish line, a young man with a prosthesis for a right leg finished strong, then he raised his arms gleefully and danced up and down like a child. A wheelchair athlete also shot across the line, where his ecstatic wife mauled him with teary kisses. One woman cried like a baby when she finally finished. Another runner dropped to his knees, looked to the sky, and gave thanks to a superior being who helped him survive the challenge. That blissful moment still awaited the Hoyts, but now they were on flat land and picking up speed. Trautwig raised his voice excitedly. "Team Hoyt bounces back again! And now they are passing runners! They could make it to the finish line before midnight. And that would be a running miracle."

A cameraman straddling the back of a motorcycle pulled alongside the Hoyts and mumbled a question to Dick. Between heavy gasps and long strides, he said, "Rick's the one that wanted to keep going. He wanted to do this, and he wanted to do it bad. This will probably be our last time to Hawaii, so he really wanted to keep going."

Dick and Rick disappeared into the darkness.

Back at the finish line, euphoric athletes dashed, walked, staggered and crawled the final yards. Suddenly, the cheering increased to a roar when Team Hoyt steamed around the final turn like a runaway train, and in a scene reminiscent of 1989, they charged past other runners on their way to another spectacular finish. When the running chair came to a stop, both men raised their right arms in unison and Russell doused them with champagne. The race clock had ticked a few seconds past 16:14; they beat the cutoff time by 45 minutes.

After a moment to absorb the exhilaration, NBC cut to the video taken back in Holland. In the final scene, they showed Rick sitting in his wheelchair and wearing a victorious smile, with his eyes glued on the blue computer screen that still displayed the letters *C-A-N*.

"They can," Trautwig concluded. "They did. They do."

The broadcast ended with a splendid, full-screen shot of the biggest, brightest moon you ever saw in your life.

* * *

Three weeks after Hawaii, another full-page spread appeared in the *Boston Sunday Herald*. Michael O'Connor titled the story

"Hoyts show their mettle." In the first of three pictures, Dick was in full stride behind the running chair. Rick held his right arm high as he checked out a spectator — a pretty lady, no doubt — from behind his one-way sunglasses. In the second picture, Dick carried Rick from the dinghy to the bike. And in the last picture, Dick strained to climb a hill while Rick huddled behind the plastic shield on their original bike-chair rig.

"Dick and Rick Hoyt again rose to the challenge of the Ironman Triathlon," said O'Connor. "They had little trouble in the running and swimming portions, but had to overcome mechanical problems with their specially designed bicycle."

He told the readers that the Hoyts had returned from Hawaii, where they had enjoyed the outdoor delights by swimming, biking, and going for a long run through pineapple groves. He said the father-and-son team had become the nation's best-known endurance-sport duo, which began when Dick pushed his disabled son in a 5-mile charity race. Dick told the reporter he wanted to get a PR on the course, and said, "You've got to be prepared physically, but more important, mentally."

O'Connor pointedly added, "He forgot *mechanically*."

"We had a bad bike stretch," Dick explained. "In fact, our bike fell apart out there in the lava fields. We were dead last off the bike." Dick told O'Connor that he had developed blood blisters on the balls of his feet only four miles into the run, and he thought they would have to give up. Matter of factly, Dick added, "But then I took off my socks and ran just with the shoes. That felt better. But when we finished, my shoes were full of blood."

O'Connor told the readers it took them two hours longer than it did ten years earlier.

"At least we finished," Dick said. "That's the main thing."

"This unique father-son tandem got its triathlon baptism on Cape Cod," O'Connor reported, "back when Boston Marathon official Dave McGillivray was staging events around Hyannis. He rigged up a primitive tug-and-tow apparatus for the water portion, fastened a high-tech basket to his bike for the cycling segment, and off they went. Ironman organizers, used to dealing with super-fit individuals, did not know how to classify the Hoyts. A man pushing 50, pushing his grown kid along a killer course. But race officials knew enough not to turn them away."

O'Connor added a couple of paragraphs about the non-athletic lives of Dick and Rick Hoyt, including their special appearances and speaking engagements on behalf of cerebral palsy research. "In addition," he wrote, "Rick works at the Boston College Computer Lab on a project called *Eagle Eyes,* which one day will enable persons in wheelchairs to operate them by eye and hand movements alone."

O'Connor ended the article with a plea by Dick. "We need a new bike. This one is 15 years old, a real dinosaur. And it weighs 78 pounds. I'm looking for a lighter one."

Counterpoint had built Dick a bike that lasted fifteen years and covered over 10,000 miles. Unfortunately, it broke down on national TV. Any bicycle manufacturers who saw the broadcast should have called immediately. Jokingly, Dick asked, "I wonder if Nike makes a bicycle?"

Al Trautwig – along with the help of two talented producers, Lisa Lax and Ken Murrah – touched millions of lives the day they aired the story about the remarkable Hoyt family. As a result, hundreds of viewers were compelled to send letters and e-mail to the network and directly to the Hoyts.

Dear Team Hoyt!

I am sure you get thousands of e-mails telling you how inspiring your story is and I am honored to join in the throng of people your story has touched. Each year my husband and I eagerly await the Ironman coverage on TV. I think we have watched faithfully for about 5-7 years now. Your story was by far the true representation of 'Ironman' spirit. I can't begin to tell you how it has blessed my life personally and in my relationship to my children. Your 'team' has redefined the word LOVE in my dictionary! I hope one day I can attain the level of love you all exemplify. I recently had to reorder a copy of the 1999 Ironman video as I have loaned mine out to so many people to see your story and I guess I loaned it to one too many and forgot who!!! But well worth it as I feel your story should be seen by EVERYONE who wants to be a parent so they can see how it SHOULD be done. Thank you for allowing us into your life so that our spirits could be lifted. God bless you!

—Mrs. Julie Wisloff
San Antonio, Texas

Mister Hoyt,

As an author of many books, I'm not usually a man without many words. However, having just seen a special on the 1999 Ironman that took place in Hawaii, I'm speechless. My wife and I were riveted to the television and at moments were engulfed in tears. Mister Hoyt, I have never witnessed such 'heroism.' I have served my country as a combat infantryman in Vietnam and still feel that all I witnessed over there pales compared to your devotion and commitment to your son. My heart goes out to the two of you. So if possible, may I contribute some funds to assist you in the purchase of a new bicycle? The documentary focused on the breakdown of yours, as well as mentioning it was many years old. Please let me know if there is something I can do in that regard.

—Scott Spiering
Spiering Asset Management, LLC

Dick and Rick Hoyt,

It was a dreary Saturday afternoon and I was channel surfing. I stumbled across the Hawaii Ironman contest and was hooked right away. By the end of the broadcast, tears of admiration and humility were streaming down my face. It was the first time I had ever heard of Dick and Rick and I was simply blown away. Such devotion between these two remarkable human beings, such commitment and trust, you have forever touched my heart, thank you so very much. Rick, you and I are close in age, and I can only imagine what treasures of insight you have on life in general! Such a courageous spirit and limitless mind, you are truly an inspiration. Dick, a father's love has found new expression through you for the world to see, you are a very remarkable man.

—Marie "Rio" Scafone

Dear Mr. Hoyt,

I was recently watching the '99 Ironman in Hawaii. I was inspired by you and your dedication to your son. I was also excited to see that there are still some people who don't just give up and who still find hope. I watched the whole race to see if you would finish. I began to cry when I saw your dedication and love toward your son and the love and admiration that he had for you. I grew up without a father, and I never had a really positive male role model. This made me realize that not all men are as heartless as my father and that there is still some common decency in this world. You have filled me with hope and inspiration, and I know now that I can accomplish anything as long as I put my mind to it. Thank you so much for restoring my faith. I would be honored to meet you and your amazingly optimistic son some time.

I am only 17 and you have been the only one who has emotionally been able to get through to me. By the end of the show I was in tears, and I haven't cried in a long time, not even at the death of my grandpa and my aunt. Thank you so much for being a positive role model for all and for passing on your hopes and inspirations to all. I believe that if you get through to one person you have succeeded, and I just wanted

to tell you that you have gotten through to me. I am also happy that you are raising awareness of disabilities and now people who have them can still live perfectly normal lives. Thank you so much. All of my love and admiration.
—Wendy from California

Mister Hoyt,
  Please accept my sincere congratulations to you and Rick on your incredible accomplishment in Hawaii. As a writer and triathlete, I am curious if anyone has approached you regarding a screenplay about your life....
—Sam Nall
Tampa, Florida

Hawaii, 1999.

Champagne shower at the finish line.

CHAPTER 22 — SPREADING THE WORD

I can't tell you how much of an impression you two left on all that heard your presentation. In a cynical and pessimistic world you represent hope, love, and determination in overcoming life's adversities. People still come up to me shaking their heads in amazement of your tremendous accomplishments.

—Tom Lambert
Needham Police Department

Dick, Rick and I raced in the Marlboro Triathlon on Sunday, the second day of my visit. Dick tended to personal business on Monday, so I hung around to view videos and read newspaper and magazine articles about Team Hoyt. On Tuesday, Dick trained by taking a three-hour bike ride on the hilly course around the Holland countryside. He invited me along.

"I'm not an Ironman," I told him. "Unless you plan to tow me, I don't ride for more than an hour."

After a half hour ride, I turned around and went back to the house to do more research for the book. Dick continued his three-hour loop alone, and when he returned home, he showered and prepared our dinner — his specialty, baked salmon. Recalling the anecdote about his friend, the culinary novice, I said, "Are you sure this salmon is done? It's still pink."

Dick chuckled and passed the potatoes.

On Wednesday afternoon, Dick went to the Auburn Health Club for a two-hour session of circuit training. "I do this exercise to strengthen my back," he said while pulling the cables on the rowing machine. "It makes it easier to lift Rick from the boat."

When Dick finished with one muscle group, he moved over to the next piece of equipment. At that moment, an elderly man sauntered into the room humming to himself. The man mounted a stationary bike and said, "How you doing, Dick? Any races coming up?"

"We have a short triathlon on Sunday," Dick answered. "And then we're doing an Ironman in Germany in a few weeks."

With a straight face, the man said, "A slow month, huh?"

Dick responded with a smile. But when he moved over to the bicep machine, he looked at me and whispered, "That guy is 85 years old. He tells everyone he's my personal trainer."

While Dick continued his strenuous routine, I meandered around the club. After briefly talking to one of the club members about the accomplishments of Dick and Rick Hoyt, I sat down and scribbled a few notes. A young woman took the seat next to me and began filling out a membership application. When she paused for a moment, I asked her if she knew the Hoyts.

"Who?" she asked.

"Dick and Rick Hoyt."

Apparently, I found the only person in Massachusetts who had not heard of the Hoyts. She shook her head. "No, I don't think so. Does he work here at the club?"

Dick ended the session with 30 minutes of stretching, but his workout did not end until he got back to the house and went for a long run. The next day, I remained in Holland while Dick went back to the club for a long swim and another run. Then, later that afternoon, we drove to Billerica to have dinner with Russell, Lisa, and two-year-old Troy Donovan Hoyt.

"I'm the director of Building Blocks," Russ said when I asked him about his profession. "It's an early prevention program for children with autism and Pervasive Developmental Disorder, and for kids who are at risk for one of those diagnoses." With a scholarly demeanor, he went on to say, "It's part of a larger agency called the North Shore Arc, which is a human service agency that serves individuals with disabilities and their families. The agency does everything from early intervention through residential and vocational services for adults."

The young man was way over my head, but I pretended to follow along. When he got into the details, I learned that Russell also had the responsibility of hiring, firing, budgeting, training and day-to-day management. He had two assistant directors, eight lead providers and thirty-three providers who work with the children and families out in the field.

"I basically run the show from soup to nuts," Russell added.

Lisa said she worked for an occupational medicine company as a Licensed Practical Nurse, where she performed drug screens, physicals and other work related medical procedures. After a great meal and enlightening conversation, we returned to Holland in a rainstorm.

On Thursday, Dick and Rick had a twelve o'clock speaking engagement at William Pollard Middle School in the town of Needham. Davin Svendsen, the tall, gray-haired administrator, greeted us in the parking lot. "Park right over there," Svendsen said after shaking Dick's hand. "Then go through that door to the auditorium. Do you need any help with your gear?"

"No," Dick answered. "We can handle it."

Svendsen said a technician would be inside to help set up the equipment. With a sincere smile, he thanked Dick and Rick for coming and excused himself to attend to other duties.

Dick parked the van and lowered Rick and the wheelchair to the ground. As we approached the double doors that led to the school auditorium, he said, "Which door was he talking about? There's no ramp at this one."

"Must be on the other side," I said.

A Needham Police Officer drove into the parking lot and waved. "That's the guy I'm looking for," Dick said. "He's the one who puts on all the DARE programs. He's a runner, too."

I observed the slender Sergeant climb out of his police cruiser. He looked like a runner.

"Morning, Dick. Morning, Rick." The congenial officer smiled broadly and exchanged a friendly handshake. "Always good to see you guys."

Dick told the officer my name and why I was there.

"I'm Tom Lambert," he said, and shook my hand. "I'll look forward to reading the book."

"How do we get inside?" Dick asked.

"Follow me. There's a ramp on the other side."

Lambert led us around the building to the main entrance. We followed him to the front of the 300-seat auditorium, where a teacher glanced at his watch and promptly dismissed a small group of music students who were rehearsing on center stage. When the technician came in to set up the projection equipment, I moved to the side of the room and sat down. As the music students scampered off to find their classmates, Svendsen returned and joined the other men at the front of the stage to talk about the format of the Hoyt presentation.

A stocky man with a crewcut came in wearing shorts and a golf shirt. He shook hands with Dick and Svendsen. They exchanged a laugh and said something about his grandchild, which surprised me because I guessed the man to be around 30 years old. His visit was short, and when he walked away, he stopped to introduce himself.

"I'm Joe O'Brien," he told me. "Are you with Mister Hoyt?" After telling him that I was, he observed my pen and note pad. "You writing about them?"

"Yes," I told him. "Do you work here at the school?"

O'Brien told me that he and Officer Lambert worked together on the D.A.R.E program.

"Oh? How do you spell your name?"

He merely smiled, handed me a business card, wished me luck, and walked out of the auditorium. I glanced down at the card: Needham Police Department. Detective.

When the doors next opened, several teachers entered and led their students down the aisles to the front rows. A female teacher stopped next to me.

"How old are these kids?" I asked.

"They're eleven and twelve."

I couldn't help but wonder if kids this young would really be interested in the Hoyt story. As I looked around the room, it was obvious that the young man sitting in the wheelchair intrigued them. In fact, some of the students pointed toward Rick and whispered their thoughts to the kids seated next to them.

Team Hoyt looked sharp in their matching black slacks and blue golf shirts with the *Fleet* logo. Rick waited patiently while Dick made final preparation. The auditorium filled quickly, so I went to the back and found a seat along the center aisle.

Svendsen stepped to the podium and said the expected. "Students, please be quiet."

He told the youngsters it would be a very special program, and exhorted them to remain quiet and listen closely. Once he had their attention, he stepped off to the side and Dick took over.

"I'm Dick Hoyt and this is my son, Rick," he told the students. "Rick has cerebral palsy."

Dick appeared a little nervous at first, but once he got started, everything went like clockwork. "Rick will tell you about himself," Dick said. "He can't talk, but he writes on the computer and then says everything though a voice synthesizer. His speech will take 15 minutes on the computer, but it took him seven and a half hours to write it. Since he can't use his arms, he uses a switch next to his head."

Dick provided his audience with some background information, including the story of Rick's birth. When he turned the show over to Rick, the synthesizer presented the recorded speech and the video screen displayed accompanying pictures. The voice, the pictures, and the image of Rick using a head switch in order to communicate completely captivated the kids. As students, they could relate when Rick told them how he took notes at school, and they were amazed at pictures of him graduating from Westfield High School.

"People stare at me wherever I go," Rick told them. "You might think it's because of my handicap, but I know it is because of my stunning good looks."

303

He got plenty of laughs with that one. Then Rick told them about his college days, and that he took only two classes each semester, but eventually graduated in nine years. His message was loud and clear: *If I can do it, you can do it.*

"I'm one of the few non-vocal quadriplegics to ever graduate from college," he said. "And now I work at Boston College two days a week on a program called *Eagle Eyes,* a system to help disabled people operate a wheelchair with their eyes."

After the students gasped and whispered to each other, Rick resumed. "On Wednesdays, I work on new programs with a speech therapist at a hospital."

Rick told them about racing with his dad, and that it began at the charity event for Doogie. The kids laughed again when he said that he cuts down on cake and candy so he won't be too heavy for his dad to push him. They sat in silent amazement when he talked about completing the Boston Marathon. Some of the kids wiped away tears when Rick told them that the first thing he would do if he were not in a wheelchair would be to "have his dad sit down in it so he could push him." Imagine the emotions evoked with the image of a miracle that could make Rick whole, and then visualize him pushing his joyous father across a finish line in the running chair.

Dick showed slides and conveyed the stories behind each of them. He included pictures of the finish line at their first race, and the biggest smile you ever saw in your life.

"They wouldn't let us race in the Boston Marathon," Dick told the children. "They said, 'No, you're different.' But they let us run unofficially."

Dick talked about qualifying at the Marine Corps Marathon, and told them Rick wore fatigues and shaved his head. After showing some shots from the World Championships in Hawaii, Dick emphasized the word "can," just as NBC had done during the Ironman.

"And we did all this without drugs," he concluded. "No drugs, no alcohol, and no cigarettes."

After his effective *Say No To Drugs* message, Dick urged the kids to ask questions. Several did, and when their curiosity was satisfied, everyone in the auditorium applauded.

"You kids will have to move out as quietly and quickly as you can," Svendsen told them. "We have another group waiting to come in."

The students moved out as quietly as anyone could expect from children that age. Some of them stopped to say "Hi" and offer Rick gifts. As one group filed out and the next group came in, a local reporter cornered Dick to ask him a few questions.

Although the second presentation was the same as the first, Dick got the biggest laugh when he said, "I want to thank you kids for being so attentive. I know it's not easy when you only have a couple more days until summer vacation."

When the cheering subsided, he concluded his presentation and the children returned to their respective classrooms. While Dick gathered up the slides and videos, Lambert opened a large box of black T-shirts with D.A.R.E printed across the back in red letters, along with a logo on the front that outlined the state of Massachusetts. He distributed the shirts to anyone who wanted one.

He tossed one over to me and said, "A shirt for you, too."

Once everything was loaded in the van and ready to leave, Dick said to Lambert, "Can we get any ice cream near here? I need to get something inside Rick."

"Sure," Lambert responded with a smile. "An officer always knows where to find ice cream or donuts. Follow me."

We trailed the officer to a small concession at a pickup point along the local commuter railway system. Everyone ordered an ice cream cone. Lambert took out his wallet and said, "These are on me." He paid the bill and we all went inside the building to sit at a table.

As Dick wrapped a bib around Rick and fed him the ice cream, I said to the officer, "Thanks for the cone. This is the first time a police department bought my ice cream."

305

Lambert promptly corrected me. "No, no. This is from my personal funds."

After a twinge of embarrassment, I said, "You're a runner, huh? Long distance?"

"Usually the short ones, but I've run Boston twice. And a few times as a guide."

"A guide?"

"Yes. For blind runners."

Lambert told me about a program for police officers who volunteer to run along with blind marathoners, and that he and some of his fellow officers had done it in the Boston Marathon. His compassion impressed me and I told him so. He shrugged and said, "Just trying to do my share."

The officer gave us directions out of the city and we headed back to Holland. Somewhere along the way, Dick said, "Rick and I have made presentations for the Needham Police before. After one of them, Tom sent us a nice letter. I'll show it to you when we get home."

The visit to Pollard Middle School presented me with additional insight to Team Hoyt. They provided inspiration in ways I had never thought of. They influenced children in many positive ways: to persevere in school; to avoid drugs; to include the disabled; to live a healthy, active life; to understand people who are "different"; to laugh in the face of hardship; to always maintain a sense of humor.

During one of their many interviews, Dick talked about the hero treatment Rick received at the races. Referring to what the specialist told them 30 years earlier, Dick humorously asked, "If Rick is a vegetable, someone will have to tell me what kind."

No one could tell him, of course. However, not surprisingly, I learned that Rick had an answer to Dick's rhetorical question about "what kind" of a vegetable he was. Some years back, as the story goes, Judy was giving a speech before a large audience. While Rob and Rick waited to join her on stage, they passed time in a nearby novelty shop, where they came across a small pillow encased in a crocheted carrot. After Rick convinced Rob they needed a pillow, Rob bought it and they took it along when they went on stage to join Judy.

Rob explained it this way. "Rick was behind Mom when she told them about his birth. When she mentioned the doctor referring to him as a 'vegetable,' Rick lifted the carrot as high as he could lift it. His humor brought down the house. Mom was dumfounded. She didn't know what everyone was laughing at until she turned around and saw Rick. She was mad at first, but she lightened up and laughed right along with everyone else."

If Rick had to be a vegetable, okay, but he would be the one to choose which kind: a carrot. And not your typical carrot, either, but a soft, cuddly one with a wicked sense of humor.

* * *

Dick went for a long bike ride on Friday and rested on Saturday. His rest included mowing the lawn, clearing the brush, branches and leaves from around his property, and hauling four loads of trash to the dump. With that out of the way, he went shopping and prepared another gourmet dinner.

The following morning, at the Massachusetts State Sprint Championships in Ludlow, Team Hoyt recorded their second consecutive win in the 60-64 age division. I placed third with the youngsters 55-59, and for that, I received a great sweatshirt along with a bronze medal.

We drove back to Holland after the race. I showered and packed my bags for the return flight to Florida. Heather rode along to Boston with us, and once we got there, we stopped at a city park by the Charles River, where a group known as Anything On Wheels sponsored a celebration and a wheelchair ride around the park. "It's a fundraising event for an organization called Partners For Youths With Disabilites," Dick told me. "They want me to say a few words, but it won't be our regular speech."

When we arrived at the park, a woman wearing jeans, a sweatshirt and a big smile welcomed us to the party. "We're so glad you could come," she said to Dick. "The band will stop in a few minutes, then you can go right up there and take the microphone. It's your show."

While Dick and the woman chatted, dozens of people in motorized wheelchairs buzzed along the walkway nearby. Rick's PCA, Yoel Shoshani, met us at the park so he could take Rick back home after the speech. When the three-piece band finished, Dick wheeled Rick up to the temporary stage, where the female vocalist handed him a microphone. The small audience gave the Hoyts a warm welcome. Dick introduced himself and his teammate, then he told them about Team Hoyt racing, with an emphasis on the importance of supporting other disabled people. He didn't talk long, but everyone appreciated the fact that two celebrities had taken the time to stop by.

We all went back to the van where Yoel prepared Rick for the ride home. "Take care of yourself," I told Rick. "Kick some butt over in Germany."

When they drove away, I realized the courageous young man had wormed his way into my heart. I didn't let it show, of course. Triathletes aren't into that sentimental stuff.

Dick drove me to the Hartford airport, shook my hand and left me standing at the curb. Before the departure time, a storm moved in and delayed my flight by more than two hours. While I sat in a corner of the Southwest lounge, I reflected over the events and emotions of the past nine days, and although I was concerned whether I had enough material for the book, and how I would go about constructing the story, I was eager to get home so I could get started.

Eventually, while we winged our way toward Baltimore, it seemed appropriate that the lyrics from a song kept running through my mind. It was a song called, "I'm leaving here a better man," and that's exactly how I felt. Before long, the man sitting next to me interrupted the song to strike up a conversation. Since I was eager to talk about the Hoyts, we got along fine; I talked and he listened. It came as no surprise when he said, "The Hoyts? Oh, sure, I've heard of them."

"Oh? Are you from Massachusetts?"

"No, from D.C."

Of course he knew the Hoyts. They owned that town. Dick resumed training on Monday morning, and three weeks later, he, Heather, a PCA, Rick and Rob took a flight to Germany to compete in another Ironman. Team Hoyt, without a doubt, was still on the fast track, kicking down barriers and speeding through life at a dizzying pace. Too fast for me, Mad Dog #727, a man who only does the short races.

When I arrived in Tampa, I kept thinking about Dick and Rick, and what would be a good title for the book. To clear my head, I went for a long run on the Gandy Bridge, and after the run, I stopped at the Banana Boat Sports Bar, which is located on the St. Pete end of the bridge. Bill Wilhite, the owner, bought me a beer. Bill had moved to Florida from a tiny town in northern Iowa. The same town, in fact, where he and I had played baseball and chased girls together, back when we were teenagers attending Corwith High School.

"Yeah, I remember seeing those guys on television," Bill said, when I told him about the Hoyts. "I want one of the books when they're out." Then, after a second thought, he added, "No, wait, I want two of them, so I can send one to my mother."

That's just the way it works with Team Hoyt. They have disseminated their marvelously inspirational message throughout America, Japan, San Salvador, Canada, Germany, and now even to rural Iowa.

For me, this compelling adventure started when I saw the Hoyts complete the Ironman in Hawaii. For Dick and Rick, it began nearly 40 years earlier. The emotions I experienced while watching that Ironman broadcast have only grown stronger and more meaningful since I met the Hoyts and learned the intimate details of their phenomenal story. My trip to Massachusetts was an unforgettable and humbling experience, and although I'm a man with few heroes, that number has grown by two.

Dick Hoyt and Sam Nall on Gandy Bridge in Tampa.

EPILOGUE

When we finished, they set off fireworks as the race director came down and had us run with him past the crowd again. After we finished that, I ate everything in sight and all I wanted was to take a bath!

—Rick Hoyt, Ironman

A word about Germany from **Dick Hoyt:**

We left for Germany on the first of July, out of Bradley Field in Connecticut, connecting to Dulles in Washington, onto Frankfurt, Germany, and finally into Nuremberg. We arrived at our hotel at midnight on the second of July. The city of Roth set up a tour of the city on the fourth, took us to lunch and drove us along parts of the racecourse.

Our race equipment did not arrive until noon that same day, so we had to drive back to Nuremberg to pick it up. The security in Frankfurt had kept the equipment in a pressurized chamber for twenty-four hours before they would release it.

On the fifth of July, we put our new bike together and Rick and I went out for a two-hour bike ride. Rick's position was not good at all — he was hanging off the side of the seat. We all worked to make him more comfortable, and finally took the molded seat cushion out of his wheelchair and attached it to the bike seat. Rick looked and felt a lot more comfortable.

311

On the sixth, we went for another two-hour bike ride, and Rick said he felt better. I did a little more training on the seventh of July, and we also registered and visited the expo. The program book for the IronMan had a feature story and photo of us. Too bad we couldn't understand what it said!

The IronMan parade was on Friday as well, and the five of us marched along. The parade ended at the "noodle party" (carbo load supper). We were guests of the race director, Detlef Kuhnel. The noodle party was held in a big tent. Saturday, July 8th, was the cycle/helmet check in, and we had a race meeting, which was conducted in English.

A total of 2,704 triathletes registered for the race, the largest field for an IronMan triathlon in the world. There were twelve waves in the swim start; we were in the first, starting at 6:10 a.m. The last wave started at 7:25 a.m. The swim was in a canal, the water was very cold and everyone wore wet suits. The weather was cloudy and cool. We did our usual zigzag up and down the canal. The TV crew said we did three miles while everyone else did 2.4! I do not have the split times yet, just the overall time. We figure the swim was really a little under two hours.

The swim to bike transition took a little while because we needed to make sure Rick was sitting as comfortably as possible. We were about seven miles out, when the race director pulled up beside us to give me some warm clothes, because he knew bad weather was coming. I put on long pants and a jacket. The weather started getting colder, rainy and windy.

The bike course had quite a few hills with four major ones. The crowds were large and very supportive, going up the major hills all you could see was people, and they would move out of the way as we passed. There were more spectators at this triathlon then any others we have competed in. It was very exciting. During the bike it would rain and we'd get soaked, then the sun would come out and I would be sweating! Then it would rain again and we'd get cold. This happened throughout the entire bike course.

The bike course was a double loop, 56 miles each loop. On our second loop they had taken all the food stations down, and I was getting very weak from hunger. Finally a man and lady appeared and gave me a banana, which helped us to make it to the bike transition. We were at the bike transition for about twenty-five minutes, because Rick was so stiff from the cold and the ill-fitting bike seat. I ate while in transition because I was so hungry and weak; I was also getting very cold, so I changed my clothes.

The weather got even worse as we headed out on the run course, and it poured rain throughout almost the entire marathon! The run was along the canal, which was all gravel, making it really tough to push Rick and the chair. The course was flat and would have been fast if not for the rain.

The finish was great! I think everyone from Roth was there to see us finish. They had bleachers set up in a horseshoe shape, and there was not an empty seat to be found. The race director had us walk around the finish area with him. The crowd was unbelievable! About twenty minutes later they had a fireworks display while the song "One moment in time" by Whitney Houston played. Our finishing time was 16:09:53. We estimate the splits at: swim: 2:00 bike: 10:00 run: 4:10.

At the awards ceremony the next morning, they presented us with flowers and awards just as they do for the age group winners. Our nine days in Germany were fantastic, the people were wonderful and it is a beautiful country. I would recommend this event to everybody. The triathlon is a sport where we have to deal with the weather. There is no roof over our heads, or dome stadiums.

Team Hoyt is not just Rick and Dick. Our support crew are the ones that make it possible for us to compete. Our support crew in Germany was: Robert Hoyt, Heather Grey and Michelle Krupski.

A word about Germany from **Rick Hoyt:**

My thoughts before the Germany IronMan were about the weather and whether or not I would fit into the seat of the new bike. I did not sit in the seat until three weeks before the IronMan. My brother Rob made a footrest out of an old lawn chair, and we had other last minute adjustments to make on the seat, right up to the day before the race.

After sitting in the Frankfurt airport for seven hours we took the short flight into the city of Nuremberg, then drove to our destination, the city of Roth.

We stayed at the Wohnstift Augustinum Roth, which was housing for the wealthy elderly. It has several guest apartments as well. I had a personal care attendant with me named Shelly. She is an occupational therapist, and her skills really helped, especially on race day.

The days leading up to the race were very busy between press conferences and doing adjustments on the bike seat, however my PCA and I were able to swim and explore the city of Roth. The weather was mostly cloudy with a few breaks of sun, and rain showers. It could be as high as the 70's during the day and as low as the 50's at night. It was daylight until 10:00 p.m.

The morning of the IronMan we got up at 3:30 am and drove to the canal where the swim was to start. I waited in the van for awhile, so my father and brother could get the equipment ready. When I got out of the van I could hear American music playing on the loudspeaker, some of the triathletes came over to wish me good luck. During the swim I heard 8 of the 12 cannons starting each wave, at this point it was not raining.

During the bike portion people would yell "pump! pump!" when we passed by. The weather was crazy, it would shower for awhile, and then the sun would shine. For a while the temperature was around 60; my body kept getting cold and warm.

In spite of all the preparation, we still had problems with the bike seat, and I began to slide forward in the seat. We had to stop twice so my father could adjust me; however, it turned into roughly ten hours of discomfort. Boy was I glad to see the end of the bike course!

During the bike transition, my PCA gave me my medication and she and my brother laid me on a table so I could be stretched out, because I was so stiff from the bike seat. It was about twenty minutes before we went out to do the marathon. When we ran by people, they again yelled, "pump!" We passed a lot of triathletes and they said "good work" to us as we went by.

The weather then turned ugly, while on the run it began to pour and pour! At about mile 22 we saw a woman talking on her cell phone while running! When we finished they set off fireworks as the race director came down and had us run with him past the crowd again. After we finished I ate everything in sight and all I wanted was to take a bath!

* * *

Rick and Dick have spread their message of inclusion all over the world, and in the year 2002, they continue to do so. After returning from Germany, they went back to California for another speaking engagement. In September, a film crew from Japan visited to shoot a special about their lives and accomplishments. They competed in the Challenged Half Ironman in San Diego in November and were subsequently honored by the Challenged Athletes Foundation (CAF) as their Most Inspirational Athletes for the year 2000.

The year 2000 ended auspiciously for the Hoyts. Russ and Lisa became parents of a second son – Ryan Hoyt was born on December 22, a healthy, vocal youngster who weighed in at nearly 10 pounds. Dick and Rick appeared as guests of the Rosie

O'Donnell Show that same month, and went back for an encore appearance in 2001.

While preparing for the 2002 season, however, the Hoyts suffered another setback. Just prior to Dick's trip to Tampa to edit his biography, his mother passed away. God rest her soul.

Anyone interested in Team Hoyt sponsorship, Hoyt Fund donations, speaking engagements, a promotional video or the purchase of IT'S ONLY A MOUNTAIN, please visit their website at www.teamhoyt.com, or you may contact Dick at teamhoyt@samnet.net.

Team Hoyt in Germany.

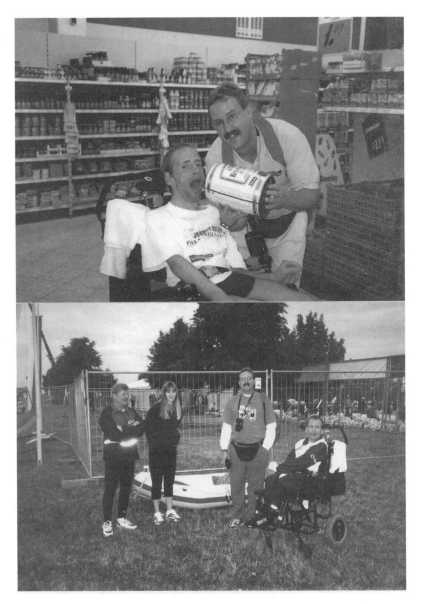

More action in Germany.

Blazing trails in Germany.

Review Team Hoyt 2001

January: Ran two 5-mile races
            Rick turned 39
            Speaking engagement in Newton

February: Ran a 10 miler in Foxboro
            Ran a half marathon in Hyannis

March: Ran a 5K in Malden
            Half marathon in Bedford
            Twenty miler from Maine to Mass.
            Presentation to AT&T in Kona, Hawaii

April: Ran two 10Ks
            Ran 21st consecutive Boston Marathon
            Three speaking engagements

May: Ran a 10K, two 5-mile races and two 5Ks
            Speaking engagement in Boston

June: Competed in two triathlons
            One 10k and a 5-mile race.
            Speaking engagement for AT&T in New York

July: Did three triathlons and one duathlon
            Received the IDEA Fitness Inspiration of the
            year Award in San Francisco.

August: Did three triathlons
            Ran in 22nd consecutive Falmouth Road Race

Review Team Hoyt 2001, continued

September: First ever triathlon in Boston
              Ran two 10Ks, one 5-mile race and 2 5Ks

October: Los Angeles County Commission on Disabilities
              Presented Team Hoyt with the first annual Billy
              Barty Inspiration Award for their unwavering
              determination and spirit.
              Made one speech and two 5-mile runs

November: Did the swim portion of the San Diego
              Triathlon Challenge
              Ran one 5-mile race and one 5K
              Spoke to AT &T in Boston
              Received the Advocacy Recognition Award
              From the Regional Employment Board of
              Hampden County in Massachusetts.

December: Appeared at Providence Seminars in San Diego
              Ran two 5-mile races

PUBLICATIONS AND BROADCAST (Partial list)

Boston Globe
People Magazine
The Boston Herald
Parade Magazine
New England Runner
Las Vegas Sun
Boston Sunday Globe
Daily Free Press
Telegram & Gazette
National Enquirer
Japanese Runner

I Witness video
ABC World News
ESPN – Arete Awards
CBS Evening News
CBS Hardcopy
ABC Wide World of Sports
Evening Magazine
WHDH-TV "Our Times"
Geraldo Rivera Show
WCBV-TV "Channel 5 News"
Good Day Show
WGGB-TV "Channel 22 News"
Cable Sports Sidelines
Las Vegas "Channel 8 News"
Montreal's World Triathlon
CBS - West 57th Street
ABC Sports "30th Anniversary Special"
BC Nightly News with Tom Brokaw
Hour Magazine with Gary Collins
Channel 22 Noon Program 5-Day Series (El Salvador)
Titan Television — "Body Stars"

TEAM HOYT AWARDS (Partial list)

Father of the Year Award
Boston, MA

Recognition Proclamation
Lambertville, NJ

True Ironman Award
Waltham Police Department, MA

Kodak Champions
Parade Magazine

Sports Personality Award
Boston Press Photographers Assoc.

George Washington Honor Medal
Freedoms Foundation

Superlative Performance for Courage in Sports
Arete Award

Certificate of Completion: Trek across America
Governor Weld, Boston, MA

Honorary Doctor of Law Degree to Dick Hoyt
Western New England College, Springfield, MA

Lifetime Achievement Award to Rick Hoyt
Western New England College, Springfield, MA

Living Legends Sports Award
Sports Museum of New England

Certificate of Achievement
President's Council on Physical Fitness

Boston Proclamation: Dick and Rick Hoyt Day
Mayor Flynn, Boston, MA

Rick - Honorary General, Air National Guard

ronman-Herausforderungen der besonderen Art. Der spastisch gelähmt Rick l
Jer querschnittsgelähmte Randy Caddell auf seinem futuristischen „Hand Cyc

A little help from friends in Germany.

Champagne at Boston Harbor.

I would like to extend my personal greetings to Lieutenant Colonel Dick Hoyt and his son, Rick, whose efforts are a statement of courage and love. May the both of you continue to work together so we may all benefit from your special relationship.
—Prime Minister Brian Mulroney
British Colombia, Canada

I can't tell you how much of an impression you two left on all that heard your presentation. In a cynical and pessimistic world you represent hope, love, and determination in overcoming life's adversities. People still come up to me shaking their heads in amazement of your tremendous accomplishments.
—Tom Lambert
Needham, MA Police Department

This is more than a story of a father's love, though it certainly speaks to all fathers, this one included. It's also a story of courage, the kind any of us could be called upon to demonstrate in our own lives. And if we were, we'd have two wonderful examples to follow in Dick and Rick Hoyt, both of whom I am proud to call friends.
—Bobby Orr
Boston Bruins

I have admired you and Rick for many years, ever since the first time I saw you compete in the Boston Marathon in the mid-1980's. The two of you have been an inspiration to me and, I am sure, to countless other people. As I told you, I have mentioned you in more than one Sunday homily as a wonderful example of courage, cooperation, teamwork, and family solidarity.
—Fr. Robin Ryan, Retreat Director
Bishop Molloy Retreat House

The session you held was outstanding and was one of the highest rated sessions of the Conference. It was not only inspiring, but it was very emotional as well. After you spoke, many people came up to me to tell me how much they enjoyed it. I would say that it is one that will always be remembered.
—T. Quinn Spitzer, Jr.
Education Chairman
Young President's Conference

IT'S ONLY A MOUNTAIN

Dick and Rick Hoyt, Men of Iron

Limited edition

ISBN 0-941072-51-7

Published by Sam Nall
Samuel E. Nall Enterprises
samnall@juno.com

Southern Heritage Press
St. Petersburg, FL
1-800-282-2823

Dedication by Dick Hoyt

I would like to dedicate this book to my mother and father, who have always supported us. They are the ones who provided me with a strong heart and body that enabled us to compete at a level beyond my own expectations and explanation.

I also dedicate the book to Judy, Rick's mother, who fought bravely and tirelessly to assure Rick an education, one that truly enabled him to be included in all daily activities.

And to my sons Rob and Russ, who selflessly accepted the fact that Rick's requirements created hardships on them at times, and frequently denied them the attention they deserved. I am very proud of who they are and what they have become.

First and foremost, however, I dedicate this book to my son, Rick. If it were not for his inner strength and determination, there would be no book. He is the one who inspires and motivates me. He is the heart and soul of Team Hoyt.

Dedication by Rick Hoyt

I would like to dedicate this book to all of the people who helped me to climb this mountain. The people number in the hundreds, from my Mom, Dad, and two brothers, to all of the teachers and professors who encouraged me to never give up and always keep trying.

Thanks to all of the doctors and therapists that have helped me. And finally, to the many people that help me live an independent life, thank you!

IT'S ONLY A MOUNTAIN

In Dick Hoyt's world, the only difference between a hill and a mountain is something called attitude, and along with their courage and determination, the Hoyt family has conquered many mountains the past forty years, literally and figuratively. They were devastated when their first son was born with cerebral palsy, a non-vocal quadriplegic, but they accepted the challenge. Rather than put Rick in an institution and forget him – as was suggested by the doctors – they gave him a life unlike any other.

ESPN, ABC and NBC brought national attention to Team Hoyt when they conquered Ironman Hawaii and again when they traversed the Rocky Mountains on a bicycle. Dick, a novice swimmer, tethers himself to a rubber dinghy and tows his adult son 2.4 miles in the Pacific Ocean. He straps him to a seat on the front of a custom-built bicycle and pedals 112 miles. Together, they then complete the Ironman events by running a marathon, 26.2 miles, with Rick seated in a "running chair." These are tremendous accomplishments, of course, but they represent only a couple of rungs in Team Hoyt's inspirational ladder.

If you are expecting a simple sports biography, or only a story about a man competing in triathlons and marathons, you are in for a pleasant surprise. That is not what you will find between the covers of this book. Instead, prepare for an emotional saga about the tremendous accomplishments of a handicapped person surrounded by a family motivated by love for one another and for humanity in general.

CONTENTS

IT'S ONLY A MOUNTAIN

Dick and Rick Hoyt, Men of Iron

INTRODUCTION

"Oh, come on. Half the guys in here have done an Ironman. It's not such a big deal."

"You've never done one," came the response.

Through all the chatter, those were the first intelligible words I heard when I entered the Sports Bar & Grill in St. Petersburg, Florida. While a handful of patrons shot pool and tossed darts in one section of the club, a pack of rowdy triathletes partied in another. The swim-bike-run crowd had spread out at rows of tables near a six-foot television screen and they were all talking at the same time. Alan Tudor and Donna Harris waved from a table directly behind the man who seemingly minimized the challenges of an Ironman, and as I walked over to join them, I overheard the man's reasoning. He said, "That's not my point. This Hoyt dude *carried* his son for the entire Ironman, and he finished it by running a sub-six mile. Try that some time."

It's unlikely the second man accepted his rhetorical challenge, however, the comment about the "Hoyt dude" became more profound as the afternoon wore on.

At four o'clock, one of the major networks would televise *Ironman Hawaii,* an event that had drawn local triathletes to the Bar and Grill in large numbers. Being a newcomer to the St. Pete Mad Dog Triathlon Club, I decided to stop by and watch the broadcast. Although the Ironman distance didn't interest me as a participant, this was an opportunity to get acquainted with some of the other club members. I had already completed my training session for the day, anyway, and felt that I had earned a break, a chance to kick back and enjoy the camaraderie.

While waiting for the telecast to begin, the party-minded Mad Dogs tossed down beers and shared personal anecdotes about racing. Their collective energies and excitement created a festive atmosphere that pulled me in. After my Coors Light arrived, I asked Donna to enlighten me about the man who had carried his son through the entire Ironman.

Her eyes lit up. "You have never heard of the Hoyts?"

"Not before today."

Donna slid closer and poured forth everything she knew about the Hoyts, but before getting into details, Rue Morgan stood and shouted, "Let the games begin!"

Morgan cupped his hand to his mouth and let loose with the traditional Mad Dog "howl." His loyal followers promptly echoed the call to order. As president and original founder of the St. Pete Mad Dogs, and as an experienced Ironman competitor, Morgan had earned their respect and unquestionably deserved this ceremonial honor. In fact, he had competed in the 1997 World Championships in Hawaii, the very race everyone had come to the Bar and Grill to watch. When Morgan led his pack of canines

ABOUT THE AUTHOR

Sam Nall was born and raised in Corwith, Iowa. After four years in the Air Force, he worked as a programmer for Univac. Upon graduation from Bakersfield College (California), he attended UCLA, where he took a course in screenwriting and now has 16 scripts registered with the Writers Guild.

While living in Bakersfield, Sam played handball, and with his partner, Kenny Eng, won many tournaments. A hip injury ended his handball career, so he began running. He eventually added swimming and biking to his training, and after moving to Florida in 1997, he competed in his first triathlon, which serendipitously led to meeting Dick and Rick Hoyt. In the USA Triathlon national rankings, Sam is currently #20 in his age division.

Last year, after interviewing NBC news anchor, Bob Hite, and Eckerd College search and rescue instructor, Bill Covert, Sam wrote a screenplay titled THE SKYWAY IS DOWN – a true story about the Skyway bridge disaster in Tampa Bay – and he is now writing a screenplay for the Hoyt story.

Sam has many friends to thank, not only for their contributions to IT'S ONLY A MOUNTAIN, but also for their encouragement and support throughout the years. He thanks Scott and Tina Matthews, Alan and Donna Tudor, Professor Bill VanHouten, Debbie Berry, Gary and Sandy Meeks, Judge Richard Oberholzer, Kenny Eng, Stan and Margaret Coombs, Paul and Dorothy Scheffelman, Barbara Durham and Greg Kaputa.

A very special thank you to Marie Johnson, his fiancée, for her patience and understanding.

With love and respect, he thanks Doris and Edward Nall, his sweet mother and late father, for their love and support. But above all, he would like to thank Dick and Rick Hoyt for their trust, confidence and inspiration. They opened their hearts and lives to Sam, and he is forever grateful.

Jogging at Pismo Beach, CA